Streaming Databases
Unifying Batch and Stream Processing

Hubert Dulay and Ralph M. Debusmann

Beijing · Boston · Farnham · Sebastopol · Tokyo   **O'REILLY**®

Streaming Databases

by Hubert Dulay and Ralph M. Debusmann

Printed in the United States of America.

Published by O'Reilly Media, Inc., 1005 Gravenstein Highway North, Sebastopol, CA 95472.

O'Reilly books may be purchased for educational, business, or sales promotional use. Online editions are also available for most titles (*http://oreilly.com*). For more information, contact our corporate/institutional sales department: 800-998-9938 or *corporate@oreilly.com*.

Acquisitions Editor: Aaron Black
Development Editor: Rita Fernando
Production Editor: Katherine Tozer
Copyeditor: Emily Wydeven
Proofreader: Krsta Technology Solutions

Indexer: BIM Creatives, LLC
Interior Designer: David Futato
Cover Designer: Karen Montgomery
Illustrator: Kate Dullea

August 2024:   First Edition

Revision History for the First Edition
2024-08-08:   First Release

See *http://oreilly.com/catalog/errata.csp?isbn=9781098154837* for release details.

978-1-098-15483-7

[LSI]

Table of Contents

Foreword

Pioneering a new category of software systems is the dream of many software engineers. I feel very fortunate for the opportunity to work on ksqlDB early on, even before it was called ksqlDB, and before the category of streaming databases was generally known. When I first heard that Ralph and Hubert were writing a book dedicated to streaming databases, I was naturally interested right away.

So what is a streaming database? Database systems have many different flavors, from traditional relational databases to XML, graph, object, vector, and NoSQL databases. Many of these are well known and have been established for many decades. Streaming, or stream processing, is much less established, although it has seen a steep adoption rate in the industry over the past decade or so, led by the rise of Apache Kafka as the de facto streaming platform.

Historically, stream processing was considered difficult, and only larger organizations with dedicated teams of streaming experts could master it. The same was true for data processing and computing 50 years ago, before SQL and relational database systems were invented to allow nontechnical users to work with data stored in computer systems. Now, SQL is the *lingua franca* of data processing.

Streaming databases are the next step in the evolution of stream processing. They unify well-established techniques from database systems with the new paradigms from the streaming world to simplify stream processing and enable nontechnical users to work with data in motion, similar to what we are used to when we query data at rest.

Database systems are designed to solve specific problems. The two main categories of database systems, online transaction processing (OLTP) and online analytical processing (OLAP) systems, were not originally designed for internet-scale applications.

With the rise of "big data" at the beginning of the third millennium, new systems such as MapReduce were invented to meet the increased scaling requirements. However, those new systems were developed by technical experts for technical experts, and they moved us away from the familiarity of SQL.

With the invention of data lakes, the first child of the "big data" era, it was quickly realized that SQL was needed to enable nontechnical users to make the most of these new technologies. As a result, SQL was reintroduced, and nowadays, all modern data lakes use SQL to query the stored data.

Data streaming, as the second child of the "big data" era, followed the same trend: first, stream processing systems were built by experts for experts without the support of SQL. It wasn't long until SQL and database technologies were introduced to enable nontechnical users to use these new streaming systems. This development led to streaming databases and the waves of innovation that followed.

As more people realize the significance of streaming databases in the world of stream processing and database technology, they will need guidance on how to use them with their existing systems. Stream processing, as this book puts it, adds a new plane between the operational plane (OLTP) and the analytical plane (OLAP). The streaming plane opens up a rich area of possibilities for the future of data systems.

In this book, Hubert and Ralph discuss the three different starting points for streaming databases:

- Stream processing systems that adopt database technologies and SQL
- Database systems that are extended to incorporate streaming concepts
- Data lakes (which already adopted SQL) that are extended to use streaming capabilities

These three gave rise to a variety of different streaming databases, each with its own limitations and optimized for different use cases. This raises the question: which system should we use for what use case, and what are the trade-offs?

Following Jay Kreps' prediction that "companies are becoming software," we have an exciting future in data processing ahead of us with streaming databases at its very core. The simplifications that streaming databases and streaming SQL offer allow many more nontechnical users to adopt stream processing, which will lead the way for streaming to become ubiquitous.

We are still early in the era of streaming databases, and it's exciting to observe the current trends and discover newly built systems.

This book provides an excellent entry point for learning about all these cutting-edge innovations and the zoo of options, which is typical for the early days of a new era. If you want to learn even more about streaming databases, check out Hubert and Ralph's podcast on Spotify, simply called "Hubert's Podcast." They interviewed many different people in the streaming and data space in preparation for this book, and it's a gem by itself.

— Matthias J. Sax
Technical Lead,
Kafka Streams Engineering Team at Confluent
Apache Committer and PMC member
(Kafka, Flink, Storm)
Reno, NV, May 2024

Preface

In this book, we go beyond the boundaries of traditional batch processing and seamlessly integrate the dynamic world of streaming data. If you come from the streaming world, we provide a database perspective for stream processing. Streaming databases bridge the gap between data at rest and data in motion.

Drawing inspiration from Martin Kleppmann's seminal work on "turning the database inside out," we flip the narrative to "bringing streaming systems back into the database." Through this paradigm shift, we can first unravel the intricate layers of stream processing before we find familiar abstractions that make real-time streaming more accessible and understandable to developers, regardless of their familiarity with streaming technologies.

Our exploration delves into the core principles of streaming databases, exposing how they empower developers to take on real-time data processing use cases within the familiar confines of a database environment. Focusing on practicality and usability, we unveil how streaming databases democratize real-time data analytics, paving the way for innovative applications and insights.

Whether you're a seasoned database engineer or a novice developer, this book guides you to unlocking the full potential of streaming databases and embracing the future of data processing.

Conventions Used in This Book

The following typographical conventions are used in this book:

Italic
    Indicates new terms, URLs, email addresses, filenames, and file extensions.

`Constant width`

> Used for program listings, as well as within paragraphs to refer to program elements such as variable or function names, databases, data types, environment variables, statements, and keywords.

`Constant width bold`

> Shows commands or other text that should be typed literally by the user.

`Constant width italic`

> Shows text that should be replaced with user-supplied values or by values determined by context.

> This element signifies a general note.

> This element indicates a warning or caution.

Using Code Examples

Supplemental material (code examples, exercises, etc.) is available for download at *https://github.com/hdulay/streaming-databases*.

If you have a technical question or a problem using the code examples, please send email to *support@oreilly.com*.

This book is here to help you get your job done. In general, if example code is offered with this book, you may use it in your programs and documentation. You do not need to contact us for permission unless you're reproducing a significant portion of the code. For example, writing a program that uses several chunks of code from this book does not require permission. Selling or distributing examples from O'Reilly books does require permission. Answering a question by citing this book and quoting example code does not require permission. Incorporating a significant amount of example code from this book into your product's documentation does require permission.

We appreciate, but generally do not require, attribution. An attribution usually includes the title, author, publisher, and ISBN. For example: "*Streaming Databases* by Hubert Dulay and Ralph M. Debusmann (O'Reilly). Copyright 2024 Hubert Dulay and Ralph M. Debusmann, 978-1-098-15483-7."

If you feel your use of code examples falls outside fair use or the permission given above, feel free to contact us at *permissions@oreilly.com*.

O'Reilly Online Learning

O'REILLY® For more than 40 years, *O'Reilly Media* has provided technology and business training, knowledge, and insight to help companies succeed.

Our unique network of experts and innovators share their knowledge and expertise through books, articles, and our online learning platform. O'Reilly's online learning platform gives you on-demand access to live training courses, in-depth learning paths, interactive coding environments, and a vast collection of text and video from O'Reilly and 200+ other publishers. For more information, visit *https://oreilly.com*.

How to Contact Us

Please address comments and questions concerning this book to the publisher:

O'Reilly Media, Inc.
1005 Gravenstein Highway North
Sebastopol, CA 95472
800-889-8969 (in the United States or Canada)
707-827-7019 (international or local)
707-829-0104 (fax)
support@oreilly.com
https://www.oreilly.com/about/contact.html

We have a web page for this book, where we list errata, examples, and any additional information. You can access this page at *https://oreil.ly/streaming-databases*.

For news and information about our books and courses, visit *https://oreilly.com*.

Find us on LinkedIn: *https://linkedin.com/company/oreilly-media*.

Watch us on YouTube: *https://youtube.com/oreillymedia*.

Hubert's Acknowledgements

I'd like to first thank my wife, Beth, and the kids, Aster and Nico, for supporting me while I wrote this book. It would not have been easy without them. Second, I'd like to thank Ralph for being a great technologist, teacher, and capable coauthor, making us an excellent writing pair.

When we first started writing this book, we interviewed many experts and leaders in the streaming space who were driving innovation in streaming, real-time analytics, and, more importantly, its adoption. Thanks to Seth Wiesman, Arjun Narayan, and Frank McSherry for the insights and Nikhil Benesch for seeking me out at Current. Thanks to Will Plummer for initially reaching out, Jove Zhong for reviewing the book, and Gang Tao and Ting Wang for continually supporting us. I'd also like to thank Yingjun Wu for your wisdom and for reviewing the book. Thank you to Adrian Kosowski, Anup Surendran, and Bobur Umurzokov for their continued partnership and support. Thanks to Hojjat Jafarpour, and Monish, for all the enjoyable conversations. Thanks to Mihai Budiu and Leonid Ryzhyk for speaking to us initially and for the quote, "All databases are streaming databases." Thanks to Micah Wylde, Richard Artoul, and Ryan Worl for your interesting conversations. Thanks to Robin Fehr and Nico Kruber for also reviewing the book. Thank you, Matthias Sax, for writing the forward to this book. Thanks to Rita Fernando for making writing for O'Reilly easy and fun. Lastly, thanks to the other streaming and database technologists who bring streaming and real-time analytics to customers.

Ralph's Acknowledgments

I would firstly like to thank Bea for supporting me (not only with finishing this book), my parents, and my kids, Sophie, Stella, and Selene. A huge thank you goes to Hubert for having been able to coauthor this book and for the great time writing it together. I would also like to thank his colleagues at Migros, with whom I have had the pleasure to collaborate on and discuss topics related to this book, especially Martin Muggli, Jason Nguyen, Simon Hofer, Alexander Rovner, André Pechstein, Erik Vido, and Philipp Jud de Capitani. Thanks also go to all those who further took part in our book's genesis by providing valuable insights and feedback and engaging in inspirational discussions. In addition to those mentioned already, this includes (in alphabetical order) Jamie Brandon, Pavan Keshavamurthy, Giannis Polyzos, Florent Ramiere, Michael Rosam, and Yaroslav Tkachenko, noting that this list is far from complete.

## CHAPTER 1

Streaming Foundations

The hero's journey always begins with the call. One way or another, a guide must come to say, "Look, you're in Sleepy Land. Wake. Come on a trip. There is a whole aspect of your consciousness, your being, that's not been touched. So you're at home here? Well, there's not enough of you there." And so it starts.

—Joseph Campbell, *Reflections on the Art of Living: A Joseph Campbell Companion*

The streaming database is a concept born from over a decade of processing and serving data. The evolution leading to the advent of streaming databases is rooted in the broader history of database management systems, data processing, and the changing demands of the digital age. To understand this evolution, let's take a historical journey through the key milestones that have shaped the development of streaming databases.

The rise of the internet and the explosive growth of digital data in the late 20th century led to the need for more scalable and flexible data management solutions. Data warehouses and batch-oriented processing frameworks like Hadoop emerged to address these challenges of the size of data during this era.

The term "big data" was and still is used to refer not only to the size of data but also to all solutions that store and process data that is extremely large. Big data cannot fit on a single computer or server. You need to divide it up into smaller, equal-sized parts and store them in multiple computers. Systems like Hadoop and MapReduce became popular because they enabled distributed storage and processing.

This led to the idea of using distributed streaming to move large volumes of data into Hadoop. Apache Kafka emerged as one such messaging service that was designed to handle big data. Not only did it provide a way to move data from system to system, but it also provided a way to access data in motion—in real time. It was a development that led to a new wave of demand for real-time streaming use cases.

New technologies, such as Apache Flink and Apache Spark, were developed and were able to meet these new expectations. As distributed frameworks for batch processing and streaming, they could process data across many servers and provide analytical results. When coupled with Kafka, the trio provided a solution that could support streaming real-time analytical use cases. We'll discuss stream processors in more detail in Chapter 2.

In the mid-2010s, simpler and better paradigms in streaming emerged to increase the scale of real-time data processing. This included two new stream processing frameworks, Apache Kafka Streams (KStreams) and Apache Samza. KStreams and Samza were the first to implement materialized views, which made the stream look and feel more like a database.

Martin Kleppmann took the pairing of databases and streaming even further. In his 2015 talk, "Turning the Database Inside-Out" (*https://oreil.ly/EPsaz*), he described a way to implement stream processing that takes internal database features and externalizes them in real-time streams. This approach led to more scalable, resilient, and real-time stream processing systems.

One of the problems of stream processing was (and still is) that it's harder to use than batch processing. There are fewer abstractions, and much more deep-down tech is shining through. To implement stream processing for their use case, data engineers now had to consider data order, consistency for accurate processing, fault tolerance, resilience, scalability, and more. This became a hurdle that deterred data teams from attempting to use streaming. As a result, most have opted to continue using databases to transform data and running the data processing in batches at the expense of not meeting performance requirements.

In this book, we hope to make streaming and stream processing more accessible to those who are used to working with databases. We'll start, as Kleppmann did, by talking about how to turn the database inside out.

Turning the Database Inside Out

Martin Kleppmann is a distinguished software developer who gave the thought-provoking talk "Turning the Database Inside-Out." He introduced Apache Samza as a newer way of implementing stream processing that takes internal database features and externalizes them in real-time streams. His thought leadership led to the paradigm shift of introducing materialized views to stream processing.

> Really it's a surreptitious attempt to take the database architecture we know and turn it inside out.
>
> —Martin Kleppmann, "Turning the Database Inside-Out" (*https://oreil.ly/EPsaz*)

However, stream processing is still hard, and hence, many data engineers have, over time, opted to continue using databases to transform data and run it in batches even if it meant not meeting SLA requirements.

As we move forward in this book, we will attempt to make streaming and stream processing more accessible to data engineers by bringing them back into the database. But before we can do this, we need to understand why Kleppmann decided to take apart the database and why he chose the specific database features in his new paradigm to achieve real-time data processing.

Externalizing Database Features

Kleppmann identified two important features in the database: the write-ahead log (WAL) and the materialized view. As it turns out, these features naturally have streaming characteristics that provide a better way of processing data in real time.

Write-Ahead Log

The WAL is a mechanism that allows databases to ensure data durability and consistency. The spinning disks that databases write data upon don't offer transactions. So databases are challenged to provide transactionality atop a device that doesn't offer transactions. WALs are a way for databases to provide transactionality without having transactional disks.

A transaction in a database refers to a sequence of one or more database operations executed as a single unit of work. These operations can include data insertion (INSERT), data modification (UPDATE), or data deletion (DELETE) (see Figure 1-1).

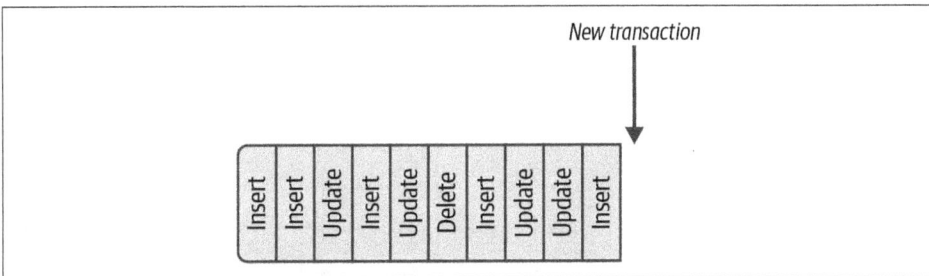

Figure 1-1. A write-ahead log that captures change events in a database

The WAL acts as a buffer that can be overwritten as new changes are made. The WAL persists the change to disk, as shown in Figure 1-2.

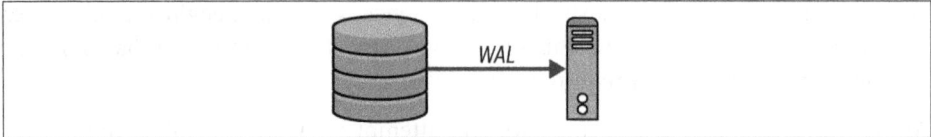

Figure 1-2. Database writing to disk through the write-ahead log

When saving transactions on disk, the database follows these steps:

1. The client starts a transaction by issuing a BEGIN statement.
2. The database writes a record to the WAL indicating that a transaction has started.
3. The client makes changes to the database data.
4. The client commits the transaction by issuing a COMMIT statement.
5. The database writes a record to the WAL indicating that the transaction has been committed.
6. The changes made by the transaction are written to disk.

When a transaction starts, the database will write a record to the WAL indicating that the transaction has started. The database will then proceed to make changes to the database data. However, the changes will not be written to disk until the transaction commits. Also, if the database crashes or loses power, the changes can be *replayed* from the log, and the database can be restored to a consistent state.[1]

The WAL provides a mechanism to capture database transactions in real time by allowing external systems to subscribe to it. One of these use cases is for database disaster recovery. By reading the WAL, data can be replicated to a secondary database. If the primary database were to suffer an outage, database clients can failover to the secondary database, which is a replica of the primary database (see Figure 1-3).

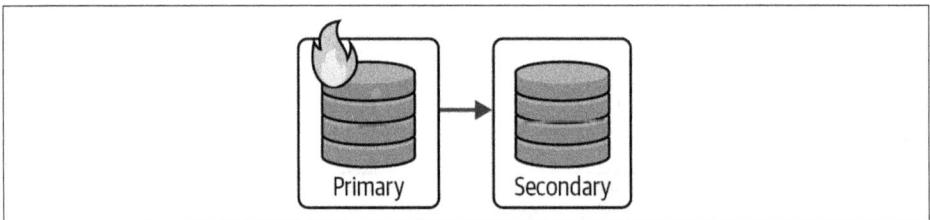

Figure 1-3. The WAL is used to replicate data from a primary database to a secondary in the case of a primary database outage

---

1 There are other types of recovery algorithms in addition to what we describe (roll forward/replay). Changes to the actual data could be also applied before the COMMIT is done (given that the WAL contains the old value), and uncommitted transactions could then be rolled back.

Since WALs are receiving transactions in real time, they naturally have perfect semantics for streaming. Clients can subscribe to the WAL and forward their transactions to a streaming platform for other systems to consume. These other systems can also build replicas that represent the original primary database. The semantics of the WAL construct are mimicked in streaming platforms like Kafka in their storage implementation. Streaming platforms extend the database WAL externally for other applications and systems to use.

There are other streaming-related concepts about the WAL. After the transactions are committed, the WAL is not cleared immediately. Instead, it follows a process called *checkpointing*, which involves periodically flushing the transactions of the WAL to the main data files. Checkpointing serves several purposes, one of which is ensuring that some committed changes have been permanently written to the data files, reducing the amount of data that needs to be *replayed* during recovery after a crash. This helps speed up the recovery process. Also, as transactions are committed, the WAL grows over time. Checkpointing helps control the size of the WAL by flushing some of its contents to the data files. This prevents the WAL from becoming excessively large and consuming too much disk space. Checkpointing and replaying transactions are features you will also find in stream processing for very similar reasons.

We mentioned that the WAL construct that normally lives internally in the database can be represented externally in streaming platforms like Kafka, which provide WAL-like semantics when replicating data from system to system.

Streaming Platforms

Streaming platforms like Apache Kafka are distributed, scalable, and fault-tolerant systems designed to handle real-time data streams. They provide a powerful infrastructure for ingesting, storing, and processing large volumes of continuous data from various sources.

Most streaming platforms have a construct called *partitions*. These constructs mimic WALs in a database. Transactions are appended to partitions like transactions to a WAL. Streaming platforms can hold many partitions to distribute the stream load to promote horizontal scaling. Partitions are grouped in abstractions called *topics* to which applications either publish or consume transactions.

By publishing the transactions to the streaming platform, you've published it to all subscribers who may want to consume it. This is called a *publish and subscribe model*, and it's critical to allow multiple disparate consumers to use these transactions.

For other streaming platforms, the names of these constructs may be different. Table 1-1 lists some alternative streaming platforms. Apache Kafka is the most popular streaming platform used today. In Apache Kafka, the abstraction of these constructs is called a topic, and the lower-level partitions are called partitions.

Table 1-1. Alternative streaming platforms

Streaming platform name	Description	Implementation	Topic name	Partition name	Kafka compliant
Memphis	Memphis is an open source next-generation alternative to traditional message brokers.	GoLang	Station	Stream	No
Apache Pulsar	Apache Pulsar is an open source distributed messaging and streaming platform that was originally developed at Yahoo!	Java	Topic	Ledger	Yes—currently, the Pulsar Kafka wrapper supports most of the operations offered by the Kafka API.
Redpanda	Redpanda is an open source streaming platform designed to provide a high-performance, scalable, and reliable way to handle real-time data streams.	C++	Topic	Partition	Yes
WarpStream	WarpStream is a Kafka-compatible data streaming platform built directly on top of S3.	GoLang	Topic	Partition	Yes
Gazette	Gazette is a lightweight open source streaming platform.	GoLang	Selector	Journal	No
Pravega	Pravega is a stream processor that provides streaming storage abstraction for continuously generated and unbounded data.	Java	Stream	Stream Segment	Kafka adapter available

> In this book, we'll use the terms "topic" and "partition" as the names of the streaming platform constructs that hold real-time streaming data.

Since Kafka is the most popular streaming platform used today, the last column in Table 1-1 indicates if the streaming platform supports Kafka clients. This will allow applications to swap out Kafka for another Kafka-compliant streaming platform.

As stated, a partition is a mechanism that streaming platforms use to scale themselves out. The more partitions a topic has, the more it can distribute the data load. This enables more consumer instances to process the transactions in parallel. The way transactions get distributed across partitions is by using a key assigned to the transaction. In Figure 1-4, the WAL in the database is read and stored into a topic in a streaming platform—on a higher level of abstraction than just a disk.

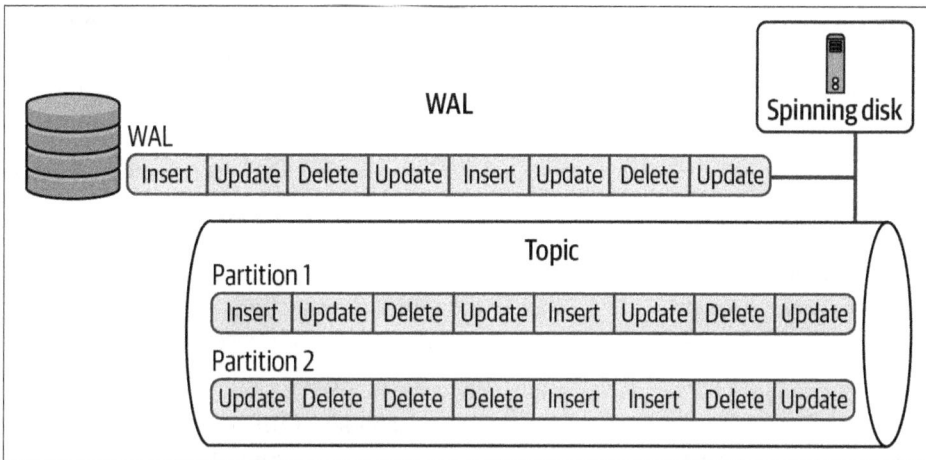

Figure 1-4. Topics in streaming platform can mimic a WAL and externalize it for other systems to build replicas of the original source database

Instead of storing the data for others to query, the streaming platform reconstructs the WAL and distributes the transactions onto separate partitions.[2] Reconstructing the WAL exposes the transactions to other data systems to build replicas of the primary database.

Partitions are immutable append-only logs that streaming platforms use to capture and serve transactions. Many consumers can subscribe to them utilizing offsets. Offsets correspond to the index or position of a transaction in the partition.[3] Every consumer of the topic has an offset pointer to keep track of their position in the partition. This allows consumers to read and process the transactions in the partition at their own pace. A side effect of this is that the streaming platform will have to retain transactions in the partitions for a longer time than databases retain their transactions in a WAL. The default retention in Kafka is 7 days. This gives a lot of time for slow consumers to process the transactions in the topic. This property is also configurable to allow even longer retention time as well.

Regarding Figure 1-4, the way you should think about publishing transactions to a topic should be a lot different than writing to disk. The important fact about topics in a streaming platform is that when transactions are published into them, they are still considered streaming. Let's use a water metaphor to help explain this. When you consume water from a faucet, you would consider that fresh water. This is the same with streaming platforms. When you consume transactions from a topic, they too

---

2 Transactions can span multiple records. In this case, the key for distributing the data onto partitions does not directly correspond to the primary key in the source database.

3 Again, for simplicity, our transaction here only holds one record.

are considered fresh. Conversely, if you bring a liter of water into your home and don't drink it for a while, it's considered stale. Stale or stagnant water is susceptible to bacterial growth and is unclean. The stale liter of water is more akin to batching of data.

On the other hand, if you don't use your faucets in over a month, the water sourced from faucets may contain rust or debris, indicating the water has become stale. In this case, water coming from faucets will not always be fresh. Streaming platforms tend to have a mechanism that protects them from stale transactions. To avoid publishing stale transactions, retention is applied to the topics. Transactions can be purged after a retention period configured by the user of the streaming platform.

To recap, primary OLTP databases naturally write to a WAL when storing to spinning disks. WALs can be used to replicate data to a secondary OLTP database for disaster recovery scenarios. Streaming platforms like Kafka can be used to externalize the database WAL using partitions abstracted by topics to provide the transactions that were originally in the WAL to other systems. These systems subscribe to the topic so that they can build their replica of the tables in the original primary OLTP database just like the secondary OLTP database did (see Figure 1-5). Hence, streaming platforms can be used to make the WALs previously hidden in your OLTP database systems publicly available—becoming a tool for synchronizing your database systems across your entire organization.

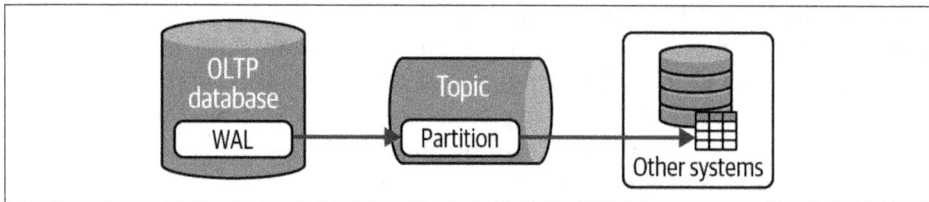

Figure 1-5. The partitions in a topic can hold the transactions from a source OLTP database and publish the transactions for other systems to build replica tables

With a similar approach, we can build materialized views in stream processing platforms.

Materialized Views

In typical OLTP databases, materialized views are special types of database objects that store the results of a precomputed query or aggregation. Unlike regular views, which are virtual and dynamically generate their results based on the underlying data, materialized views store the actual data, making them physically stored in the database.

The purpose of materialized views is to improve the performance of complex queries or aggregations by precomputing and storing the results. When a query references a materialized view, the database can quickly retrieve the precomputed data from the materialized view instead of recalculating it from the base data tables. This can significantly reduce the query execution time and improve overall database performance, especially for large and resource-intensive queries.

The materialization process in databases usually needs to be refreshed manually to keep the stored results fresh. Example 1-1 shows an example of how to refresh a materialized view in a Postgres database, a popular OLTP database.

Example 1-1. Refreshing a materialized view in Postgres

```
REFRESH MATERIALIZED VIEW CONCURRENTLY product_sales;
```

By enabling materialized views to be updated, the stored data will always be fresh; that is, the stored data is real-time data. This characteristic makes materialized views fit naturally into streaming frameworks.

In the previous section, streaming platforms could hold transactions from OLTP WALs. These partitions mimic the WAL construct, so other systems can build replicas of tables in the original OLTP database. This same approach can be applied in stream processors to build tabular structures (see Figure 1-6).

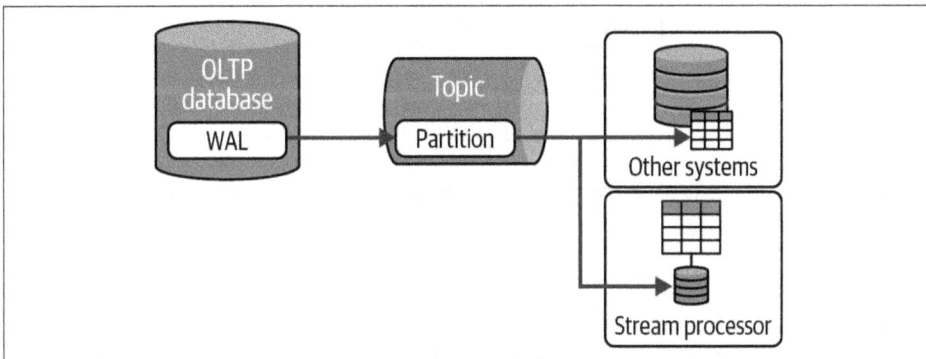

Figure 1-6. Replicas can also be built in stream processors the same way other systems can build replicas

We'll talk more about stream processing in Chapter 2. We also have dedicated Chapter 3 to materialized views because their importance to streaming databases is substantial. To best explain streaming databases, it helps to set up a simple use case that we can follow to the end. Along the way, we'll identify each system needed to accomplish the goal of the use case.

Use Case: Clickstream Analysis

Let's start by defining a simple use case. This use case will help create a path to a better understanding of streaming databases, how they can resolve a real-time use case, and the advantages they bring when architecting a real-time solution.

Our use case will involve clickstream data. Clickstream data refers to a sequence of recorded events that capture the actions and interactions of users as they navigate through a website, application, or digital platform. It provides a detailed record of the clicks, page views, and other interactions performed by users during their online sessions.

Clickstream data can be used for various purposes, like personalization, targeted advertising, user segmentation, fraud detection, and conversion rate optimization. It plays a crucial role in web analytics, marketing analytics, user experience research, and other data-driven disciplines. In Figure 1-7, a customer clicks on a product, generating a click event that is captured by a microservice. That click event is sent to downstream analytical consumption.

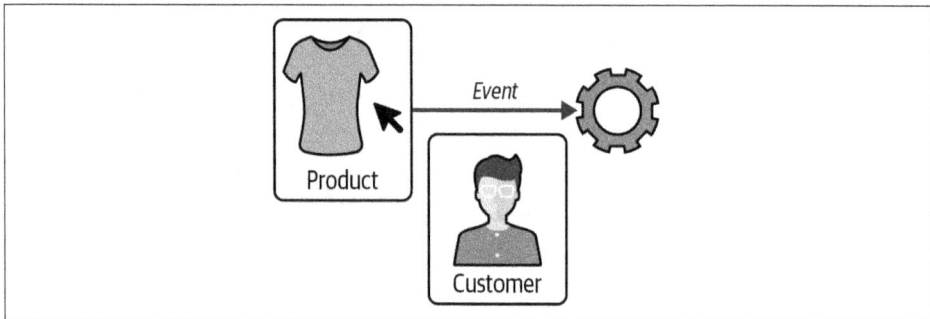

Figure 1-7. A user clicks on a green T-shirt, generating a click event captured by a microservice

In our use case, a 24-year-old male customer who lives in Woodstock, NY, clicks on a green T-shirt using a phone application. Our goal is to provide clickstream data to end users so that they can perform analytics and derive insights that help make data-driven decisions.

Let's say in this example, we want to capture click events and associate them with existing customers. This will help analytics to provide targeted marketing and to create a more personalized experience.

We call the data going into a WAL in an OLTP database *transactions*. We call the clicks we capture from a user-facing application in our use case *events*. They both will eventually end up in a streaming platform like Kafka so that we can eventually join them together.

Understanding Transactions and Events

So far, we have called the data that originated from a database a transaction. These are the inserts, updates, and deletes that have occurred and got written to the WAL and subsequently got written into a topic in a streaming platform. We can also call these transactions *change events* or just *events*. They are *insert events*, *update events*, and *delete events*, just like a click on an application is an event.

Even though they are both events, it's extremely important to understand that they are still different types of events. One comes from changes to tables in a database, and the other comes from the actions taken on an application. To discern their differences, we'll need to briefly go over domain-driven design.

Domain-Driven Design

In software, engineers will model their applications using objects that exist in their business domain. For example, if part of your business includes customers, then you will create an object in the application that represents a *customer*. You would do this for every object included in the business domain.

Let's build a model that describes the objects in our use case. Customers and products are objects that would be part of the domain model that defines this application. These objects are called entities. Entities live in the OLTP database and undergo change events like inserts, updates, and deletes.

Events like click events capture the interactions between the entities in the application. In our example, a customer clicks on a product. The *customer* and *product* are the objects, and the action is the *click* of the product. This is represented in Figure 1-7.

We can use the structure of a sentence to describe this relationship. A sentence contains a *subject*, *verb*, and an *object*. The *subject* in a sentence generally is the entity that's carrying out an action. The *verb* describes the action. Lastly, the *object* is the entity upon which the action is being applied. In our use case, the sentence is:

```
The customer clicked on a product.
```

Click events tend to provide a lot more information, so we can expand this sentence with more description:

```
The customer with IP 111.11.1111 clicked on product 12345 on 07/21/2023 at
11:20 am Eastern time.
```

Notice that we don't know the name of the customer or product, nor do we know the customer's location or age. We also don't know the product type or its color. We have to enrich the clickstream event with customer and product information before delivering it for analysis.

One question you could ask is, "Why can't the click event also be stored in the database?" This is a valid question. Why not use the WAL to read the click events together with the entities? One major reason is the OLTP database could run out of space. If you think about how many times a customer clicks on items in an application, it would not be sensible to store all that data in an OLTP database. While entities tend to change very slowly, they can be deleted or updated. In contrast, click events are immutable and would be inserted only into a table. This pattern is also called append-only. Click events are better captured using a microservice that writes to a streaming platform directly.

Another difference to note is that the action event is being enriched, and the entity events are being used to enrich. Knowing the differences between action events and entity change events will be significant throughout this book. Each type will be handled differently as they flow through the streaming data pipeline until they are served to the end user.

Context Enrichment

All forms of analytical consumption need a context in which the event occurred. The click event, as noted earlier, only contains the information related to the click but neither the customer nor the product information. Typically, entity information is not available at the time of the click event. If it were, collecting and enriching clickstream data in the application would not be economical or scalable because of the size of the data and the latency it would generate.

The better way to enrich the click event is to perform it downstream of a real-time data pipeline. Having this additional information will help make more informed decisions. For example, if the customer likes green shirts and is a male in his 20s, knowing that information will help enable smarter decisions and make the application more personalized.

In our use case, the click event is associated with two other entities in the business domain: the customer and the clicked product. Combining these details of the entities with the click event will create a more compelling context needed for real-time analytics. Compelling analytics can tell us more about the event and how to quickly react to issues like deciding to increase the inventory of men's green shirts.

We know entities that are part of the domain of the application exist in the OLTP database. We also know that changes to these entities are written to the WAL. But we did not talk about how the events in the WAL make it into a topic in a streaming platform, where other systems can consume change events and build their replica of the entities in the application. The replica will enable this enrichment of the click event with product and customer information in a stream processor downstream. The process of creating this replica is called *change data capture*.

Change Data Capture

Change data capture (CDC) is a technique used in databases and data integration systems to capture and track changes made to the data in real time. The primary goal of CDC is to identify and capture any change transactions (inserts, updates, or deletes) made to specific tables and make the changes events available for consumption by downstream systems or processes.

When performing CDC, you can either subscribe to a stream of transactions that have been executed or you can capture a snapshot. Snapshots are not change events as you would see in WAL. In database terminology, a snapshot refers to a copy of a database (or table in a database) taken at a particular point in time, just like taking a snapshot with a camera. Streams sourced from databases are akin to compressed videos, where each frame of the video isn't a picture (or snapshot) but pixel changes from one frame to the next.

> The type of video that provides only changes in each frame versus snapshots to save processing time is called delta encoding. Delta encoding is a video compression technique that stores only the differences between consecutive frames. This can significantly reduce the size of the video file while still preserving the original video quality.

CDC can be implemented in a few ways:

Listening to the WAL
> This is the approach we've been discussing in this chapter and the preferred way of capturing changes in a database. It's done in real time and naturally is streaming.

> The WAL approach to capturing change transactions is typically used by relational OLTP databases like PostgreSQL and MySQL. We talk about it because of how similar it is to the constructs that hold streams in streaming platforms. Some NoSQL transactional databases may not follow this approach but have some other mechanism to capture changes.

Comparing snapshots
> This involves taking a snapshot of a table and comparing it to a previous snapshot to filter out changes. This act can be process intensive, especially if the table is large. Also, this approach is not true real time. Snapshots are taken in intervals. Changes that include a reversion that occurs in between intervals would be lost. Suspicious change and reversion events might sometimes go undetected.

Comparing update timestamps

This approach saves the timestamp of the last batch of changes and filters for records with update timestamps that occur after it. This approach requires an update column included in the table that needs to be updated anytime the record is changed. This approach is also not in real time.

Fortunately, most OLTP databases have some way of reading their WAL. Some OLTP databases also have native support for submitting events to streaming platforms or other systems. For example, CockroachDB provides a way to create a change feed from itself to:

- Kafka
- Google Cloud Pub/Sub
- Cloud Storage (Amazon S3, Google Cloud Storage, Azure Storage)
- Webhook

This avoids requiring a client to subscribe to the WAL in CockroachDB and, instead, CockroachDB pushes change events to Kafka directly (see Example 1-2). This is a preferred pattern because it significantly reduces the architectural complexity of the streaming data pipeline.

Example 1-2. Creating a change feed from CockroachDB to Kafka

```
CREATE CHANGEFEED FOR TABLE customer, product INTO 'kafka://localhost:9092';
```

Having this feature natively in OLTP databases fundamentally brings them closer to streaming databases. We'll discuss streaming databases in Chapter 5.

> Even if you were Martin Kleppmann himself, Chapters 1 to 4 are critical reading before Chapter 5. Please don't skip ahead because they provide foundational information supporting the introduction of streaming databases in Chapter 5.

As stated, this push mechanism reduces architectural complexity. Other OLTP databases that don't have this feature require additional components called *connectors* to extract data and publish them into a topic in a streaming platform.

Connectors

In streaming, we distinguish two main types of connectors:

Source connectors
> Source connectors read data from a data source system (e.g., a database) and make that data available as an event stream.

Sink connectors
> Sink connectors consume data from an event stream and write that data to a sink system (a database again or a data warehouse, a data lake, etc.).

The two types of connectors are depicted in Figure 1-8. In most cases, source connectors either transform *data at rest* into streaming data (aka *data in motion*), whereas sink connectors transform streaming data into data at rest.

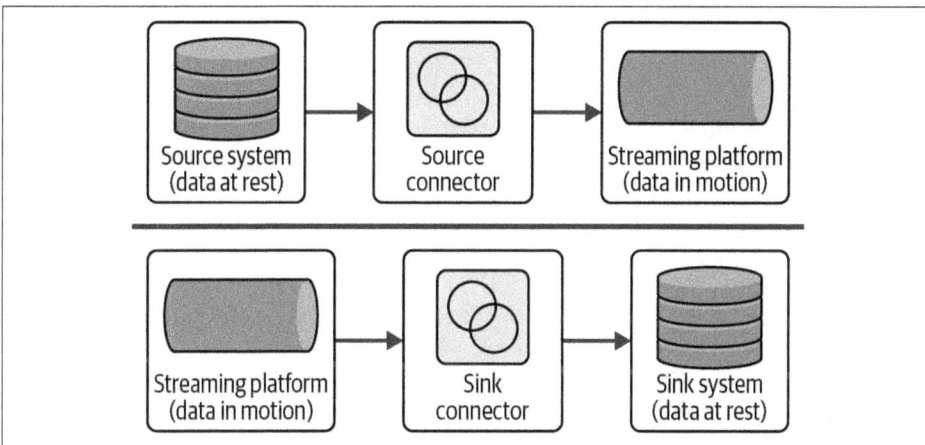

Figure 1-8. Source connectors (top) and sink connectors (bottom)

With data at rest, we mean that the data is sitting in a database or a filesystem and not moving. Data at rest tends to get processed using batching or microbatching techniques.[4] A dataset batched from one source system to another has a beginning and an end. The applications that process batched data can be started using a job scheduler like cron, and the data processing ends when the dataset ends.

This is the opposite of streaming, or data in motion. Data in motion implies that there is neither a beginning nor an end to the data. Applications that process streaming data are always running and listening for new data to arrive on the stream.

Now let's dive into how source and sink connectors can be implemented.

---

4 It's debatable whether microbatching is actually closer to streaming or batch.

Connector Middleware

Connector middleware solutions such as Kafka Connect, Meroxa, Striim, or Stream-Sets already provide a large number of connectors out of the box and are often extensible to serve further sources and sinks. Connector middlewares also offer horizontal scaling, monitoring, and other required features, especially for production deployments.

Kafka Connect is part of the Apache Kafka project. It is a distributed cluster in which Kafka connectors are deployed to run in parallel. These types of deployments create complexity in the streaming architecture. These clusters are bulky and maintenance of them is arduous.

If you have a large amount of data sources and sinks, these clusters often become costly and consume a lot of resources. Delegation of this integration is better solved by embedding the connectors into the systems themselves.

Embedded

An increasing number of databases offer embedded connectors to streaming platforms. As we stated earlier, CockroachDB is an example of this. An even larger set of databases has implemented embedded connectors; that is, they can consume data off the event stream themselves. Examples are Apache Druid, Apache Pinot, ClickHouse, StarRocks, Apache Doris, and Rockset.

As we stated, having databases solve the integration to streaming platforms gets them closer to becoming streaming databases. If you enable databases with the ability to pull and push data into streaming platforms, streaming will naturally become a first-class citizen in the database.

Custom-Built

Connectors can be custom-built, for example, by implementing a dedicated microservice. The advantage of this approach is its flexibility; the downside is clearly the need to "reinvent the wheel"—it often doesn't make sense to implement connectors from scratch, especially in light of the plethora of existing powerful and scalable open source connectors (e.g., the Debezium source connectors for the Kafka Connect middleware).

In Figure 1-9, we have illustrated the three ways of implementing connectors (the illustration only shows source connectors for simplicity; the corresponding sink connector implementations would just be a mirror image of this illustration).

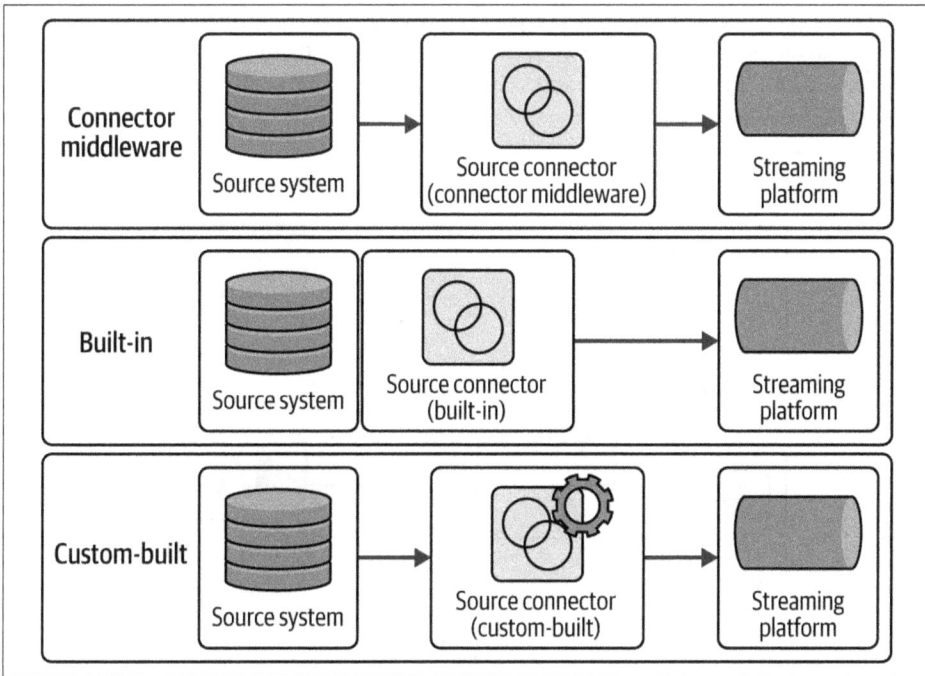

Figure 1-9. Ways of implementing connectors via connector middleware, built-in connector, or custom-built connector

> In the remainder of this book, we'll abstract away from the actual implementation of the connectors. When we speak about a "connector," this can be a connector based on a connector middleware, a built-in connector, or a custom-built one.

Back to our example use case. Here, we want to enrich click events with product and customer information. Most likely, this data would reside in a transactional database or online transactional processing (OLTP) database. To make this data available as an event stream, we need to use a source connector for that database.

> An OLTP database is also called an operational database, and it refers to a type of database designed to handle a high volume of transactions. OLTP databases are designed to provide fast data access and updates, which is important for applications that require real-time data processing.

In Figure 1-10, you can see that the product and customer information is stored in an OLTP database. Two database source connectors read from this database and write them to topics ("Product topic" and "Customer topic"). The click events are written to the "Click event topic."

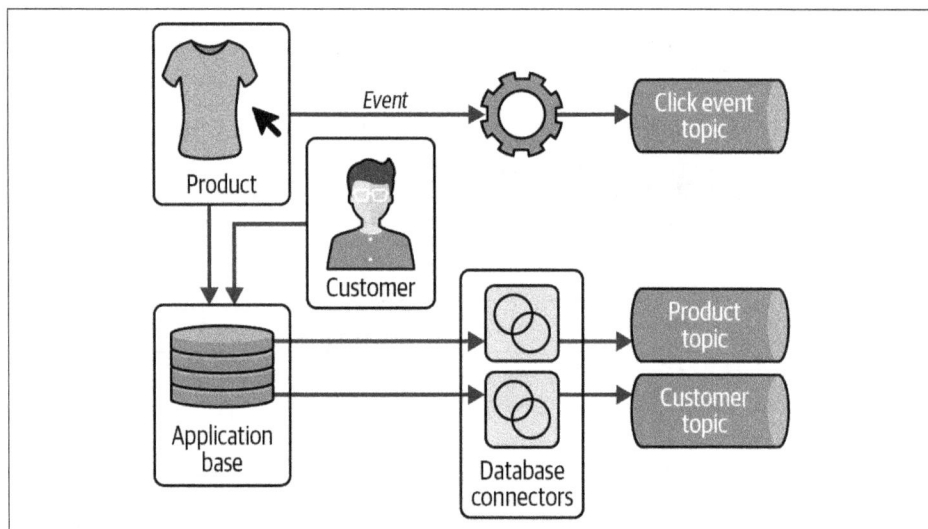

Figure 1-10. Customer and product data in the database

Summary

In this chapter, we introduced some foundational streaming concepts by introducing Martin Kleppmann and his approach to turning the database inside out. By doing so, we identified two features that lay the foundation for streaming and stream processing: the database WAL and the materialized view.

We learned that the topics in streaming platforms are externalized database WALs for other systems to subscribe to. These other systems can then build replicas of tables from the source database using, for example, CDC (or other forms of connectors) and perform their processing of the real-time data.

In the next chapter, we'll continue with the clickstream use case example and bring it to the next step—the stream processing platform where the enrichment will occur.

## CHAPTER 2

Stream Processing Platforms

In Chapter 1, we introduced a simple use case of getting real-time data to consumers. We also introduced connectors and how they can convert data at rest into data in motion (or event streams) and then publish them into topics in streaming platforms.

The event streams can now be read, but they most likely aren't yet in a format consumers can use. Events tend to need cleansing and preparation before they undergo analytical processing. Events also need to be enriched with context for them to be useful enough to derive insights. Analytical processing heavily relies on the accuracy and reliability of the data. By addressing issues such as missing values, inconsistencies, duplicates, and outliers, data quality is improved, leading to more reliable and accurate analytical results.

In Figure 2-1, event data preparation can also significantly impact the performance of analytical queries. By optimizing the data layout, indexing, and partitioning, the efficiency of data retrieval and processing can be improved. This includes techniques such as data denormalization, columnar storage, and indexing strategies tailored for the analytical workload. Well-prepared data can reduce the processing time and enable faster insights. We will cover denormalization, columnar storage, and indexing strategies in Chapter 4 when we discuss how to serve analytical data to consumers.

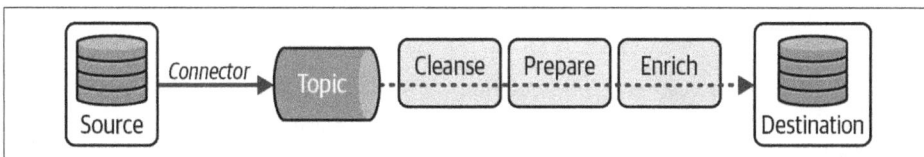

Figure 2-1. Cleanse, prepare, and enrich event data prior to reaching the destination

Event data preparation also plays a crucial role in ensuring data governance and compliance. This involves enforcing data security measures, anonymizing sensitive information, and adhering to privacy regulations. By properly preparing the data, organizations can maintain data integrity, protect privacy, and comply with legal and ethical requirements.

Overall, data preparation in a data pipeline is essential to ensuring that the data is accurate, consistent, and well-structured for effective analytical processing. It enhances the reliability of analytical results, improves performance, and enables the extraction of meaningful insights.

In Figure 2-1, the dotted line from the "Topic" to the "Destination" represents the stream processing platform. The role of the stream processing platform is to take on the tasks of cleansing, preparing, and enriching event data as a preprocessing step before reaching the destination data store.

> In this book, we will call the tasks of cleansing, preparation, and enrichment of event data "transformations" that get executed in a streaming data pipeline.

Transformation tasks tend to be resource consuming and process intensive. It's best to complete transformations as part of a preprocessing step in a data pipeline before writing to a data store that serves it to consumers. The earlier the transformations can be done, the better—as executing them incrementally, seeing only small amounts of data at once, is much less resource consuming than having to scour through large amounts of data already at rest later.

The destination data stores are typically online analytical processing, or OLAP, data stores. OLAP data stores allow users to invoke analytical queries on the data. Real-time OLAP (RTOLAP) data stores are also OLAP but are optimized for serving real-time analytical data.

It's best practice to avoid process-intensive tasks in the OLAP that serve analytics to the consumers. OLAPs need to reserve their resources for quickly responding to analytical queries that answer questions related to the business or provide fast insights to customers—another reason for executing the preprocessing as early as possible in the pipeline.

> OLAPs are data stores optimized for analytical reads. They tend to be columnar-based data stores used to power user-facing dashboards and applications. OLTPs are databases that capture information from applications from which events originate. They are optimized for writing and single-row lookups. OLTP databases tend to be the source for CDC extraction mentioned in Chapter 1.

In our clickstream use case, we will enrich the clickstream with customer and product information. This will provide context to the click analytics, like the location of the customer, the type of product, its color, and more. This information can enable more precise predictions that can help businesses reduce costs immensely in time, lost inventory, and customer satisfaction.

Some transformations are complex enough to require remembering information, for example, if they require joining (like our use case) or for aggregations. That information needs to be saved somewhere to be remembered. That place is called the state store. These complex transformations are then called stateful transformations.

Stateful Transformations

In Chapter 1, we ended the data pipeline with events being written to a topic in a streaming platform. This kept the events in a stream for consumers to subscribe to. Do not confuse this with *loading*, or the "L" in ELT. At this point, all we've technically done is extract the events from their source and put them into a topic. As for ELT, this still keeps us in the "E" (*extract*) phase.

Streaming platforms like Kafka do not transform data in such a way that it can hold state. Hence, more complex transformations, like aggregations, and joins cannot be performed on Kafka directly—you need additional components like Kafka Streams.

Data pipelines follow two types of patterns that are common approaches for data integration and processing, but they differ in the sequence of their operations and can be limited in streaming capabilities:

- Extract, transform, and load (ETL)
- Extract, load, and transform (ELT)

In ETL, data is first *extracted* from the source systems, which could be OLTP databases, files, devices, or other data sources. The extraction process involves retrieving the required events from these sources. Extraction is the job of the source connectors we mentioned in Chapter 1.

In ETL, the "T" requires the streaming data to be temporarily held in a store. This store holds the *state* of a transformation. In other words, stateful transformations require maintaining and updating some information or context between multiple input data elements. Here are a few examples:

Rolling averages
    To calculate a rolling average, you need to keep track of the sum and count of previous data elements. As new data arrives, you update the state by adding the new value and removing the oldest value, allowing you to compute the average over a sliding window.

Sessionization

In web analytics or event processing, sessionization involves grouping related events into sessions based on a certain set of criteria (e.g., user activity within a specific time threshold). To accomplish this, you need to maintain state information about ongoing sessions, such as start time, end time, and the list of events belonging to each session.

Deduplication

Removing duplicate events from a stream often requires maintaining a record of previously seen events. As new events arrive, you compare them (typically using their primary keys) against the stored state to identify and filter out duplicates.

Windowed aggregations

Aggregations such as sum, count, or maximum that operate over windows of data are required to hold the state to accumulate values within each window. As new data points arrive, you update the state accordingly and produce aggregated results periodically.

Machine learning models

In scenarios where you continuously update and refine machine learning models using streaming data, the models themselves require state. The model state holds information about the learned parameters, weights, or other relevant data, which gets updated with each new data point.

These examples demonstrate how maintaining state in streaming transformations enables computations that span across multiple data elements, allowing for more complex and meaningful analysis of streaming data. Pure streaming platforms like Kafka, again, do not have this ability without deploying additional ecosystem components like Kafka Streams–based microservices.

> Some streaming platforms have stateless transformations built in. These are called functions or single message transforms—transformations that don't require maintaining state. These would include string transformations like capitalization or simple math operations between columns. They do not qualify as stateful transformations in ETL or ELT.

As stated earlier, we have only completed the "E" for the extraction of data. Simply putting events in a topic does not qualify as "load" in ETL or ELT because the pure streaming platform cannot execute stateful transformations. Also, the pure streaming platform cannot directly serve user-facing consumers or applications. Remember, these consumers require cleansing, preparation, and enrichment of the events—and none of these steps has yet been completed when the events have initially landed on the streaming platform.

This is where stream processing platforms come in. Note that we use the terms *stream processing platform, stream processing system, stream processing framework,* and *stream processor* interchangeably throughout the rest of this book. Stream processing platforms have mechanisms to hold state and perform complex transformations.

These stateful transformations live within a data pipeline. We call the extraction, transformation, and loading (ETL) into an OLAP data store a data pipeline. In our case, it's a streaming data pipeline (streaming ETL). Data pipelines play a crucial role in real-time analytics. They are responsible for collecting data from various sources, transforming it into a format that can be analyzed, and promptly delivering it to analytics tools and applications.

Data Pipelines

Continuing the water metaphor introduced in Chapter 1, streaming data pipelines are like the pipes in your home. In Figure 2-2, water in your pipes can contain minerals and need to be filtered or heated for user consumption. Just like water pipes, streaming data pipelines route event data through a series of transformations before reaching the analytical consumer.

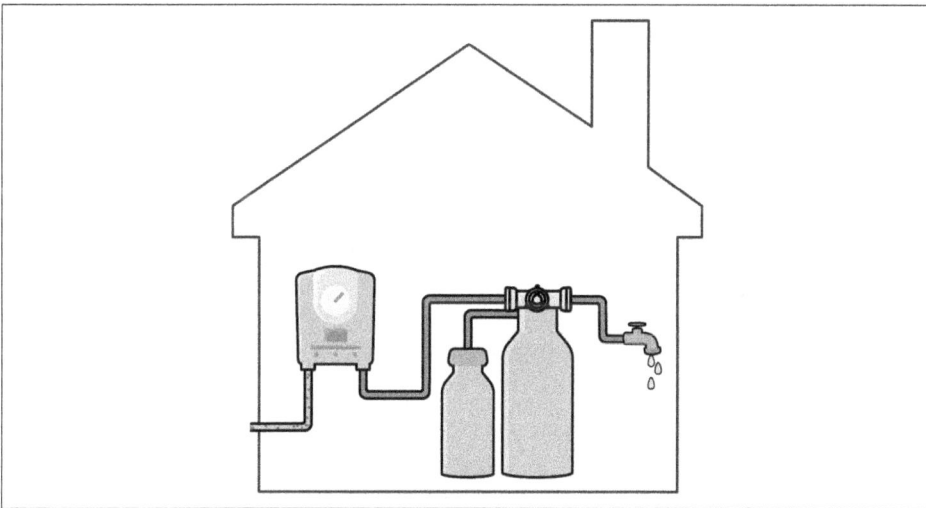

Figure 2-2. Streaming data pipelines follow the plumbing metaphor

One of the roles of the data pipeline is to move the data from the operational data plane to the analytical data plane. The operational data plane is where the applications live, including microservices and OLTP databases. The analytical data plane is where the analytical systems live—like data warehouses, data lakes, lakehouses—all kinds of OLAP data stores. Data pipelines live in between the operational and analytical data planes, transforming and integrating data from one to the other, respectively. See Figure 2-3.

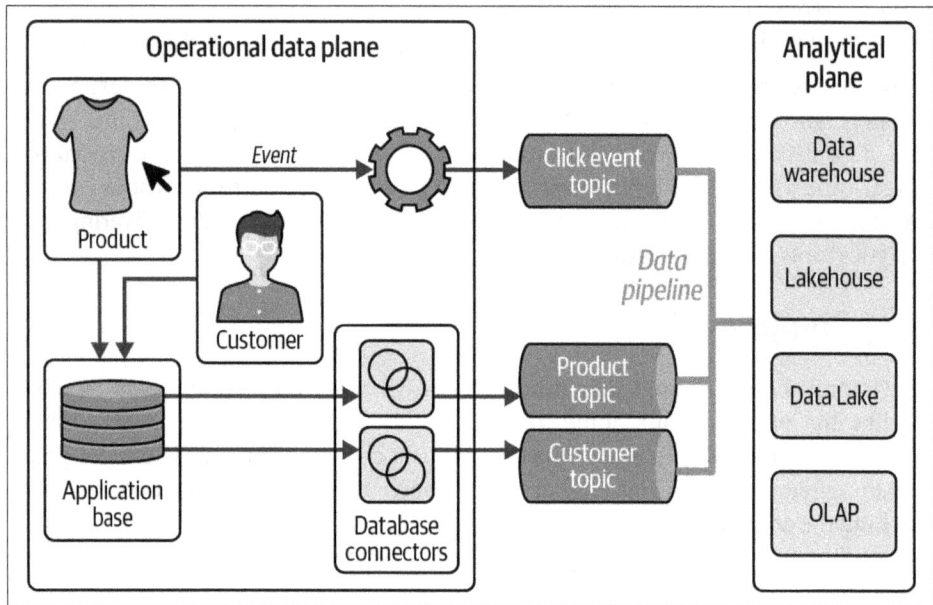

Figure 2-3. How data moves from operational to analytical planes using streaming data pipelines

Once the data is extracted, it undergoes *transformation* tasks previously mentioned to convert it into a suitable format for the target system or data warehouse, or OLAP data store (see Figure 2-4). The transformed data is typically stored temporarily in an intermediate store.

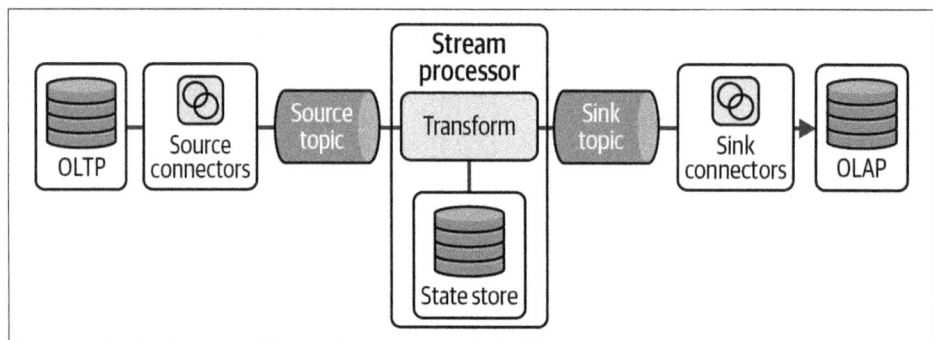

Figure 2-4. An ETL data pipeline that extracts from an OLTP source database, performs stateful transformations, and writes to an OLAP datastore

Lastly in ETL, the *load* operation loads the transformed data into the target system, such as a data warehouse. This involves inserting the data into the appropriate tables or structures within the target system.

Let's return to our simple use case where a customer clicks on a green T-shirt on an application. Figure 2-5 shows where we are now. On the left side, we capture data coming from a phone application. The click events go to a microservice that forwards the event to a topic in a streaming platform ("Click event topic").

The product and customer information gets sent to the OLTP database. The arrow that emits from the phone to the OLTP database would represent transactions made on the customer or product. Transactions would either be an insert, an update, or a delete. These transactions are the same transactions that are associated with CDC, which we talked about in Chapter 1. The transactions in the WAL in the OLTP database are consumed by a connector and are published to their corresponding topics ("Products topic," "Customers topic").

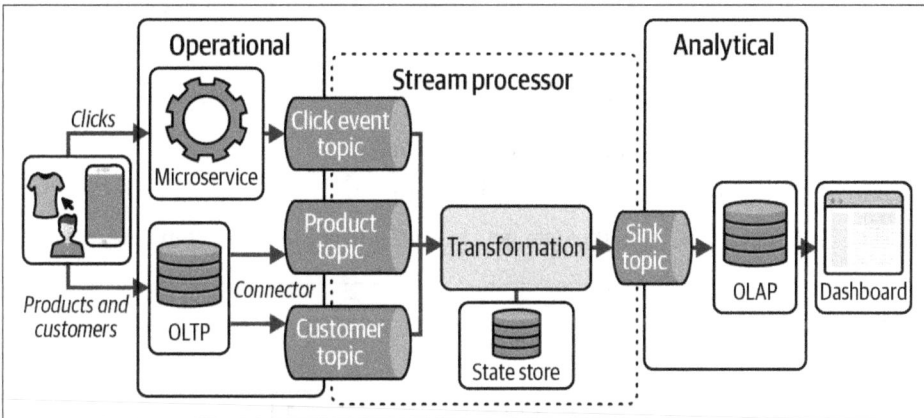

Figure 2-5. An ETL streaming data pipeline with connector and source and sink topics

All three topics—for click events, products, and customers—are consumed by the stream processor that implements the stateful transformations of the events. The result of the stream processor is published to a sink topic that is then consumed by the OLAP data store. The OLAP data store then serves the analytical data to the dashboard for data analysts.

As you can see in Figure 2-5, ETL supports streaming nicely because the transformation is done in the stream processing platform. After all, the data is kept in motion. The transformation is performed before loading the data into a destination store (or OLAP) that serves the data to the consumers. This approach avoids executing the (pre-)processing in the destination data store again and again for each served query. Remember, preprocessing tasks are resource consuming and process intensive. In the data-serving data store, we need to reserve these resources to serve the data and not to transform it.

ELT Limitations

In ELT, the transformation and load tasks are transposed, which makes this approach more flexible but also causes some limitations. The transformation is executed in the target system instead of transforming in the data pipeline. Without needing to hold the state of the transformation, ELT data pipelines are much simpler and do not use stateful stream processing. By loading the data into the target system (most likely a database that can perform transformations), the data has been removed from the stream and placed at rest. The data pipeline is no longer considered real time because the transformation needs to be either scheduled or triggered to run at a time interval. This approach is considered batching.

A SQL statement is triggered to run on the destination data store. The SQL statement has transformation logic, hence the "T" at the end of ELT. Let's look into this in depth.

Figure 2-6 illustrates the ELT process:

1. The data gets extracted from the OLTP database.
2. The data gets loaded into the OLAP datastore.
3. The SQL that transforms the data gets executed when the load completes.

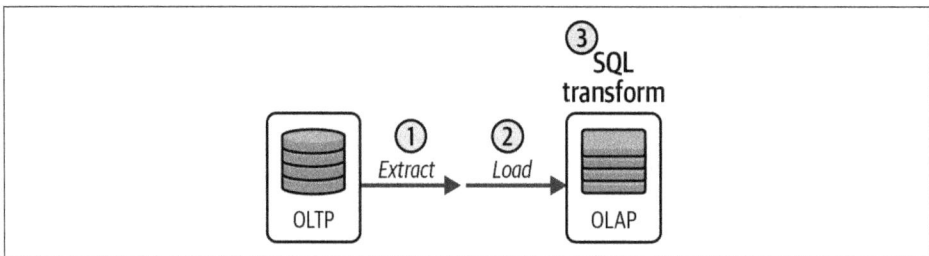

Figure 2-6. An ELT data pipeline that forces transformations in the destination data store

The invocation of the SQL statement in the destination data store would only get triggered after the "load" has been completed. This implies that the data flowing through the data pipeline is batched because batches have an end. If the data was a stream, it would never end, and thus, it would become hard to find out when the SQL would have to be executed. See Figure 2-7.

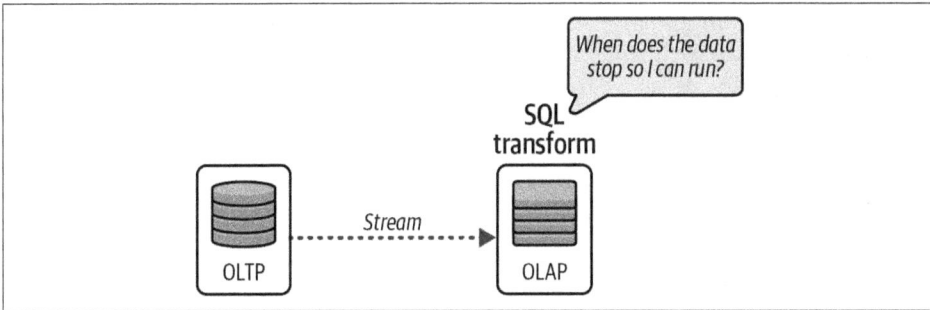

Figure 2-7. An ELT data pipeline failing to transform events

In real-time streaming use cases, the data pipeline should delay persisting data into the destination until the transformations are complete and the data ready for serving. At first glance, ELT is not at all a good fit for streaming.

Stream Processing with ELT

However, there is a way that ELT can support streaming real-time use cases. This can only be done by leveraging the capabilities of modern streaming platforms and real-time data processing frameworks. Here's how ELT can be applied to streaming real-time use cases:

Extract
> In ELT, the extraction step involves retrieving data from streaming sources, such as message queues, event streams, or real-time data feeds. These sources continuously produce data in real time, and ELT can extract this data stream for further processing.

Load
> The extracted data is loaded into a target system that supports streaming data ingestion and storage. This could be a streaming platform or data store designed to handle high-velocity and high-volume data streams in real time. The target system should be capable of ingesting the streaming data efficiently and storing it in a manner that allows for real-time processing.

Transform
> In ELT, the transformation step occurs after the data is loaded into the target system, such as real-time data processing frameworks like Apache Flink, Apache Kafka Streams, or any stateful stream processing platform.

Figure 2-8 shows how ELT can work using a stream processing platform as its target. In this case, the stream can either be a connector extracting data from an OLTP database, or the stream can be a streaming platform like Kafka. However, as many stream processing platforms like Flink do not have a persistence layer (counting out their state stores), the result of the transformation step would have to be brought to, for example, a database to enable queries. Streaming databases do have a persistence layer and could also be a target system enabling this architectural pattern. We will revisit this when we finally talk about streaming databases in Chapter 5.

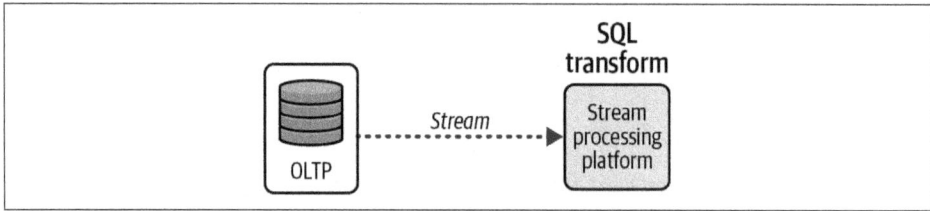

Figure 2-8. ELT with a stream processing platform as the target

By adopting streaming platforms and stateful stream processors, ELT can effectively handle streaming real-time use cases. The key factors for deciding between ETL and ELT include the scalability and performance of the target system, efficient streaming data ingestion, and the ability to perform stateful transformations and analytics on the streaming data.

Stream Processors

Stream processors are software platforms or tools that enable the processing of continuous data streams in real time. Most importantly, they can perform stateful transformations because they have a built-in state store.[1] These transformations of event data are necessary for consumers to derive the analytical insights that they need.

Popular Stream Processors

Here is a selection of popular stream processors:

- Apache Kafka Streams is a stream processing library for JVM-based programming languages that is part of the Apache Kafka project. It allows developers to build real-time applications and microservices that consume, process, and produce streams of data from/to Kafka.

- Apache Flink is a stream processor that supports both batch and stream processing and can be connected to a large variety of sources and sinks, including Kafka, Pulsar, and Kinesis, as well as databases like MongoDB and Elasticsearch.

---

1 There are (typically older) stream processors like Apache Storm that don't have built-in state support, but we are focusing on the majority of stream processors here that do.

Flink views batch as a special case of streaming (streaming with bounded data). Contrary to Kafka Streams, Flink is not a library but runs on its own cluster.

- Spark Structured Streaming is a component of Apache Spark that enables stream processing. It supports a large variety of connectors and is also cluster based. It is set apart from other stream processors like Kafka Streams, Flink, and Samza by making use of mini-batching instead of native stream processing—for Spark, streaming is a special case of batch rather than the other way around, as in Flink.

- Apache Samza is a stream processor developed by LinkedIn. It supports Kafka, Azure Event Hubs, Kinesis, and HDFS and is also cluster based like Flink.

- Apache Beam is not a stream processor itself but a unified programming model and set of software development kits (SDKs) for building data processing pipelines. It provides an abstraction that allows developers to write data-processing jobs that can be executed on various distributed processing engines, such as Apache Flink, Apache Spark, Apache Samza, and Google Cloud Dataflow.

Newer Stream Processors

We continue with a selection of newer stream processors:

Quix Streams
> A C#/Python-based stream processing library comparable to Kafka Streams for the JVM. Quix Streams also supports streaming data frames that behave similarly to data frames in, for example, Pandas or Spark while being incrementally updated under the covers.

Bytewax
> A Python-based stream processing library—comparable to Kafka Streams—making use of timely dataflow as the underlying stream processing engine.

Pathway
> A Python-based stream processing library. It is based on Differential Dataflow (DD) as the underlying stream processing engine.

Estuary Flow
> A stream processor that supports a large variety of connectors. It is cluster based.

These stream processing frameworks provide features like event-time processing, windowing, state management, fault tolerance, scalability, and integration with various data sources and sinks. They empower developers to build real-time data processing pipelines and enable applications that can react to data as it arrives, making them valuable tools for handling streaming data in a variety of use cases.

These lists only include stream processors but not streaming databases. Streaming databases can also perform stateful transformations. We will introduce streaming databases in Chapter 5.

Although these stream processors are very powerful, not all of them support materialized views. Materialized views represent data in a way that is reminiscent of a database. This capability is very useful for the implementation of real-time analytics use cases.

At the time of writing, the following stream processors from the aforementioned list support materialized views:

- Kafka Streams (KTable, GlobalKTable)
- Samza (Table)
- Pathway (Table)

Emulating Materialized Views in Apache Spark

As of the release of this book, to our knowledge, Apache Spark doesn't have built-in support for creating materialized views. However, Apache Spark offers various features and optimizations that can help achieve similar benefits to materialized views. For example:

- You can leverage Spark's caching mechanism to cache intermediate or final results of expensive computations. By caching the results in memory or disk, subsequent queries can access the precomputed data, potentially improving performance.

- Another approach in Spark is to use DataFrames or Datasets to define reusable views or transformations that can be applied to input data. These views can be saved and reused across multiple Spark applications, providing a form of data abstraction and optimization.

- Additionally, like Flink and other stream processors, Spark integrates with external data stores and systems, such as Apache Hive, Apache HBase, or other databases, which might have native support for materialized views. In such cases, you can leverage the capabilities of the underlying data store to create and manage materialized views while using Spark for data processing and analytics tasks.

It's worth noting that the Apache Spark ecosystem is constantly evolving, and new features and enhancements may be introduced in newer versions that extend its capabilities. Therefore, it's always recommended to refer to the official Apache Spark documentation and release notes for the latest information on materialized views or similar optimizations.

Two Types of Streams

To better understand materialized views, you will need to understand the types of streams in a stream processor. There are two types of real-time streams of data that flow through stream processors—*change* and *append-only* streams. The best way to describe these streams is to provide examples of how they get created. See Figure 2-9.

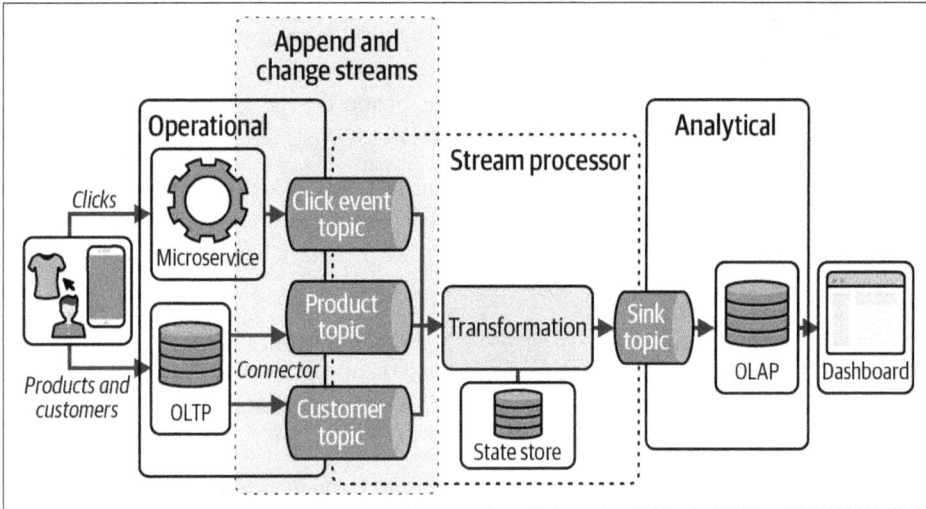

Figure 2-9. Click events are append streams, and change streams come from CDC streams

In Figure 2-9, the topics are highlighted: Click event, Product, and Customer. The click event stream is append-only, which means it contains discrete, distinct events. Why do we know this? Clicks are always unique. Every click event is different, even if it's done on the same T-shirt by the same customer. The only difference is the time it was clicked. In an append-only stream, the events are associated with a timestamp that indicates when each event occurred. The timestamp provides temporal information, allowing for the ordering and sequencing of events within the stream. This also applies to other types of events, not just click events.

Append-only streams tend to be *not* sourced from databases. In our use case in Figure 2-9, the clickstream data is sent to a microservice that acts as a proxy for the topic. If clicks were written to an OLTP database, the database would run out of space very quickly because every click event is a unique event; that is, we would trigger an *insert* into the OLTP table for every click on the application. Hence, using an OLTP database for click events would be bad design—it's clearly better to use an append-only stream of events here.

Conversely, change stream data almost always comes from CDC events. If you recall, these events are the transactions applied to a table in the OLTP database. These transactions are inserts, updates, and deletes. These records will not grow as fast as clickstream data because some events will include updates or deletes of existing records in a table.

Also, customer data may not change a lot. Customers may change their names, emails, or phone numbers, but probably not that often. Products would have a lot more changes, but still not many compared to clicks on an application. Also, change streams tend to represent changes to dimensional data. Dimensions change slowly in a database because they typically represent properties that do not frequently or rapidly change for the entities they describe.

If the product and customer datasets fit in the OLTP database, this means they should fit in the state store in the stream processing platform if the state store is sized appropriately. This provides a way to create a materialized view in the stream processor, which we could use to enrich the clickstream data.

In Chapter 1, we talked about how OLTP databases can support disaster recovery by replicating the primary database to a secondary database. This is exactly what we've done here—we've replicated a table in the OLTP database into the state store in the stream processing platform.

In the stream processing platform, both change and append-only streams will reside in structures that have different names depending on the stream processor you are using. For append-only streams, these structures may be called *streams*. For change streams, they may be just called *tables*. We can perform our enrichment of the clickstream by using SQL.

Append Stream

First, Example 2-1 ingests the clickstream data from Kafka into a hypothetical stream processor (for the example, we use a syntax similar to existing stream processors). This statement will create a source table called *click_events* that is an append-only stream.

Example 2-1. Create a source table from a Kafka topic

```
CREATE SOURCE click_events (
  id integer,
  ts long, ❶
  url varchar, ❷
  ipAddress varchar, ❸
```

```
    sessionId varchar,
    referrer varchar,
    browser varchar
)
WITH (
    connector='kafka',
    topic='clicks',
    properties.bootstrap.server='kafka:9092',
    scan.startup.mode='earliest'
)
ROW FORMAT JSON;
```

❶ Timestamp.

❷ Contains product ID to be parsed out.

❸ The `ipAddress` that identifies a customer.

Debezium Change Data

The SQL statements in Examples 2-2 and 2-3 also ingest data from Kafka—but in this case, it's Debezium CDC data for products and customer information. Debezium is a popular connector that can read the WAL of an OLTP database and capture changes to a table and publish them to Kafka. Notice in the SQL statements, there is a `before`, `after`, and op that provide the before and after values of the changes as well as the type of operation that was performed to the record.

Example 2-2. Ingest and create a table for the products

```
CREATE SOURCE products (
    before ROW<id long, name varchar, color varchar, barcode long>,
    after ROW<id long, name varchar, color varchar, barcode long>,
    op varchar,
    source <...>
)
WITH (
    connector='kafka',
    topic='products',
    properties.bootstrap.server='kafka:9092',
    scan.startup.mode='earliest'
)
ROW FORMAT JSON;
```

Example 2-3. Ingest and create a table for the customers

```
CREATE SOURCE customers (
    before ROW<id long, name varchar, email varchar, ipAddress varchar>,
    after ROW<id long, name varchar, email varchar, ipAddress varchar>,
```

```
    op varchar,
    source <...>,
)
WITH (
   connector='kafka',
   topic='customers',
   properties.bootstrap.server='kafka:9092',
   scan.startup.mode='earliest'
)
ROW FORMAT JSON;
```

To enrich the clickstream data with product and customer information, we will need to join these three tables together. A lot of transformations will need to be done to get the CDC data into a structure that allows us to easily join them with the clickstream data. For now, let's assume we've done this work. We will go over this more specifically in later chapters, when we start using a streaming database.

If we've transformed the product and customer tables from the Debezium format to a standard table, we still cannot join them with the clickstream table. The product and customer tables will contain duplicate records for each ID caused by multiple changes made to a single record. This means that joining these tables together will result in even more duplicate records. In Table 2-1, you can see that the color value was changed multiple times. We want this table to only project the latest record. This will project only one record per ID.

Table 2-1. Products table that contains previous changes to the color column

ID	Name	Color	Barcode
1	T-shirt	Green	123456
1	T-shirt	Greenish	123456
1	T-shirt	Lime green	123456

Materialized Views

The term "materialize" is defined as something that creates itself. The "something" doing the materialization usually does it on its own. This concept is important in understanding materialized views.

In Example 2-4, we create materialized views for each of the CDC datasets: products and customers. Each materialized view will only hold the latest version of every record.[2] The materialized view reduces the count of records, keeping only the latest record for each product or customer ID. That is, in essence, what a materialized view does—it's a reduction of the change stream. The reduction is an aggregation, like

---

2 We assume that we have flagged the product id and the customer id as primary keys here.

count, average, min, max, etc. In our case, the materialized view is reducing records by their ID, capturing the latest state of the record.

Example 2-4. Create a source table from a Kafka topic

```
CREATE MATERIALIZED VIEW mv_products AS select * from products;
CREATE MATERIALIZED VIEW mv_customers AS select * from customers;
```

The materialized views allow us to JOIN them with the clickstream events by only projecting the latest records for each product and customer change streams. We do not create a materialized view on the clickstream because it cannot be reduced. Remember that append-only streams are discrete, unique events like clickstreams. Click events cannot be reduced any more. Example 2-5 shows how we join the three tables and write them out to a sink topic.

Example 2-5. Create a source table from a Kafka topic

```
CREATE SINK http_enrich AS
SELECT
  E.*,
  C.*,
  P.*
FROM click_events E
JOIN CUSTOMERS C ON C.ip=E.ip and
JOIN PRODUCTS P ON P.product_id=E.product_id ❶
WITH (
    connector='kafka',
    topic='click_customer_product',
    properties.bootstrap.server='kafka:9092',
    type='upsert',
    primary_key='id'
);
```

❶ The product ID value was extracted from the click URL and placed into a separate column called product_id.

Since the change streams can be reduced, their results are small enough to fit in a state store in the stream processing platform.

It's advantageous to perform these transformations on the streams before loading them into the OLAP data store for serving. Consumer queries that are invoked on the OLAP should only contain analytical business logic and not any of the transformations implemented in the preprocessing.

Query logic that transforms events should be separate from queries that focus on business analytics. We will use this practice to separate transformation logic from analytical logic in queries using push and pull queries. We will talk more about materialized views and push versus pull queries in Chapter 4.

From now on, we will be focusing only on stream processors that support building materialized views. Materialized views in a stream processor can be treated like materialized views in a database. The primary difference between materialized views in a stream processor and those in a database is that in the stream processor, the data is sourced from streaming data, and the materialized views are updated continuously rather than periodically/manually.

In Figure 2-10, we can see what transformations have been done. These transformations were defined in SQL and executed in a stream processing platform. The materialized views for the product and customers are always running, producing the latest records from the Debezium change streams.

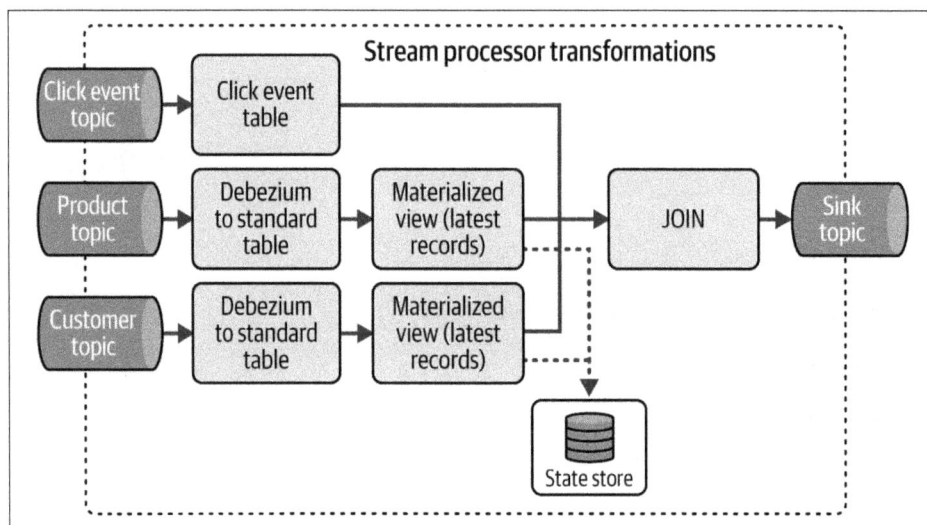

Figure 2-10. The transformations executed in the stream processor

Summary

In this chapter, we covered the common ways to transform data and how these transformations get executed in different data pipeline patterns: ETL and ELT. We indicated that to perform more complex transformations, the stream processor will need to be able to store state.

- Stream processing platforms need to support stateful stream processing to hold the state of complex, stateful transformations.

- ETL naturally fits streaming use cases by preprocessing data before it reaches the serving data store.

- ELT writes the events in the destination data store before transforming the data. Transformations are defined as SQL statements that need to be triggered to execute in the destination database, which forces batching semantics.
- ELT can support streaming by changing the target system to a stream processing platform.
- Materialized views are what make nontrivial, stateful transformations in stream processing platforms possible. Materialized views require a stream processing platform that can hold the state of a transformation.
- The stateful stream processing platform writes the result of the transformations into a sink topic.

In the next chapter, we will discuss different ways of serving the transformed data to consumers.

## CHAPTER 3

Serving Real-Time Data

In Chapter 2, we had the stream processing platform transform the data and place it into a sink topic. The preprocessed data is now residing in a topic in the streaming platform. In Figure 3-1, the sink topic and OLAP data store are highlighted in the analytical plane.

The next thing we need to do is to serve real-time data to the consumers. In this chapter, we'll talk about delivering enriched real-time data to the end user. This stage of the real-time data pipeline is the last mile streaming data takes before it's presented to the end user.

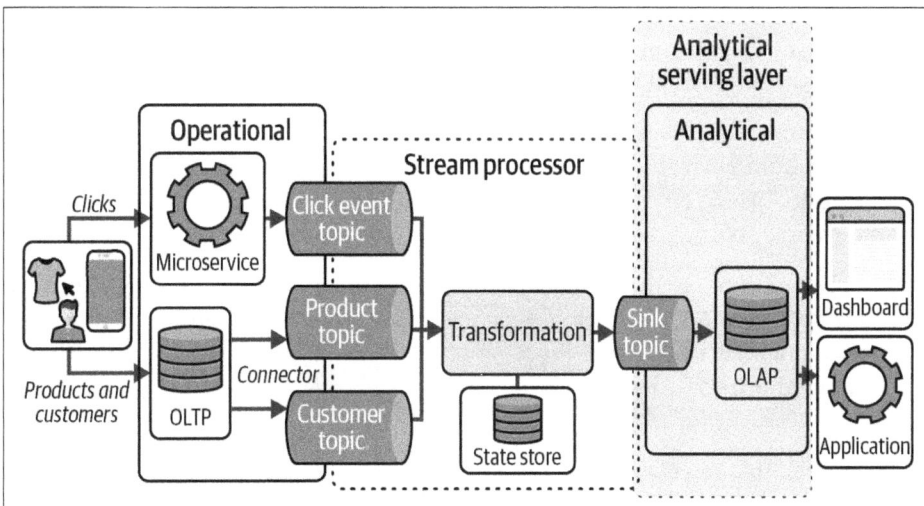

Figure 3-1. The preprocessed data is available in the sink topic for real-time analytical serving to user-facing dashboards or applications

Real-Time Expectations

To serve real-time analytics to the consumers we've identified (humans and applications), a set of service-level agreements (SLAs) should be considered. In our clickstream use case, we didn't specify requirements for the end user or application. However, since we want to serve analytics in real time, we should consider some metrics:

Latency
> Measures the time it takes for an analytics query or computation to complete and return results. In real-time analytics, low latency is crucial to provide near-instantaneous insights to users. SLA metrics may define acceptable latency thresholds, such as average response time or maximum response time, to ensure the timely delivery of analytics results.

Throughput and concurrency
> Measures the number of analytics queries or computations that can be processed within a given time frame. It indicates the system's capacity to handle concurrent requests and is especially important for high-volume scenarios. SLA metrics may specify a target throughput, such as queries per second or computations per minute, to ensure sufficient capacity for real-time analytics workloads.

Data freshness
> Indicates how up-to-date the analytics results are in relation to the underlying data streams. It measures the delay between when the data is generated and when it becomes available for analysis. SLA metrics may specify acceptable data freshness requirements, such as a maximum delay in seconds or minutes, to ensure that users have access to the most recent information.

Accuracy
> Measures the correctness and precision of the analytics results. SLA metrics may define acceptable error rates, confidence intervals, or validation criteria to ensure the accuracy of real-time analytics.

In serving real-time analytics to the consumers, the preceding metrics affect the real-time requirements the most. Other metrics are related to capacity sizing, data resilience, and security. We will focus more on them in later chapters of this book. These other SLA metrics include:

Availability
> Measures the percentage of time the real-time analytics system is operational and accessible to users. SLA metrics may define the desired uptime or downtime allowance for the system, taking into account planned maintenance windows and unexpected outages. High availability is critical for providing continuous access to real-time analytics capabilities.

Consistency

Metrics ensure that results are consistent across different query executions and system replicas.

Scalability

Measures the ability of the real-time analytics system to handle increasing data volumes, user requests, and computational complexity. SLA metrics may specify performance benchmarks or capacity thresholds, ensuring that the system can scale horizontally or vertically to meet growing demands.

Security and privacy

SLA metrics may include security and privacy requirements to ensure data protection, access controls, encryption, and compliance with regulations. This includes measures to prevent unauthorized access, safeguard sensitive information, and maintain data integrity.

We need to choose the most appropriate database for serving the data that meets the real-time-related SLAs: latency, concurrency, freshness, and accuracy.

Choosing an Analytical Data Store

Several types of data stores can satisfy the SLAs for real-time analytics, depending on the specific requirements and constraints of the use case. Again, our use case did not specify SLAs for real-time analytics, but clickstream use cases require very-low-latency queries to keep track of and react to changes in inventory, like dynamic replenishment, dynamic pricing, inventory redistribution and allocation, and predictive analytics, to name a few.

Here are some examples of data stores that can satisfy these strict real-time SLAs:

- In-memory databases, such as Redis, SingleStore (formerly MemSQL), Hazelcast, or Apache Ignite, store data in memory for fast access and processing. These databases offer extremely low latency and high throughput, making them suitable for real-time analytics that require near-instantaneous responses.

- RTOLAP data stores, such as Apache Pinot, Apache Druid, ClickHouse, StarRocks, and Apache Doris. These data stores tend to be column-oriented distributed data stores. They organize data by column rather than row, enabling efficient analytics and query processing. These databases can handle large volumes of data and offer excellent scalability and high availability, making them well-suited for real-time analytics at scale.

- Hybrid transactional/analytical processing (HTAP) data stores such as TiDB or SingleStore (formerly MemSQL) support both real-time transactional processing and analytics within a single system. These databases provide the capability to serve real-time analytics directly on operational data, minimizing data movement and reducing latency.

Serving data from a data warehouse, data lake, or lakehouse will not achieve the real-time SLAs needed for some of the inventory-related use cases stated earlier.

> It has been debated that the term "database" refers to OLTP databases. If you recall, OLTP databases are usually transactional and row-based and exist on the operational data plane that serves records to user-facing applications. Those who agree with this premise like to use the term "data store" for systems that serve analytical queries. We will adhere to these definitions and may interchange them throughout this book.

Some of these data stores previously stated are commonly deployed in the analytical data plane, which would coincide with OLAP-style data stores. Others would be deployed only in the operational data plane, like HTAP databases, which we will talk about more in depth in Chapter 7. In this chapter, we will use what has been traditionally used in real-time analytical use cases, which are RTOLAP data stores. What makes them real time is that they are able to source data from a topic in a streaming platform like Kafka.

Sourcing from a Topic

In Figure 3-1, you see that the real-time data for our use case was preprocessed and placed into a sink topic in a streaming platform like Kafka. Streaming platforms provide a publish and subscribe model for distributing streaming data, which means other systems, domains, and use cases can be consuming the same data from the sink topic. The preprocessing work done in the stream processing platform may have prepared the data only to the point where all consumers can use the data, in a data format that corresponds to a common denominator for them. This leaves any consumer-specific data preparation up to the consumer to implement. Figure 3-2 shows this scenario.

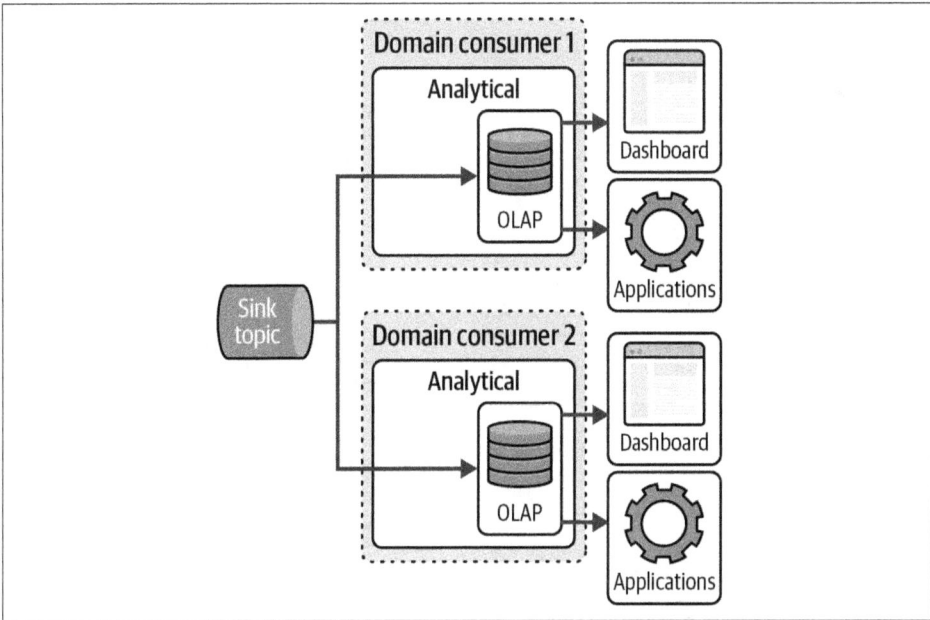

Figure 3-2. The sink topic can be consumed by multiple domain consumers requiring differing timestamp formats

Let's say, for example, *Domain consumer 1* needs the timestamps in the data to be seconds while *Domain consumer 2* needs the data to be in the YEAR-MONTH-DAY format. The engineer who implemented the transformation in the stream processing platform could decide to serve the timestamp in milliseconds so that both consumers can derive their preferred timestamp values. This would also satisfy any future consumer who needs the data in milliseconds.

These scenarios require queries to implement the transformation to get the timestamp value to their required format. Unfortunately, this transformation will slow the query down. It would also need to be executed for every run of the query and could eventually break the SLA for latency. This would eventually cause the application or dashboard to slow down and create an unsatisfactory experience for the data consumers. Any consumer-specific data preparation left for the consumer to implement will always affect the SLAs for serving real-time analytics.

This scenario is illustrated in Figure 3-3.

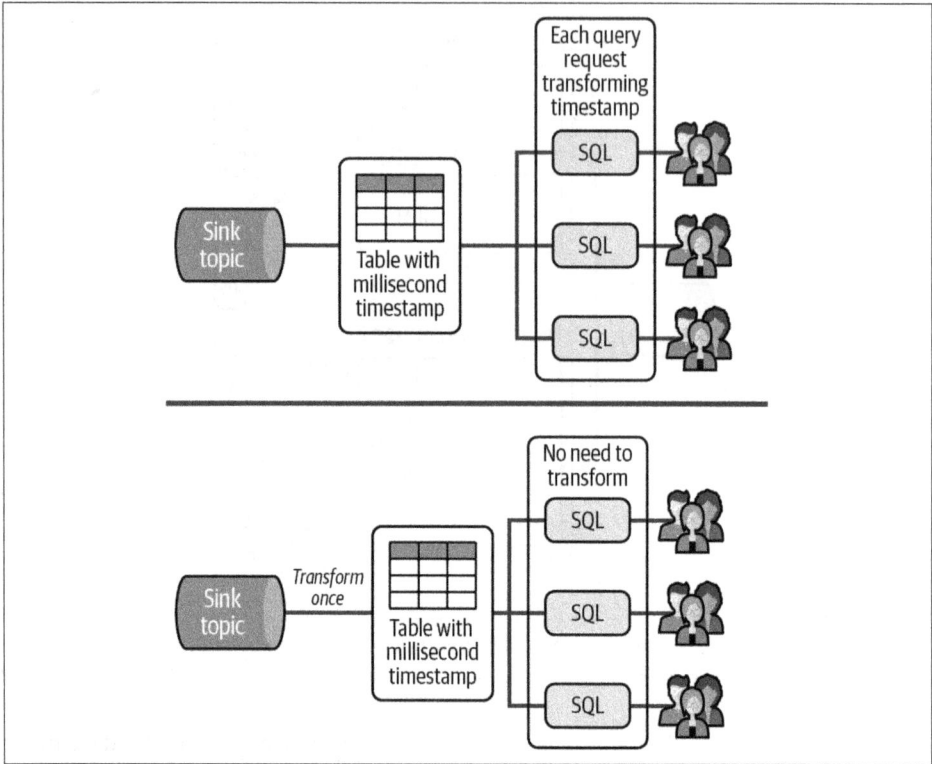

Figure 3-3. On the left, the timestamp transformation is done per query request, and on the right, the timestamp transformation is done only once

Ingestion Transformations

In many RTOLAPs, a feature exists where streaming data can be preprocessed before it reaches the persistent storage. It provides a way for RTOLAPs to transform the streaming data while data is still in flight. In the timestamp use case, the data consumed from the topic can travel through a set of stateless transformations, like converting milliseconds to a YEAR-MONTH-DAY format.

Ingestion transformations are akin to a stateless stream processor. This is important to keep in mind in subsequent chapters as we talk about materialized views. Consumers of the data in the topic are forced to treat said data as a base format from which to derive their preferred formats.

Most of these RTOLAP data stores can only perform stateless preprocessing of real-time data before it's stored, although some are already considering doing stateful transformations as part of the ingestion process.

Apache Pinot is an example of an RTOLAP data store that has the ability to perform stateful transformations at ingestion. Pinot has a comprehensive list of indexes that makes Pinot queries to perform at very low latency. One of the indexes is named *star-tree index*. The advantage of the star-tree index is its ability to preprocess aggregations, requiring to hold state. This, in effect, is a stateful transformation that occurs at ingestion. We will talk more about indexes and their importance later in this chapter.

In RTOLAP data stores, stateful ingestion transformation is becoming more common to get data from a base format into a preferred one. In future use cases, stateful ingestion transformations in RTOLAPs could join with other tables to provide a denormalized view in the RTOLAP. Denormalized views are a lot more performant when serving analytical queries because the join is performed only once prior to persisting the data. This is more optimal than the user submitting a join query, which would happen at every query request.

> A denormalized view, also called One Big Table (OBT), refers to a way of organizing data that combines and consolidates information from multiple tables into a single table or view. Typically, data is divided into multiple tables, each representing a specific entity or relationship to ensure data integrity and minimize redundancy and, ultimately, storage. However, in certain analytical scenarios, it can be more efficient to combine related data into a denormalized view. A denormalized consolidated view simplifies querying and analysis because all the necessary information is available in one place, eliminating the need for complex joins between tables. Denormalized views will introduce redundancy and potentially impact data integrity if not carefully managed.

Ingestion transformations and stream processing behave very much the same in that they are both asynchronous processes that run in the background. Asynchronous processes are not interactive with a user and, instead, are defined and run by the user but do not wait for the results to return. We'll return to asynchronous and synchronous processes later in this chapter.

Not only do ingestion transformations format the data, but they also optimize it for fast analytical queries. One such optimization is to use columnar (or column-based) formats, which many OLAPs like Pinot take advantage of. Columnar formats are typically not used in OLTP databases, which employ row-based formats. We'll cover this in more detail in this chapter.

OLTP Versus OLAP

It's illustrative to compare OLTP databases and OLAP data stores to understand how data can be served.

Recall that OLTP databases are used for transactional workloads on the operational plane. They serve records back to the user-facing application and are designed to efficiently handle and manage transactional operations in real time. They are primarily used to support day-to-day business activities that involve frequent data interactions, such as creating (inserting), retrieving, updating, and deleting data records. This is also known as CRUD: creation, retrieval, update, deletion.

The main purpose of an OLTP database is to ensure the integrity and consistency of data during transactional processing. It provides fast and reliable access to data for operational tasks like order processing, inventory management, financial transactions, and customer interactions. OLTP databases are optimized for handling a large number of concurrent transactions, often with multiple users accessing the system simultaneously.

These databases typically have normalized data structures, meaning they minimize data redundancy and maintain data consistency. They prioritize transactional capabilities, supporting ACID (atomicity, consistency, isolation, durability) properties to ensure reliable and secure data processing.

ACID

ACID is an acronym that defines a set of properties that ensure the reliability and consistency of data when performing transactions in an OLTP database:

Atomicity
> Imagine a transaction as a single, indivisible action. Atomicity means that a transaction is treated as a whole, and either all of its changes are applied successfully, or none of them are. It ensures that the database remains in a consistent state even if something goes wrong during the transaction.

Consistency
> Consistency ensures that a transaction brings the database from one valid state to another. It means that any rules, constraints, or relationships defined in the database are maintained during and after the transaction. In simpler terms, the database remains in a sensible and expected state, so when many clients are retrieving records from the database, they all have the same view of the database, and the records are all the same and, thus, consistent.

Isolation

Isolation means that multiple transactions can occur concurrently without interfering with each other. Each transaction is isolated from the others until it's completed, preventing conflicts and ensuring that each transaction sees a consistent view of the database.

Durability

Durability guarantees that once a transaction is successfully completed, its changes are permanently saved and will survive any subsequent system failures or crashes. The changes become a permanent part of the database, and the data is reliably stored for future use.

ACID compliance ensures that database transactions are reliable, consistent, isolated from each other, and durable, providing a strong foundation for data integrity and reliability.

Conversely, OLAP data stores are used for analytical workloads on the analytical plane. They employ different optimization techniques than OLTP databases. Each type of data store is optimized for the role they are supposed to play.

Row- Versus Column-Based Optimization

We introduced row-based versus column-based formats earlier in this chapter. These formats are two different ways of organizing and storing data in a database.

In a row-based format, data is stored and organized row by row. It means that all the columns of a particular row are stored together, and then the next row's data is stored, and so on. This format is similar to how data is traditionally represented in spreadsheets. It's optimized for transactional processing, where individual rows are frequently updated or inserted.

In a column-based format, data is stored and organized column by column. It means that all the values of a particular column are stored together, and then the next column's values are stored, and so on. This format is optimized for analytical processing, where queries often involve aggregations, filtering, and analysis of specific columns or subsets of data. See Table 3-1 for more differences.

When real-time streaming data reaches the serving layer, it's expected to have been prepared for fast analytical queries since the serving layer lives in the analytical plane. Columnar storage will provide the best query performance and efficiency for analytical queries.

Table 3-1. Row- versus column-based optimization differences

Properties	Row-based	Column-based
Data storage	In row-based format, each row is stored together. Row-based formats impact how the data is accessed and read during queries. Analytical queries are not recommended.	In column-based format, each column is stored together. Column-based formats provide better optimizations that support analytical queries.
Query performance	Row-based formats are generally better suited for transactional operations that involve retrieving entire rows or updating individual rows.	Column-based formats excel in analytical operations, as they allow for faster data retrieval and processing of specific columns or subsets of data.
Compression	Row-based formats offer some compression techniques like *null value compression, run-length encoding, dictionary compression,* and *data type–specific compression.* Compression techniques introduce additional computational overhead during data read and write operations and, therefore, the choice and configuration of compression algorithms need to be balanced based on the specific workload and performance requirements of the database system.	Column-based formats often offer better compression ratios than row-based formats. Since columns typically contain repetitive information, compression techniques can be applied more effectively, resulting in reduced storage requirements.
Query efficiency	Row-based formats may need to read entire rows, even if only a few columns are needed, which can lead to higher disk I/O and slower query performance.	Column-based formats are designed to read and process only the columns required for a particular query, minimizing disk I/O and improving query performance.

Queries Per Second and Concurrency

Queries per second (QPS) is the measure of how well an OLAP data store can return the results of a query. This in turn indicates the volume of queries the OLAP can process within a second and, ultimately, the number of concurrent queries that can be invoked.

In our clickstream use case, we did not specify how many end users may be viewing the analytics. The assumption is for every end user, there will be at least one query. We did indicate that this is a real-time use case. Hence the data freshness on the dashboard is expected to be real time. Real-time dashboards tend to require a high rate of refreshes to keep the charts in the dashboard as real time as possible. There is a query for every refresh of the dashboard.

For 1,000 users viewing clickstream analytics with a 5-second dashboard refresh rate, you will get the following formula:

$$1,000 \text{ users} \times \frac{1 \text{ query}}{5 \text{ second refresh}} = 200 \text{ QPS requirement}$$

This means the query needs to have a latency of 5 milliseconds. We can convert 200 queries/second to milliseconds/query by taking the inverse:

$$\frac{1}{200 \text{ queries/second}} = 5 \text{ ms/query}$$

You'll need to test a single query to see if the OLAP data store can return the result within 5 milliseconds. This is a hard requirement to meet for only 1,000 end users. If the dashboard is used by external users or on a phone application, you might exceed 1,000 end users. You probably also don't want to limit your business to only 1,000 users. You'll need to scale your OLAP cluster out to accommodate more users or simplify the query so that it can return in under 5 milliseconds. You can also apply better indexing strategies.

Indexing

Indexing plays a crucial role in improving QPS for OLAP databases. Applying indexes strategically will help improve QPS without scaling out the OLAP cluster, which requires more hardware and higher costs.

All RTOLAP data stores employ a set of indexes to help with QPS. They help in several ways. For instance, indexing allows the database to locate and retrieve relevant data more quickly. By creating indexes on frequently queried columns, the database can avoid scanning through the entire dataset and directly access the indexed values, significantly reducing query response time and, thus, improving QPS.

Indexes also provide valuable statistics and metadata that the query optimizer can use to determine the most efficient query execution plan. This aids in optimizing resource allocation, data retrieval strategies, and join operations, ultimately enhancing overall query performance and increasing QPS.

Pruning is a performance technique that allows the OLAP to prune away chunks of data where results don't exist. This approach narrows down the search space based on specific column values. This selective access eliminates the need to scan the entire dataset (or omit large subsets of data), allowing the database to handle a higher volume of queries within a given time frame, thereby also increasing QPS.

Indexes also provide a data structure that organizes the data in a way that reduces disk I/O operations during query processing. By reducing the number of disk reads required, indexing minimizes the time spent on accessing data, leading to improved QPS.

As a concrete example for indexes in an RTOLAP data store, Apache Pinot supports several types of indexes to optimize query performance. Table 3-2 shows some of the most commonly used indexes in Apache Pinot.

Table 3-2. Row- versus column-based optimization differences

Index	Description	Use
Bitmap index	Bitmap indexes are efficient for low-cardinality columns (columns with a small number of distinct values). They create a bitmap for each distinct value, indicating the presence or absence of the value in each row. Bitmap indexes are highly effective for filtering and aggregation operations.	Low-cardinality columns
Sorted index	Sorted indexes store the values of a column in a sorted order. They are particularly useful for range-based queries and enable efficient filtering and sorting operations.	Date, timestamps
Inverted index	Inverted indexes are suitable for high-cardinality columns (columns with a large number of distinct values). They map each unique value to the corresponding set of rows that contain that value. Inverted indexes are efficient for equality and prefix searches.	High-cardinality columns
Forward index	Forward indexes store the raw values of a column in the order they appear in the data. They are useful for queries that require fetching the raw values without any specific filtering or aggregation.	For columns not used for filtering or aggregations
Text index	Text indexes are designed for full-text search scenarios. They enable efficient searching based on keywords, phrases, or other textual criteria.	Text columns for efficient searching

These indexes can be used individually or in combination, depending on the nature of the data and the specific query patterns. Choosing the appropriate index for each column plays a crucial role in optimizing query performance in Apache Pinot.

It's important to note that while indexing can significantly enhance query performance and QPS, it's essential to strike a balance between the number and size of indexes, as excessive indexing can negatively impact insert, update, and delete operations. A proper indexing strategy and periodic index maintenance are crucial for optimal performance of OLAP databases.

As stated earlier in this chapter, the star-tree index can preprocess aggregations that require a holding state. It is, in effect, a stateful transformation that occurs at ingestion time.

Star-tree is an indexing technique used to sort and preaggregate data across multiple fields based on its cardinality. It's designed to speed up aggregation and computation-heavy queries on large datasets. The star-tree index operates like a tree structure, where each level corresponds to fields used to filter and aggregate data in your dataset (see Figure 3-4). The root of the tree represents the *star* (or wildcard), which aggregates metrics across these fields. Each path from the root to a leaf node represents a combination of field values and their corresponding aggregated metrics.

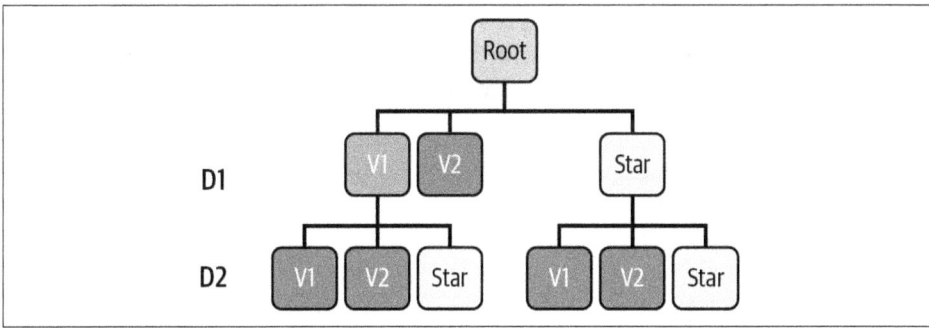

Figure 3-4. The preprocessed data is available in the sink topic for real-time analytical serving to user-facing dashboards or applications

Let's perform a simple example of how the star-tree index works:

- The query starts from the root node and walks down to the first dimension, or D1. The star-tree dimensions are ordered by cardinality top-down. In this case, D1 is a column with the highest cardinality.

- If the SQL predicate is where D1 = V2, the records are aggregated under V2 node on D1 dimension:

    Query path = Root → V2 scan

- If the SQL predicate is where D1 = V1, then the query goes to the star node in the second dimension under "V1" and returns the preaggregated value:

    Query path = Root → V1 → Star preaggregated

- If the SQL predicate is where D1 = V1 and D2 = V1, the query scans the V1 records under the D2 dimension:

    Query path = Root → V1 → V1 scan

- If the predicate is where D2 = V2, the query path goes to the star node on the D1 dimension because D1 isn't filtered. Then it drops to the V2 node and scans its records:

    Query path = Root → Star → V2 scan

- Lastly, for queries where there isn't a predicate:

    Query path = Root → Star → Star

Part of the star-tree configuration is providing a split threshold limiting the number of records to scan. If you provide a split threshold of 100,000, the star-tree index will ensure that your queries will never scan more than 100,000 records.

The star-tree index gets built after the segment has been created during the segment generation phase. A segment in Apache Pinot is a logical abstraction that represents a chunk of table data with some number of rows. The segment stores data for all columns of the table in a columnar fashion, along with dictionaries and indexes for these columns.

> Segments are similar to shards or partitions in relational databases and can also be seen as time-based partitions. They allow Pinot's distributed architecture to scale horizontally by breaking down large amounts of data into smaller, manageable chunks, which are then distributed across multiple nodes.

The star-tree aggregates data as it's being ingested so that incoming queries can take advantage of it. This optimization activity is akin to the preprocessing work done in a stream processing platform. Preprocessing built into OLAP data store is becoming more common because the work to optimize into columnar formats, index optimizations, and simple transformations like timestamp reformatting is very hard to avoid. OLAPs are *extremely dependent* on implementing stateful stream processing for real-time data.

By providing a way to define stateful ingestion transformations in the OLAP, users can author additional preprocessing logic that will execute once instead of at every invocation of an analytical query (see Figure 3-5).

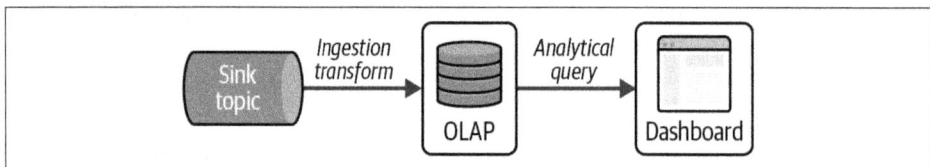

Figure 3-5. Users of the OLAP data store can define both the ingestion transform and the analytical query

Users can define a separate command for ingestion in either SQL or a set of functions during the ingestion phase so that the SQL in the analytical query stage is simplified, executes with lower latency, and ultimately increases the QPS of the OLAP data store. This technique will also decrease the need to scale the OLAP cluster since you've reduced the work the analytical queries have to perform.

Serving Analytical Results

As mentioned, QPS is a metric that indicates good performance for queries that are invoked by users or applications. Especially for real-time use cases, analytical queries will have a high refresh rate. High refresh rates can strain the OLAP system. This is also called *polling*.

Synchronous Queries

The type of analytical polling queries we've been describing is also called *pull queries* because the user or application (client) submits a query and pulls data from the OLAP system. It follows a request-response pattern.

The clients submit the queries through a driver and a dialect. The dialect provides a way for the client and OLAP to communicate using a variant of SQL specific to the OLAP system.

Asynchronous Queries

Analytical data can also be served in an asynchronous manner. This type of query is called a *push query* because the data is being pushed to the clients. The advantage of push queries is that QPS is no longer a needed measurement because it's strictly a pull query performance measurement. Clients of push queries get notified of new analytical data such that no polling is necessary.

Push queries are most likely served from topics in a streaming platform. Clients can subscribe to the topics and (re-)populate their real-time applications or dashboards when notified.

Services like Aklivity/Zilla provide asynchronous APIs that allow clients to subscribe to asynchronous analytical data using either Server-Sent Events (SSEs) or WebSockets. SSEs and WebSockets are technologies used for real-time communication between clients (usually web browsers) and servers. While they both enable real-time updates, there are key differences between them:

Unidirectional communication
SSEs allow the server to push data to the client browser, providing a one-way communication channel. The client receives updates or events from the server, but it cannot send data back using the same connection.

Event stream format
SSEs use a specific event stream format for delivering data to the client. The server sends data as a series of events, and the client processes these events using JavaScript. The event stream format includes event types, data, and optional fields like IDs or timestamps.

HTTP protocol
> SSEs are built on top of the HTTP protocol and use standard HTTP connections. This establishes a long-lived connection between the client and the server, typically using a single HTTP connection for multiple updates.

Browser compatibility
> SSEs are supported by most modern web browsers, but there might be limitations in older browsers or specific configurations. SSEs don't require additional browser plugins or libraries for basic functionality.

Bidirectional communication
> WebSockets support full duplex communication, allowing both the client and the server to send data to each other over a single connection. This enables real-time communication in both directions.

Arbitrary data format
> WebSockets have a flexible data format that supports arbitrary binary or text-based data transmission. They don't enforce a specific event stream format like SSE.

WebSocket protocol
> WebSockets use a specialized WebSocket protocol built on top of TCP. It provides a persistent, low-latency, and bidirectional communication channel.

Browser compatibility
> WebSockets are supported by most modern web browsers, but there might be limitations in older browsers or specific configurations. WebSocket functionality requires native WebSocket support or the use of WebSocket libraries or frameworks.

SSEs are suitable for scenarios where the server needs to push periodic updates or events to the client, such as real-time notifications, live updates, or streaming data feeds. WebSockets are well suited for applications that require bidirectional, interactive, and real-time communication, such as chat applications, multiplayer games, or collaborative editing tools.

The choice between SSEs and WebSockets depends on the specific requirements of the application. SSEs are simpler to implement and boast broader browser support, while WebSockets offer more advanced functionality and bidirectional communication capabilities.

Push Versus Pull Queries

Synchronous queries are similar to pull queries, and asynchronous queries correspond to push queries. It's important to understand this now because it will become more apparent in Chapter 4 when we talk about materialized views.

With push queries, the data is actively pushed to the client or application when changes occur in the database. This allows for real-time updates and immediate access to new information without the need for continuous polling or manual requests.

Since data is pushed as soon as it becomes available, push queries can provide lower latency than pull queries. There is no delay in waiting for the client to request the data; it's delivered proactively.

Push queries align well with event-driven architectures. They enable systems to react to events and trigger actions based on the received data, providing a more responsive and event-oriented approach.

Pull queries, on the other hand, provide more flexibility because they allow the client or application to retrieve data on demand whenever needed. The data is fetched when requested, which gives more control over the timing and frequency of data retrieval.

Pull queries help reduce unnecessary network traffic because the client only retrieves data when necessary. This can be beneficial in scenarios where network bandwidth is limited or when the data being retrieved is not frequently changing.

Pull queries can be more resource efficient because the server doesn't need to actively push data to all clients or applications. It eliminates the need for continuously monitoring and pushing data, which can reduce server load and resource consumption. On the other hand, frequent pull queries can lead to very high resource consumption since the data store may need to scour large amounts of data too often.

The choice between push queries and pull queries depends on the specific requirements and use case. Push queries are generally preferred when real-time updates and immediate data availability are critical, while pull queries provide more flexibility and efficiency in scenarios where data retrieval can be done on demand and not too frequently.

But what if we can take advantage of both push and pull queries? Using a combination of both pull and push queries could play out as follows:

1. The client submits the query as a pull query to fetch the current state of the table in the OLAP system.
2. The client then subscribes to the changes in the table, that is, only updating records that have changed.

Just like a WAL in an OLTP database, the client can first invoke a pull query to get a snapshot of the data and then subscribe to the table's WAL to get incremental changes. This idea is depicted in Figure 3-6 and will be important in Chapter 5 when we start talking about streaming databases.

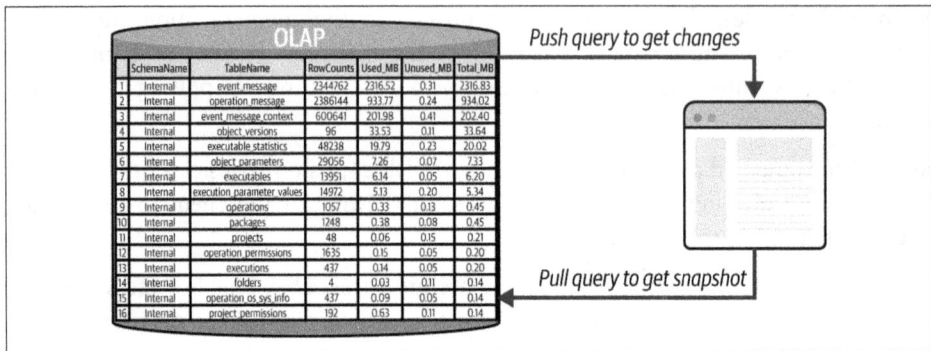

Figure 3-6. A pull query is invoked by the dashboard and automatically subscribes to changes to the view

Unfortunately, OLAP data stores don't support asynchronous push queries. OLAP data stores typically are dead ends in the sense that it's hard to extract raw values from them. They are optimized for serving analytical results, which are aggregations or summaries of the data.

Summary

In this chapter, we introduced OLAP data stores and compared them to OLTP databases. We also covered many of the optimization techniques for OLAP data stores, which are used to serve analytical queries with low latency. Two of the most important concepts to take away are:

- The importance of stateful ingestion transformations and how they prepare data for optimized analytical queries.
- Push and pull queries and the different ways in which they serve analytical data.

In Chapter 4, these concepts will be important to understand as we go into the concept of materialized views in detail.

Materialized Views

In the previous chapters, we only talked briefly about materialized views. Materialized views will be the most important concept to understand before you can begin to appreciate streaming databases. Materialized views in databases were first introduced in the early 1990s. They were initially developed as a feature in some OLTP databases to improve query performance by precomputing and storing the results of complex queries. Materialized views provide a way to store the results of a query as a physical table, which can be refreshed periodically or on demand to keep the data up-to-date. This approach helps to reduce the overhead of executing expensive queries repeatedly by allowing users to retrieve data from the materialized view instead.

In stream processing, materialized views are not only updated periodically or on demand. They're always refreshed asynchronously in the background. As new data comes in, the materialized view gets updated immediately and the results are stored. We've highlighted this pattern in previous chapters. The asynchronous refresh closely corresponds to streaming, and synchronous refresh to batch.

Martin Kleppmann's video titled "Turning the Database Inside-Out" describes materialized views as not only being preprocessed data but also directly built from writes to the transaction log. Materialized views have had a significant impact on stream processing by introducing the concept of precomputed and continuously, incrementally updated query results. Materialized views address some of the challenges in stream processing and provide benefits such as improved query performance, reduced data duplication, and simplified analytics.

Views, Materialized Views, and Incremental Updates

With materialized views, the processing logic for generating certain query results is separated from the mainstream processing pipeline. This separation can lead to more modular and manageable code, making it easier to maintain and extend the stream processing system.

To understand materialized views, we first need to understand *traditional views*. Both traditional views and materialized views live in a database. Traditional views (or just "views") are defined by a SQL statement that gets executed when the client selects from the view. The results of a view don't get stored. This increases the latency for queries that select from the view because the results are not preprocessed. To better understand this, let's again use an analogy: you have a smart chipmunk named Simon (see Figure 4-1).

Figure 4-1. Chipmunk counting nuts, illustrating a traditional view

You ask Simon, "How many nuts are currently in my yard?" Simon runs out into your yard and counts the nuts, then comes back and tells you the number. When you ask Simon again what the count of the nuts in your yard is, he again runs out a second time to count all of the nuts and gives you a number. Both times, you had to wait for Simon to count the nuts before you received the number even if it did not change. This is akin to a traditional view and is represented mathematically in Figure 4-2.

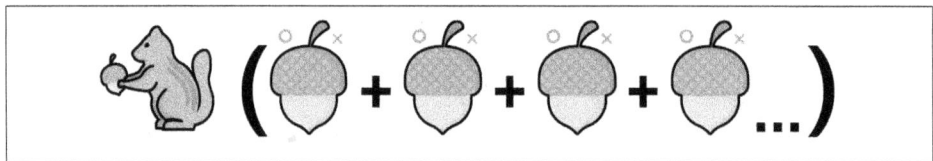

Figure 4-2. The smart chipmunk can be represented as a function that aggregates the nuts in the yard and returns the count

You decide this isn't efficient. Instead, you instruct Simon to write the total number of nuts on paper and store it in a box. You then ask Simon how many nuts there are, but he can't answer because he's too busy looking for changes in the number of nuts in the yard. So you employ another chipmunk that isn't as smart as Simon to just tell you the number in the box. Let's name him Alvin. This analogy is akin to a materialized view.

In this analogy, the chipmunks are SQL statements. The box in the second scenario is the storage that materializes views to save the results that have been precounted. In this same scenario, Simon (precounting the nuts) is smarter than Alvin presenting the value in the box (see Figure 4-3). Alvin presenting the value does so with low latency and can serve it to many clients concurrently without great effort.

Figure 4-3. Two chipmunks are used to describe a materialized view

An important part of the materialized view analogy is that Simon isn't counting the nuts from the first to the last nut; he's looking for incremental changes in the number of nuts. This includes how many were removed from the yard and how many were added (or fell from the trees).

Incremental changes refer to the process of making small, targeted changes to existing data rather than recomputing the entire dataset from scratch. These updates are typically applied to keep data consistent and up-to-date over time without incurring the computational overhead of reprocessing the entire dataset.

The incremental function is represented mathematically in Figure 4-4. X represents the current state of the nuts in the yard, and Δ^* represents the incremental change to the nuts in the yard. X is already stored while the smart chipmunk captures ΔX and then adds to it the current state, X, to get to the next state.

To capture incremental changes, Simon always needs to be watching for new changes asynchronously—similar to what we have in a streaming setting.

Figure 4-4. The smart chipmunk adds incremental changes to the total nuts in the yard

Recall CDC (change data capture) from Chapter 1. CDC is a prime example of incremental changes. To review, CDC is a technique used to capture and track changes made to a database or data source over time by reading the WAL in an OLTP database. Instead of processing the entire dataset from scratch, CDC identifies and captures only the incremental changes: inserts, updates, and deletes.

Change Data Capture

There is a relationship between CDC and materialized views. Materialized views do the hard work of precomputing by watching for incremental changes and storing the results. Beforehand, CDC provides the incremental changes it captures from the WAL in an OLTP database. This means we can use a materialized view to preprocess the CDC containing incremental changes.

Going back to our chipmunk analogy, we had Simon provide a count of nuts in a yard. Let's extend this example a bit to say there are many types of nuts in the yard. Each nut has these attributes:

- Color
- Location (latitude, longitude)

Nuts can change color as they age and may be moved or removed by other animals. Simon keeps track of these changes by inserting, updating, or deleting each nut on the list of nuts on the paper in the box. So when a client queries the list, the client only sees the latest status of each nut in the yard.

We illustrate this scenario technically in Figure 4-5. Here are some important points in the diagram:

- The WAL in the primary/OLTP database on the far left is replicated to create a replica of the primary database.
- Using a CDC connector, the WAL is also written into a topic in a streaming platform. The topic publishes the WAL of the primary database for other systems to subscribe to.

- Sink connectors can consume from the topic and build replicas in other database systems.
- Stream processors can build the same database replica in their cache.

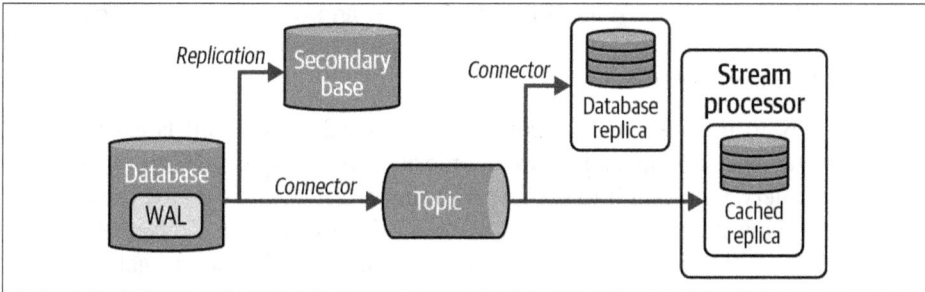

Figure 4-5. Replication using incremental changes

With this technique, you can build a replica of the original OLTP database from a user-facing application in any downstream data store or stream processing engine. We will focus on the stream processing engine primarily because it satisfies the real-time use case and doesn't force batch semantics.

In Chapter 3, we introduced push and pull queries. If we apply the chipmunk analogy, Simon is the push query and Alvin is the pull query.

> When we speak of smart (Simon) and simpler (Alvin) chipmunks, we're talking about the complexity of the SQL statement. Simon can do complex transformations and aggregations, while Alvin performs simple SQL lookup queries with low complexity.

Push Versus Pull Queries

Let's expand on the chipmunk analogy. By leveraging the push query (aka Simon), we can query the result from Alvin without having to incur the latency we get when we compute the result synchronously.

We return to the original use case, where Simon is counting the number of nuts in the yard. To review, Simon works asynchronously, watching for changes in the nut count and storing any updates in the box. In a sense, Simon pushes the result into the box. Alvin serves the contents of the box to the client synchronously. Similarly, at query time, Alvin pulls the result from the box and serves it to the client. To summarize:

- Simon is a push query that runs asynchronously.
- Alvin is a pull query that runs synchronously.

Simon does most of the work calculating the result so that Alvin can focus on serving results with low latency as soon as he is queried. This works very nicely, but there's one drawback: the client invoking the pull query doesn't have much flexibility in asking more compelling questions. It only has the count of nuts to work with for building real-time insights. What if the client wants an average count, the maximum count, or to join multiple tables? In this case, the push query negates the ability of the client to ask deeper questions.

In Figure 4-6, to increase query flexibility, you'll need to trade off latency because you're forcing the serving engine to do more work. If a user-facing application invokes the query, you want it to execute with the lowest latency because the assumption is that many more end users will be using the application. Conversely, if you want the highest flexibility so that you can slice and dice the data to gain insights, then you should expect only a few expert end users to execute these queries.

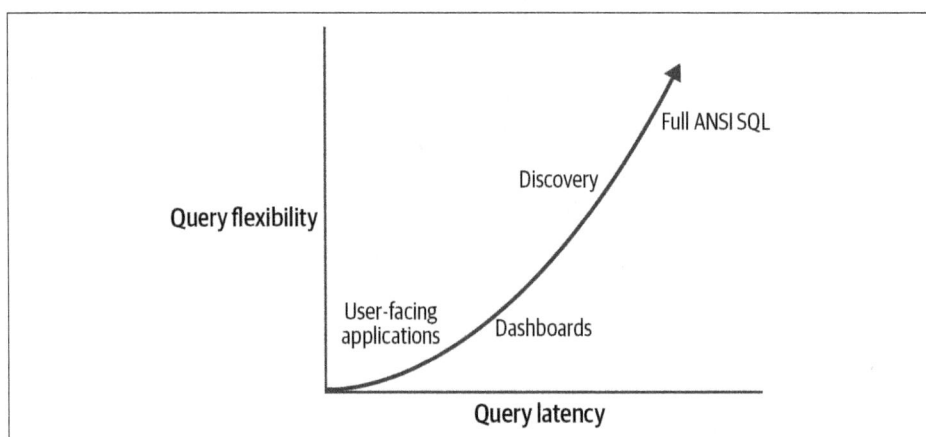

Figure 4-6. A diagram showing pull queries trade-off when adding flexibility and the corresponding use cases

If you think about it, applications that require the lowest latencies would benefit the most from using push queries instead of pull queries. Figure 4-7 shows how you can balance between push and pull queries.

The box in the middle represents the materialized view. It balances the heavy lifting of push queries with the flexibility of the pull query. How you balance push and pull queries is up to your use case. If the box moves down along the line, the materialized view provides less flexible queries but is more performant. Conversely, as the box moves up, the more flexible the pull queries become, but the queries execute at higher latencies. Together, push and pull queries work to find the right balance between latency and flexibility (see Figure 4-8).

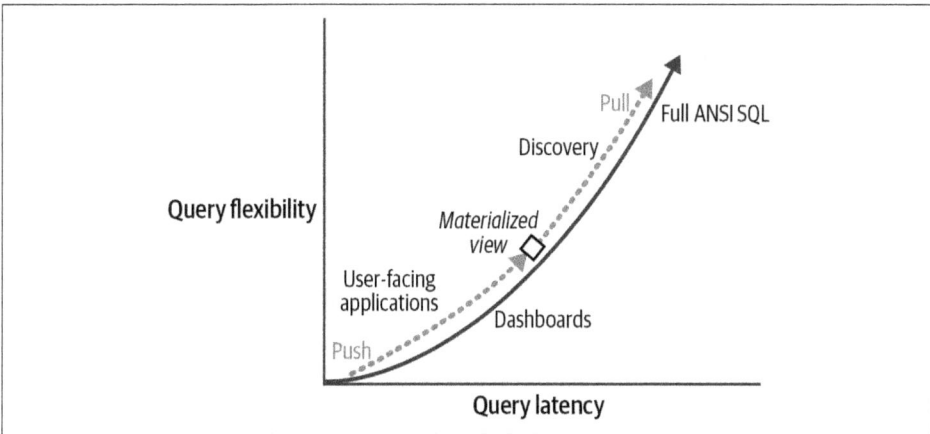

Figure 4-7. As query latency nears zero, push queries are preferred

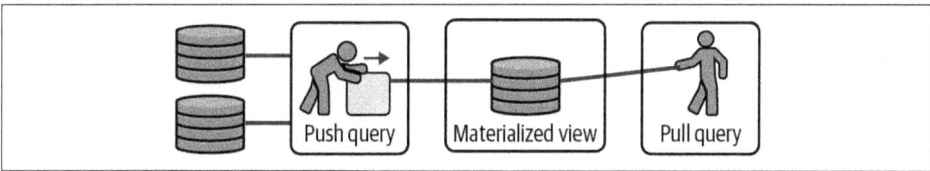

Figure 4-8. Pull and push queries working together to balance latency and flexibility

But is there a way for us to have both high flexibility and low latency and without needing two SQL queries? We can do this by using materialized views that emit changes to a WAL. This would be the client experience:

1. The client submits a push query. This query creates a materialized view.

2. The client then subscribes to the changes in the materialized view just like subscribing to a WAL.

With this approach, the client is submitting a push query instead of a pull query. By allowing the client to also make changes to the push query, you get the flexibility needed for ad hoc queries. Also, by subscribing to the materialized view's changes, query latency is no longer an issue because the incremental changes are being pushed to the client as they arrive. This means that the client no longer needs to invoke a pull query and wait for its result, bringing down latency. Only one SQL query is needed for the client to start receiving real-time analytical data.

This pattern is difficult today because push and pull queries are typically executed in separate systems. The push query is usually executed in the stream processor, while the pull query is executed in the OLAP system that serves to end users. Moreover, push and pull queries are typically authored by different teams of engineers. Streaming data engineers would write the push query, while analysts or the developers of user-facing applications invoke pull queries.

To get out of this dilemma, you'll need a system that has:

- Stream processing capabilities like building materialized views
- The ability to expose the materialized views to topics in a streaming platform, akin to a WAL
- The ability to store data in an optimal way to serve data
- The ability to provide synchronous and asynchronous serving methods

These features are only available in streaming databases. They have the ability to marry stream processing platforms and databases together, using the same SQL engine for both data in motion and data at rest. We'll talk about this in greater detail in Chapter 5.

The most common solution for real-time analytics is running a stream processing platform like Apache Flink and a RTOLAP data store like Apache Pinot (see Figure 4-9).

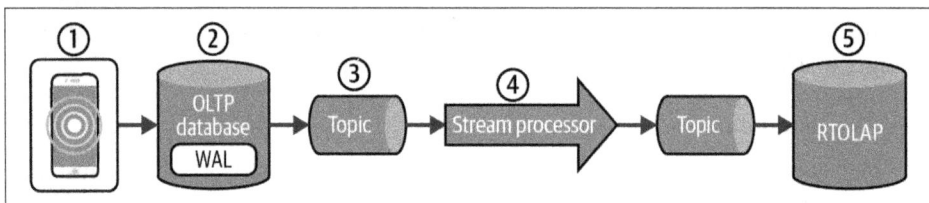

Figure 4-9. Common solution for real-time analytics

Figure 4-9 shows the path by which data in an OLTP database travels to an RTOLAP system for serving to a client. Let's look closer at this architecture:

1. The entities are represented as tables in the OLTP database following domain-driven design.

2. The application inserts, updates, or deletes records in the table. These changes are recorded in the database WAL.

3. A CDC connector reads the WAL and writes the changes to a topic in a streaming platform. The streaming platform externalizes the OLTP WAL by publishing the changes into topics/partitions that mimic the WAL construct. These can

be read by consumers to build replicas of the tables from the original OLTP database.

4. The stream processor is one such system that reads the topic and builds internal replicas of tables by using materialized views. As the materialized view gets updated asynchronously, it outputs its changes into another topic.

5. The RTOLAP data store reads the topic that contains the output of the materialized view and optimizes the data for analytical queries.

In Figure 4-9, the stream processor executes the push query at step 4 and the pull query gets invoked at step 5. Again, each query gets executed in separate systems and authored by different engineers.

Figure 4-10 drills down to show more of the complexity and division between the push and pull queries. The push query performs the arduous task of complex transformations and stores the result in a materialized view. The materialized view records its changes to its local store to a topic in a streaming platform that exposes the materialized view to the serving layer that holds the RTOLAP system.

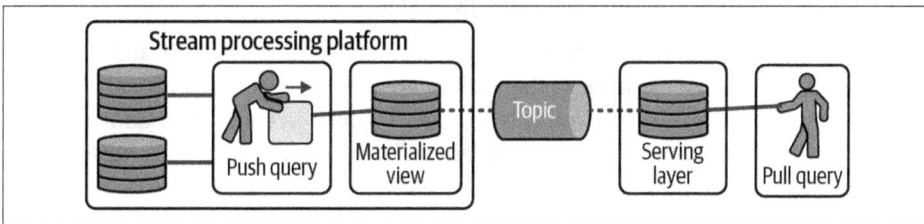

Figure 4-10. A pull query pulling the result from two persisted tables through a view

As a result, the end user that interfaces with the RTOLAP system doesn't have the flexibility to define the preprocessing logic needed to make the pull query run at low latency (see Figure 4-11).

Figure 4-11. End user trying to get a data engineer to optimize a query

Having the end user that authors the pull query also provide optimization logic to the streaming data would help avoid these scenarios. Unfortunately, these situations occur very often because of the current state of streaming architectures.

The problem is exacerbated when we try to directly replicate CDC data into an RTOLAP system.

CDC and Upsert

The term *upsert* is a portmanteau of the words *update* and *insert* to describe the logic an application employs when inserting and/or updating a database table.[1] Upsert describes a logic that involves an application checking to see if a record exists in a database table. If the record exists by searching for its primary key, the record then invokes an update statement. Otherwise, if the record does not exist, the application invokes an insert statement to add the record to the table.

We learned that CDC data contains incremental changes like inserts, updates, and deletes. The upsert logic handles two out of the three types of changes in a CDC stream (we'll come back to the delete change later).[2]

Upsert operations can indirectly improve select query performance and accuracy in certain scenarios. While upserts themselves are primarily focused on data modification, they can have positive impacts on select query performance and accuracy by maintaining data integrity and optimizing data storage. Here's how upserts can contribute to these improvements:

Data integrity and accuracy
> Upserts help maintain data integrity by preventing duplicate records and ensuring the data is accurate and consistent. When select queries retrieve data from a database with proper upsert operations, they are more likely to return accurate and reliable information.

Simplified pull queries
> Selecting from a table with proper upsert operations simplifies the queries upon lookup. Having to perform deduplication or filtering for the latest records complicates the SQL and adds latency to its execution.

Upsert operations behave like a push query to help optimize and simplify the pull query. It is one of the factors to control the balance between push and pull queries. Let's walk through a CDC scenario to help better understand this in Figure 4-12.

---

1 A portmanteau is a word that results from blending two or more words, or parts of words, such that the portmanteau word expresses some combination of the meaning of its parts.

2 In many database systems the UPDATE operation consists of a DELETE and INSERT step; hence in these systems, UPSERT also involves a DELETE operation.

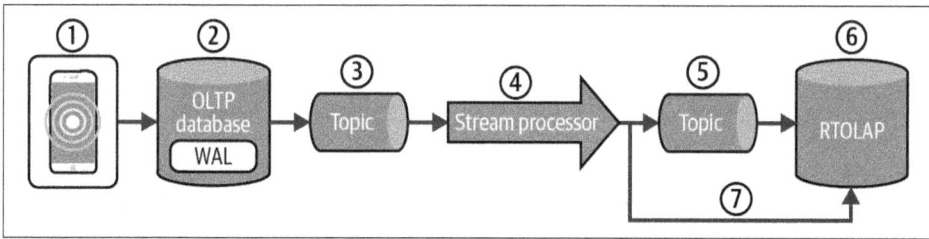

Figure 4-12. Steps outlining the replication to an RTOLAP data store

1. A transaction is sent from an application to either insert, update, or delete a record in a table in an OLTP database. Let's assume the use case is updating the inventory of green T-shirts, so the table in question is the Products table.

2. The update is written into the WAL of the OLTP database.

3. Let's assume that the connector reading the WAL was just started. This would require the connector to take a current snapshot of the Products table to get the current status.

   a. If the connector doesn't have this snapshot, the downstream systems cannot build an exact mirrored replica of the Products table.

   b. By taking a snapshot of the table, the connector creates seed events that are logically equivalent to an insert for every record in the Products table.

   c. Once this snapshot is available in the topic, we can build a table replica. You cannot build replicas with only incremental changes.

4. When the stream processor starts up, if it's the first time consuming the topic, it reads it from the beginning. Otherwise, it starts reading from a stored offset. Reading the topic from the beginning allows the stream processor to build a replica of the Products table. Again, you cannot build a table replica with only incremental changes.

   a. Complex transformations are implemented in the stream processor. They will require the stream processor to build a materialized view that represents a replica of the Products table.

   b. Transformation operations are done on or between tabular constructs like materialized views. If no transformation is needed, creating a materialized view is not necessary, and the stream can pass through directly from the input topic to the output topic.

5. The output topic is similar to the input topic in that it holds a snapshot of the data to seed any downstream replicas. However, it has undergone transformations executed within the stream processor. For CDC data, the contents of the topics in this pipeline need to be able to seed downstream replicas.

6. If the RTOLAP data store reads from the topic directly, it will need to handle the upsert logic itself. To do so, it will also need to understand the data in the topic to identify insert, update, and delete operations so that it can subsequently apply them to the existing internal table.

7. This step is an alternative to step 6. In this case, the stream processor sends the data directly to the RTOLAP data store. For RTOLAPs that do not support upsert, the stream processor will have to execute the upsert logic instead of the RTOLAP system.

Since upsert operations, by definition, only support inserts and updates, deletes tend to be omitted. Some systems will implement upsert to also include delete logic. Others, like Apache Pinot, will only flag a deleted record so that its previous versions can be recovered. In these cases, it's important to use the RTOLAP implementation of upsert, which requires the RTOLAP to read directly from the output topic. Some RTOLAPs may not expose the delete feature, and the work would have to be done in the stream processor.

> Step 3 talks about holding the snapshot of the Product table in the topic. In Chapter 1, we talked about topics having a retention period after which older records are truncated. A different type of topic is necessary for CDC data called a *compacted topic*, where the truncation process preserves the latest record of each primary key. This allows older data to be preserved, enabling materialization of downstream table replicas, including the historical records.

In summary, there are two locations where the upsert logic can be implemented—in the RTOLAP system or the stream processor. The simpler and preferred approach is to have the RTOLAP read from the output topic and apply the upsert logic itself. The output topic also provides a buffer in cases where the stream processor produces data faster than the RTOLAP can consume.

Upsert highlights the pain of having two real-time systems *grapple over* or *dodge ownership of* such complex logic. These pains will create further contention between data engineers and analytical end users.

CDC can be hard to conceptualize in streaming because it takes part in so many constructs and complex logic. For example, it's related to WALs in an OLTP database, it requires compacted topics in streaming platforms to keep history, it needs upsert to simplify and speed up pull queries, and it needs to be materialized in views. The difficulties go on when multiple systems are involved between the original OLTP source and the RTOLAP data store just to build a replica of the Products table. As we noted, there can be ways to consolidate these systems and help reduce redundancy and complexity. Streaming databases are one way to achieve this consolidation.

Transformations that include enrichment will require joining multiple streams in the stream processor. Recall the two types of streams: change streams and append-only streams. Change streams contain change data for entities in the business domain, like products and customers. Append-only streams contain events like the clickstream data from the application. Let's walk through the streaming data pipeline again to see how to implement this.

Joining Streams

As previously stated, transformation operations are done on or between tabular constructs that hold change streams (materialized views) and append-only streams. Append-only streams are like change streams where the only changes allowed are inserts. In fact, you could consider all tabular constructs in databases to be sequences of changes going into and out of the tabular structure.

One of the main reasons you would not represent an append-only stream in a materialized view is that materialized views have to store results. Since append-only streams are inserts only and ever-growing, you would run out of storage space at some point, just like you would not write click events into a database because it too would run out of storage.

Since both change streams and append-only streams are represented as tabular constructs, many different streaming systems name these constructs differently. In this book, we will use the following terms with regard to tables in a stream processor:

Append tables
   A tabular construct that holds append-only streams. These constructs are not backed by a state store. These constructs represent data that passes through the stream processor.

Change tables
   A tabular construct that represents a materialized view. Change tables are backed by a state store.

We also need to differentiate topics in a streaming platform in the same way. Knowing the type of streaming data in the topics will indicate how they can be processed or represented in a tabular construct. We use these terms to identify topics in a streaming platform:

Append topics
   Topics containing append-only data.

Change topics
   Topics containing change events or CDC events. Some Kafka engineers would also call these "table topics."

With these terms, we can better describe how streams are joined together, as the logic can get confusing. It's important to use SQL as the language to define joins and transformations because SQL is the universal language for manipulating data, and the SQL engine needs to combine streams and databases. Sharing a SQL engine to manipulate both data in motion and data at rest leads up to having a streaming database.

Apache Calcite

Let's start with joining the append table and the change table we described in Chapter 2. The SQL in Example 4-1 is based on Apache Calcite, a data management framework used to build databases using relational algebra. Relational algebra is a formal and mathematical way of describing operations that can be performed on relational databases. It's a set of rules and symbols that help us manipulate and query data stored in tables, also known as relations.

Apache Calcite contains many of the pieces that make up mathematical operations but omits some key functions: storage of data, algorithms for processing data, and a repository for storing metadata. If you want to build a database from scratch, Apache Calcite is one building block to do that. In fact, many of the existing real-time systems use Calcite: Apache Flink, Apache Pinot, Apache Kylin, Apache Druid, Apache Beam, and Apache Hive, to name a few.

> Calcite intentionally stays out of the business of storing and processing data. ...[T]his makes it an excellent choice for mediating between applications and one or more data storage locations and data processing engines. It is also a perfect foundation for building a database: just add data.
>
> —Apache Calcite documentation

This is what we'll do here—just add data. We bring back our clickstream use case where we have three sources of data, each in its own topic in a streaming platform.

Example 4-1. Joining to table topics

```
CREATE SINK clickstream_enriched AS
SELECT
  E.*,
  C.*,
  P.*
FROM CLICK_EVENTS E ❶
JOIN CUSTOMERS C ON C.ip=E.ip and ❷
JOIN PRODUCTS P ON P.product_id=E.product_id ❸
WITH (
    connector='kafka',
    topic='click_customer_product',
    properties.bootstrap.server='kafka:9092',
    type='upsert',
```

```
    primary_key='id'
);
```

❶ CLICK_EVENTS is an append table sourced from an append topic. It contains click events from a user-facing application.

❷ CUSTOMERS is a change table sourced from a change topic. It contains change events from an OLTP database captured using a CDC connector.

❸ PRODUCTS is a change table sourced from a change topic. It also contains change events from an OLTP database via CDC connector. Here, we will assume the product ID value was extracted from the click URL and placed into a separate column called product_id.

As long as SQL is supported, stream processing platforms can represent data in topics in tabular structures, so SQL and tools like Calcite can be used to define complex transformations. Example 4-1 is an inner-join that joins together matching records that exist in all three tables—CLICK_EVENTS, CUSTOMERS, and PRODUCTS.

The output of any streaming SQL that aggregates or joins streams is a materialized view. In this case, we are joining:

CLICK_EVENTS
    An append table containing click events

CUSTOMERS
    A change table/materialized view of all customers

PRODUCTS
    Another change table/materialized view of products

Here are the properties of different types of table joins:

Append table to append table
    This is always windowed, or else the state store will run out of space.

Change table to change table
    A window is not required because the join result could fit in the state store if it's appropriately sized.

Change table to append table
    This is also windowed, or else the state store will run out of space.[3]

---

3 In Kafka Streams and ksqlDB, you can use materialized views (KTable or GlobalKTable) for the append table. In this case, a window is not required because the output is again a stream.

Notice that whenever an append-only stream is part of a join, a window is needed to limit the data held in the state store.

In stream processing with SQL, when you perform a left join operation between streams corresponding to an append table and a change table, the result is driven by the append table.

In SQL, such a join looks as follows:

```
SELECT ...
FROM append_table_stream
LEFT JOIN change_table_stream ON join_condition;
```

Here, `append_table_stream` and `change_table_stream` represent the two input streams you want to join, and `join_condition` specifies the condition that determines how the two streams are matched.

The left stream (`append_table_stream`), which is specified first in the FROM clause, drives the result of the join. The result will contain all the events from the left stream, and for each event in the left stream, it will include the matching events from the right stream (`change_table_stream`) based on the `join_condition`.

Let's illustrate this with two streams from our clickstream example: *clicks* and *customers*. Each event in the *click* stream represents a click with a customer ID and each event in the *customers* stream represents a customer with a customer ID. To join the two streams on the customer ID, you would write the SQL query as follows:

```
SELECT k.product_id, c.customer_name
FROM click k
LEFT JOIN customers c ON k.customer_id = c.customer_id;
```

In this example, the `click` stream is the left stream, and it drives the result of the join. For each customer event in the `click` stream, the query retrieves the corresponding customer name from the `customers` stream based on the matching customer ID.

It's important to note that in stream processing, the join is continuous and dynamic. As new events arrive in the input streams, the join result is continuously updated and emitted as the result stream. This allows you to perform real-time processing and analysis on streaming data with SQL.

Clickstream Use Case

Let's step back to be able to clearly understand the full diagram in Figure 4-13 step by step.

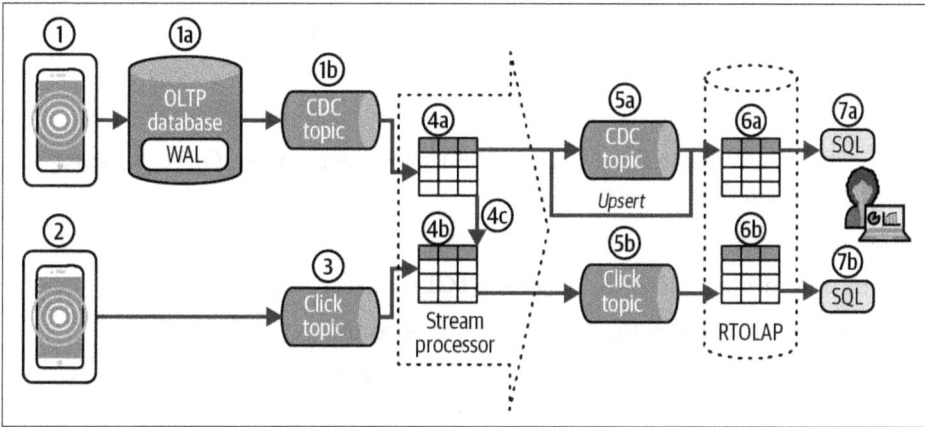

Figure 4-13. Path of CDC and append-only events from the application to the RTOLAP

1. A customer updates their information.

   a. The information is saved in an OLTP database.

   b. A CDC process runs on the OLTP database, capturing changes to the CUSTOM ERS table and writing them into a CDC topic. This topic is a compacted topic that can be considered a replica of the CUSTOMERS table. This will allow for other systems to build their replicas of the CUSTOMERS table.

2. The same customer clicks on a product on an e-commerce application.

3. The click event is written into a topic. We don't write click events into an OLTP database because click events are only inserts. Capturing them in an OLTP database might eventually cause the database to run out of storage.

4. The stream processor reads from the CDC and click topics.

   a. These are the messages from the CUSTOMERS change table topic in the stream processor. They are stored in a state store whose size depends on the window size (or, in the case of, for example, Kafka Streams or ksqlDB, fully stored in a KTable).

   b. These are the messages from the CLICK_EVENTS append table topic in the stream processor.

   c. A left-join is executed between the CLICK_EVENTS append table messages and the CUSTOMERS change table messages. The result of the join is CLICK_EVENTS enriched with their corresponding CUSTOMER information (if it exists).

5. The stream processor writes its output to the topics below.

   a. This is a change topic and contains the CDC CUSTOMER changes. This would be a redundant topic since the topic in 1b contains the same data. We keep it here to keep the diagram balanced.

   b. This is an append topic that contains the original CLICK_EVENT data enriched with the CUSTOMER data.

6. Topics are pulled into the RTOLAP data store for real-time serving.

   a. This is a replica of the original CUSTOMERS table in the OLTP database and built from the change topic.

   b. This contains the enriched CLICK_EVENTS data.

7. The user invokes queries against the RTOLAP data store.

   a. The user can query the CUSTOMERS table directly.

   b. The user can query the enriched CLICK_EVENTS data without having to join the data themselves, as the join has already been done in the stream processor.

As we indicated earlier, you can either implement the join in the stream processor or by the user. In this case, we decided to prejoin the CLICK_EVENTS and CUSTOMER data to improve query performance from the user's perspective. The hard work of joining is done by the stream processor so that the RTOLAP can focus on fast, low-latency queries. In this scenario, the stream processor is creating a materialized view that gets written to the topic in 5b. The RTOLAP builds a replica of the materialized view in itself from the topic in 5b. Within the RTOLAP database, we might have to implement a retention scheme that deletes older enriched CLICK_EVENTS to avoid running out of storage.

Alternatively, we could have just bypassed the stream processor and let the RTOLAP perform the joining when the user invokes the query. This would not require building a materialized view, and it would negate the need to manage another complex streaming system. But this query would be slow and put a lot of stress on the RTOLAP system.

So how can we reduce architectural complexity but still get the performance of materialized views? This is where we can converge stream processing with real-time databases—by using streaming databases.

Summary

I'm gonna make a very bold claim [that] all the databases you've seen so far are streaming databases.

—Mihai Budiu, "Building a Streaming Incremental View Maintenance Engine with Calcite," March 2023

Traditionally, stream processing and databases have been seen as distinct entities, with stream processing systems handling real-time, continuously flowing data, and databases managing persistent, queryable data. However, materialized views challenge this separation by bridging the gap between the two systems.

Materialized views enable the creation of precomputed, persistent summaries of data derived from streaming sources. These views serve as caches that store computed results or aggregations in a way that is easily queryable. This means that instead of solely relying on stream processing systems for real-time analysis, we can leverage materialized views to store and query summarized data without the need for continuous reprocessing.

By combining the benefits of stream processing and databases, materialized views offer several advantages. First, they provide the ability to perform complex analytics on streaming data in a more efficient and scalable manner. Rather than reprocessing the entire dataset for each query, materialized views store the precomputed results, allowing for faster and more responsive querying.

Moreover, materialized views facilitate the seamless integration of streaming and batch processing paradigms. They can be used to store intermediate results of stream processing pipelines, providing a bridge between the continuous flow of streaming data and the batch-oriented analytics typically performed on databases. This integration helps unify the processing models and simplifies the overall architecture of data-intensive systems.

Overall, materialized views blur the boundaries between stream processing and databases by allowing us to leverage persistent, queryable summaries of streaming data. By combining the benefits of both systems, they enable efficient and scalable real-time analytics, seamless integration of historical and real-time data, and the convergence of streaming and batch processing paradigms. The use of materialized views opens up exciting possibilities for building intelligent and responsive data systems that can handle the dynamic nature of streaming data while providing fast and flexible query capabilities.

We've now introduced two constructs in OLTP databases that bring them close to streaming technologies:

The WAL
> A construct that captures changes to database tables.

The materialized view
> An asynchronous query that preprocesses and stores data to enable low-latency queries.

In Chapter 1, we introduced Martin Kleppmann's quote: "turning the database inside out." We did, in fact, turn the database inside out by:

1. Taking the WAL construct in the OLTP and publishing it to the streaming platform, like Kafka.

2. Taking the materialized view feature and mimicking it in a stateful stream processing platform. This relinquished the need for complex transformations from the OLTP databases that needed to focus on capturing transactions and serving data by externalizing them to the streaming layer.

We now have the foundation to talk about streaming databases in the next chapter. This is where we will again turn the tables on the streaming paradigm by bringing WALs and materialized views back into the database. In other words, we'll "turn streaming architectures outside in."

## CHAPTER 5

Introduction to Streaming Databases

In a spreadsheet, you can put a formula in one cell (for example, the sum of cells in another column), and whenever any input to the formula changes, the result of the formula is automatically recalculated. This is exactly what we want at a data system level: when a record in a database changes, we want any index for that record to be automatically updated, and any cached views or aggregations that depend on the record to be automatically refreshed. You should not have to worry about the technical details of how this refresh happens, but be able to simply trust that it works correctly.

—Martin Kleppmann, *Designing Data-Intensive Applications*

In the previous chapter, we learned how to "turn the database inside out," as Martin Kleppmann has so aptly coined it. This involved externalizing the WAL of a database into *input change streams*, creating *materialized views* on top of them, and writing the processed data back into *output change streams*. Unlike materialized views in classic databases, such as Oracle or Postgres, where the refresh intervals range from a few minutes to a few hours, materialized views in stream processing platforms like Flink, Kafka Streams, ksqlDB, or Samza could be refreshed continuously—with every new change coming in.

The idea of "turning the database inside out" empowered us to build materialized views offering fresher data than ever before. However, compared to a simple classic database installation, it also required us to deal with a lot of additional complexity: to actually *make sense* of the continuously updated materialized views created by Flink, Kafka Streams, ksqlDB, or Samza, the output change streams had to be ingested into an additional external database (e.g., a RTOLAP database like Druid, Pinot, ClickHouse, or Rockset). So, architecturally, "turning the database inside out" forced us to spin up and operate three systems (the streaming platform, the stream processor, and the external database) instead of simply having one classic database.[1] And, to make matters more complicated, only expensive and hard-to-find stream processing experts could implement this—not your run-of-the-mill database expert. Consequently, from a global perspective, the "turning the database inside out" idea has been kept on the sidelines, only being applied for use cases like fraud detection, where low latency really has been of paramount importance.

We believe that the idea of "turning the database inside out" was a crucial first step toward building a bridge between the streaming and the database world and that it has paved the way for significant advances in stream processing. But it did not go all the way.

In this central chapter of this book, we'll let you jump on board a journey from stateful stream processing, stream-based materialized views, and state stores toward a new notion of materialized views re-based on their original formulation from the database world. We will show you how the new *streaming databases* like ksqlDB, Materialize, RisingWave, and Timeplus are about to start putting the final bricks on the bridge between the streaming and the database world and take the next logical step after turning the database "inside out": to turn it "outside in" again. To get started, let's review the components you're familiar with from many of the diagrams so far.

Identifying the Streaming Database

The diagrams provided thus far mainly contain the following components, also shown in Figure 5-1. For now, let's ignore the connectors that are required to read from and write to systems.

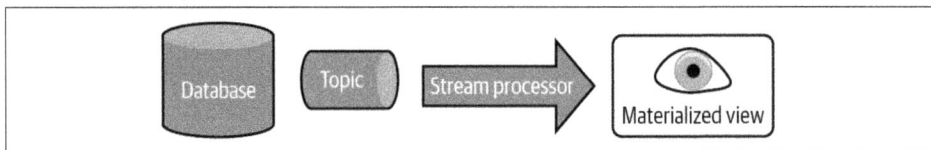

Figure 5-1. Stream processing parts

From left to right, the components in Figure 5-1 are as follows:

- The database can be one of the three types of data stores that we talked about so far: OLTP, RTOLAP, and the internal state stores in a stream processor. The differences between them dictate how data is stored and queried.

---

1 If the external downstream database does not support reading from the streaming platform out of the box, a fourth architectural component, a connector middleware (Kafka Connect, Striim, StreamSets, HVR, etc.), is required on top.

- The topic is a construct that mimics the WAL in an OLTP database. Topics publish streams of data to other databases and stream processors.

- Stream processors are the applications that transform streams of data. They hold an internal state store.

- The materialized view is a process that precomputes a result and stores it in a database. Materialized views are created in a database or stream processor, both of which need to have a persistence layer.

We can arrange these components to build a streaming topology that represents a data flow. The flow we've been suggesting thus far looks like this:

Example	Description
Database → Topic → Stream Processor → Topic → Database	Simple flow

Until now, we've been focusing on the flows in the following—a typical real-time analytical flow that we employed as the solution for our click events use case:

Example	Description
OLTP → Topic → Stream Processor → Topic → RTOLAP	OLTP database flowing to an RTOLAP
Microservice → Topic → Stream Processor → Topic → RTOLAP	Microservice that captures click events flowing to the same RTOLAP

But nothing is stopping us from doing the following, where the output is another—or even the same—OLTP database. This is an important distinction that will become apparent when we start to talk about different types of streaming databases and materialized views later in this chapter:

Example	Description
OLTP → Topic → Stream Processor → Topic → OLTP	A flow whose destination is another or the same OLTP database

In all of these flows, the exact location of the *materialized view* is ambiguous. There are three components where the result of the stream is materialized:

- The stream processor creates a materialized view and stores the result in its internal state store.

- The changes to the materialized view are pushed out to the output topic.

- Neither the stream processor's internal state store nor the output topic can be queried directly. Hence, the destination database pulls the changes to its own materialized view, which corresponds to the table. This table is optimized for end-user analytical queries.

The only thing we know for certain is that the materialized view is not a first-class citizen because it spans all three of the components in the middle of Figure 5-2.

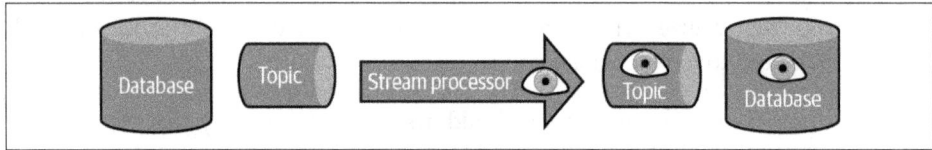

Figure 5-2. The materialized view is stretched across multiple systems

What if we could consolidate these three components? This is an example of a streaming database. If we converge the stream processor and the database, we no longer need the topic to expose the changes to the materialized view in the stream processor's state store. Instead, the stream processor's state store and the database will become one and the same (see Figure 5-3).

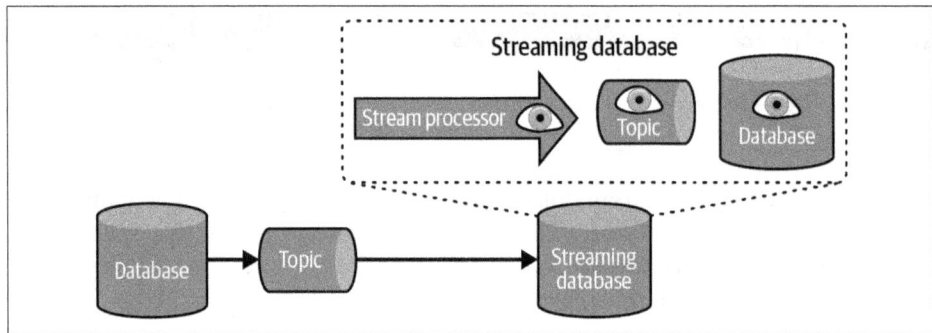

Figure 5-3. Streaming database is formed when converging the stream processor and the database

This streaming database will be able to handle both push and pull queries. If you recall, the push query is a process that runs asynchronously in the background like a stream processor, and the pull query is an analytical query requested by the end user. This implies that one and the same SQL engine needs to support both push and pull queries.

Consolidating the storage in one place solves only half of the problem. Building a single SQL engine that supports both data at rest and data in motion is even more difficult. The stream processing side of the streaming database might need to change from using its internal state store to using a real database when joining and aggregating data. Also, the objects in the streaming database may need to differentiate between data in motion tables and data at rest tables.

Column-Based Streaming Database

Returning to our clickstream use case, the destination of the streaming pipeline was an RTOLAP data store. Let's update that diagram to use a (columnar) streaming database in Figure 5-4.

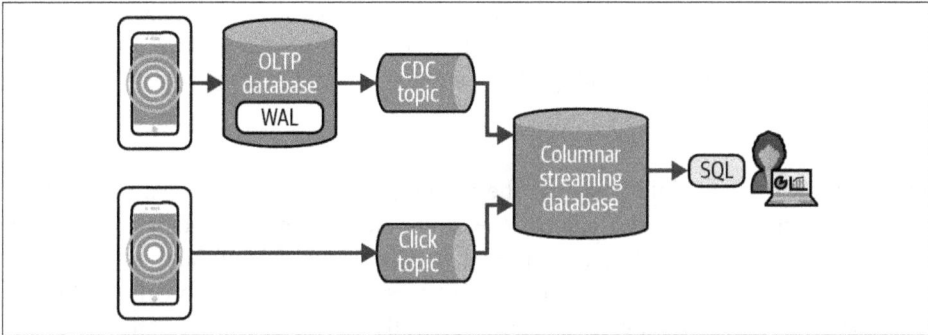

Figure 5-4. The clickstream use case that uses a streaming database for analytical queries

This solution provides a way for users of the streaming database to author both push and pull queries using SQL in one place. The push query would be a SQL query that creates a materialized view, like in Example 5-1.

Example 5-1. Creating a materialized view from two streams of data

```
create materialized view CUSTOMER_CLICKS
as select * from CLICK_EVENTS E
join CUSTOMERS C on C.ip = C.ip
```

An application could also invoke a pull query, like in Example 5-2.

Example 5-2. Application invoking a pull query that returns the customer details

```
select * from CLICK_EVENTS E
join CUSTOMERS C on C.ip = C.ip
where C.id = '123'
```

Example 5-1 gets invoked by what previously was the stream processor engine, and Example 5-2 gets invoked by what previously was the RTOLAP SQL engine for low-latency execution.

Row-Based Streaming Database

Figure 5-5 shows that a row-based streaming database can even become the destination of a streaming data pipeline. If you recall the differences, row-based databases, such as OLTP databases, are optimized for fast read and write operations associated with transactional data like CRUD (create, retrieve, update, delete) transactions. OLAP is optimized for analytical queries like aggregations. Why would you have a row-based database as the destination if the use case is to perform analytical queries against it?

> Using an OLTP database for analytical workloads is generally not recommended due to several fundamental issues like performance, locking and concurrency, and resource utilization, to name a few.

The solution to the riddle posed in the previous paragraph is that you don't have to run the analytical queries against the row-based streaming databases. You still have the option to publish the output of it to an output topic and subsequently feed an RTOLAP database for analytical queries, as you can see on the right side of Figure 5-5. But you're not reducing complexity by consolidating systems. You're only replacing the stream processor with another stream processor—this time, a row-based streaming database—and your materialized view is again stretched across multiple streaming systems: row-based streaming database, topic, and RTOLAP.

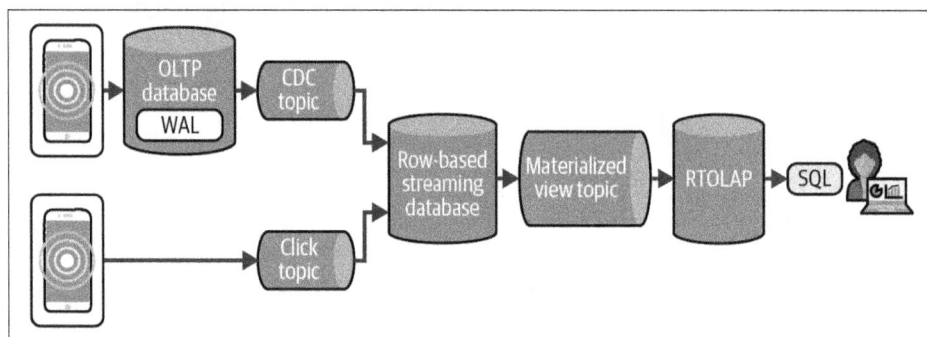

Figure 5-5. Row-based streaming database just replaces the stream processor

By nature, streaming is a row-by-row feed of data that is better suited to work with row-based streaming databases. The better solution for row-based streaming databases is to keep the transformed data within the application using a pattern called Command Query Responsibility Segregation (CQRS).

CQRS is an architectural pattern that separates the operations that read data (queries) from those that modify data (commands) into distinct components. In CQRS, the idea is to have separate models for reading and writing data. This allows for optimized performance and scalability, as the read and write operations can be independently optimized for their specific requirements. CQRS can help improve system responsiveness, enhance scalability, and enable better alignment of data models with their intended usage.

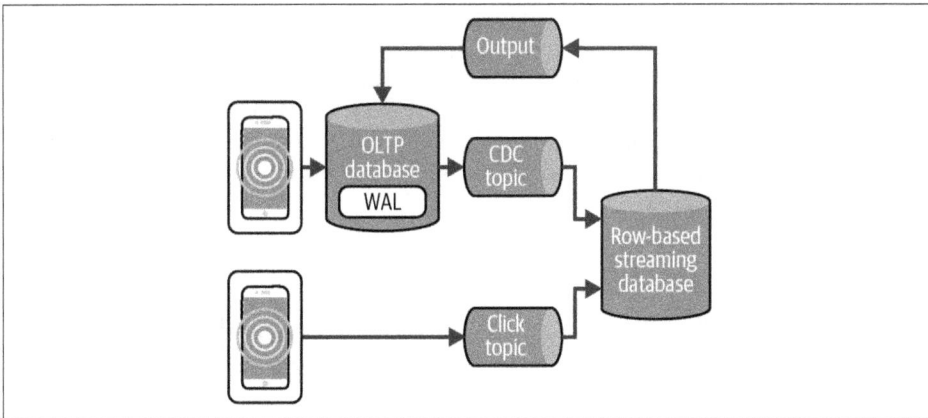

Figure 5-6. CQRS implemented with a row-based streaming database

In Figure 5-6, the data in the output topic is written back to the source OLTP database. The better solution is to have the output topic update a separate database used for only reading by the client application. This pattern provides eventual consistency between write and read OLTP databases. Plus, you can even use the streaming database accessible to the application as the read-only database in a CQRS pattern (see Figure 5-7).

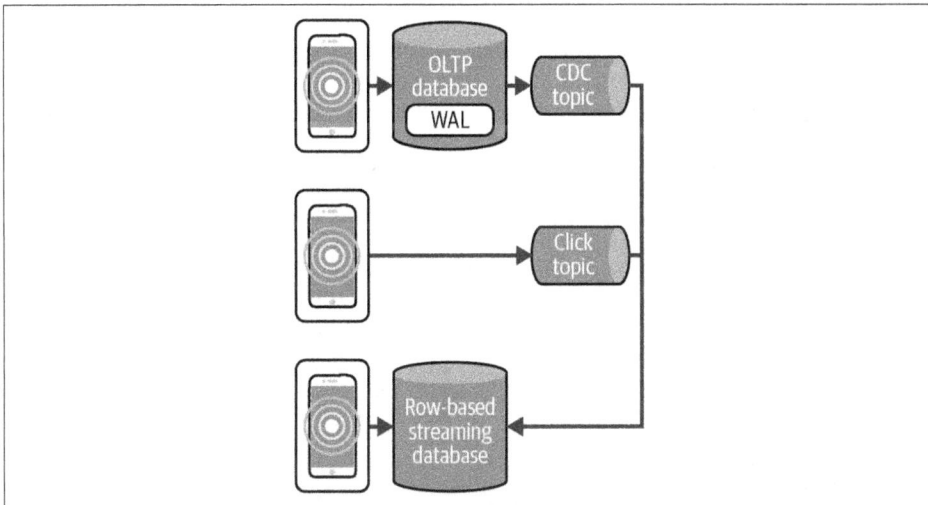

Figure 5-7. CQRS where the streaming database is used as the read-only database for the application

Row-based streaming databases bring streaming a lot closer to the edge, or what some call the *web edge*.

The term "web edge" typically refers to the outermost layer or boundary of a web application or service. It represents the point of interaction between the application and the external world, including users, clients, and other systems. The web edge is responsible for handling incoming requests, processing them, and routing them to the appropriate components within the application's architecture.

Edge Streaming-Like Databases

So far, we've consolidated the stream processor, the topic, and the destination database into a streaming database on the right side of Figure 5-8 that outlines the column-based streaming database.

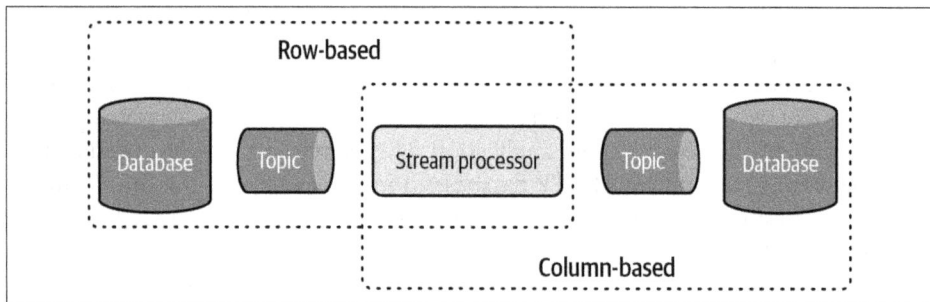

Figure 5-8. A real-time data pipeline where streaming databases can reside

Emerging databases are starting to appear, like that on the left side of this diagram, which is closer to the application and the web edge. We will discuss them more in Chapter 7, when we talk about hybrid transactional and analytical processing databases, or HTAP databases.

So far, we have spoken in detail about two types of streaming databases: row-based and column-based. Both have the difficult task of converging SQL engines in the stream processor and the destination database. The two SQL engines may have different semantics that could limit what can be expressed in the SQL because the converged SQL engine that underlies it doesn't support them.

SQL Expressivity

SQL expressivity refers to the ability of the SQL engine to succinctly and effectively represent complex data manipulations and queries using a concise syntax. In other words, it measures how well SQL can capture the intent of a query or operation in a way that is easy to understand and maintain. Merging SQL engines between a stream processor and an OLAP or OLTP database can introduce various challenges and pitfalls due to the fundamental differences in their design, use cases, and performance characteristics:

Performance mismatch

Stream processors are optimized for handling high-velocity, real-time data streams, while OLAP databases are designed for complex analytical queries on historical data. Merging their SQL engines might result in performance issues if the combined engine struggles to balance the real-time requirements of streaming data with the resource-intensive nature of OLAP queries.

Latency

Stream processing requires low latency for real-time processing, while OLAP databases often prioritize query optimization over low-latency response. Trying to achieve both low latency for streaming and high performance for analytical queries within a single SQL engine can be challenging.

Resource allocation

Stream processors and OLAP databases have different resource requirements. Stream processors need to process data as it arrives, potentially causing resource contention with OLAP queries that demand substantial compute and memory resources. Properly allocating resources becomes critical to avoid bottlenecks.

Data modeling differences

Stream processors usually work with raw or semistructured data, whereas OLAP databases require structured, preprocessed, and well-modeled data for efficient querying. Merging the two SQL engines might lead to conflicts in data modeling approaches.

Data consistency

Stream processors often operate on data in motion, while OLAP databases work with data at rest. Ensuring data consistency between these two states can be complex, especially when merging the SQL engines to handle both.

Complexity

Combining the capabilities of stream processing and OLAP databases can lead to a more complex system. This complexity can impact maintainability, debugging, and overall system stability.

Data volume and retention

Stream processors may have a shorter retention period for data due to high data volume and real-time processing requirements. OLAP databases usually store historical data for analysis over longer periods. Deciding how to handle data retention and integration can be challenging.

Query optimizations

OLAP databases often provide advanced query optimization techniques for complex analytical queries. Stream processors might not offer the same level of optimization, potentially leading to suboptimal performance for OLAP queries.

Schema evolution

Stream processors may handle schema evolution more flexibly than OLAP databases, which tend to require well-defined schemas. Merging their SQL engines can result in difficulties when dealing with evolving data schemas.

Maintenance and updates

Managing updates and maintenance for a combined SQL engine that handles both streaming and OLAP workloads can be more challenging, as updates must account for the requirements of both use cases.

To mitigate these pitfalls, careful architectural planning, thorough performance testing, and a deep understanding of the specific use cases for each SQL engine are essential.

Merging SQL engines between OLTP and a stream processor can be easier compared to merging SQL engines between OLAP and a stream processor. This is due to the inherent differences in data storage and processing characteristics between OLTP and OLAP systems:

Data format

OLTP databases typically use a row-based storage model, which is well suited for capturing individual transactional records. Stream processors also work with data in a row-based format as they process real-time events. This alignment in the data model can facilitate smoother integration and compatibility.

Real-time nature

Both OLTP systems and stream processors deal with real-time data to some extent. While the processing requirements might differ, the common focus on real-time data handling can make it easier to merge their SQL engines.

Transaction handling

Both OLTP and stream processors may involve transactional processing, albeit with different levels of complexity. This shared aspect can lead to better integration when it comes to handling data consistency and updates.

Event-driven

Stream processors are event driven by nature, which nicely corresponds to real-time updates in OLTP databases. This compatibility simplifies the integration process.

While merging SQL engines between OTLP and a stream processor might be easier due to these shared characteristics, merging SQL engines between OLAP and a stream processor is more complicated due to fundamental differences in data storage, processing, and query optimization strategies. Again, careful architectural planning and consideration of the specific requirements of each system are crucial to successfully achieve integration in either scenario.

The reduction of infrastructure complexity and unified SQL engine will make development easier for engineers, especially when debugging their materialized views.

Streaming Debuggability

Data engineers will always need to verify the logic of their SQL when writing data pipelines. Having your materialized view stretch across three different distributed systems (stream processor, topic, and OLAP) makes it very hard to debug. While it's theoretically possible to debug it by looking at the input and output topics alone, practically, the debugging needs to be undertaken by looking at both the topics *and* the external database at the same time.

Streaming databases make it easier to debug by virtue of providing a more advanced form of materialized views compared to the (key/value) state stores of classical stream processors. Streaming databases persist the materialized views in either a row-based or column-based store and thus make it easier to verify the results in one place. Debugging can also be performed faster because the data is already indexed for more complex ad hoc queries. On the contrary, stream processors like Flink first require the results to be written out to a database to test their validity via ad hoc queries.

Advantages of Debugging in Streaming Databases

The following are the advantages of debugging in streaming databases:

Familiar SQL interface
> Many streaming databases offer a SQL-like query language for defining stream processing operations. If you're already familiar with SQL, debugging can be more straightforward due to the familiarity of the language.

Simpler logic
> Streaming databases often provide a higher-level abstraction that simplifies complex stream processing tasks. This can lead to simpler logic, which, in turn, can make debugging easier.

Integrated ecosystem
> Streaming databases are often part of a larger data ecosystem. They can help to achieve a better integration with other data tools and monitoring solutions by combining a stream processor and a database in one system, compared to having to combine a separate stream processor with a separate downstream database.

This integrated environment can aid in debugging by providing a more holistic view of the data pipeline.

Built-in optimizations

Streaming databases might have built-in optimizations for common stream processing patterns. These optimizations can help improve performance and reliability and reduce the need for complex debugging in certain scenarios.

Easier deployment

Some streaming databases are designed for ease of deployment, which can simplify the debugging process by reducing potential deployment-related issues.

SQL Is Not a Silver Bullet

SQL is a very abstract language. For some use cases, it can be advantageous to be able to use a lower-level DSL (domain-specific language) in addition to SQL, such as Kafka Streams (Streams DSL and Processor API) and Flink (DataStream API) for increased expressibility. User-defined functions (UDFs) in SQL-based streaming databases can be a mitigating factor, but only to a certain extent.

For debugging and/or profiling, especially in highly performance-critical situations, it would also be desirable to observe the actual logical execution plan derived by the stream processing system, for example, to inspect the state of an aggregation operator created by a GROUP BY statement. Tooling for inspecting the execution plan of stream processing systems is, however, still in its infancy.

Streaming Database Implementations

Table 5-1 shows a list of some of the streaming databases available at the time of this book's release.

Table 5-1. Existing streaming databases

Name	License	State store implementation	Use cases
ksqlDB	Confluent Community License	RocksDB (LSM tree key-value storage)	CQRS, push queries
RisingWave	Apache 2	row-based	CQRS, push queries, single row lookups
Materialize	Business Source License (BSL)	row-based	CQRS, push queries, single row lookups
Timeplus (Proton)	Apache 2	column-based	Analytical push and pull queries

The streaming databases listed in Table 5-1 vary with respect to their underlying persistence layer. The first streaming database, ksqlDB, uses state stores based on RocksDB (LSM tree storage). ksqlDB only supports indexing by primary keys.

While primary key/value access does yield good performance, more complex queries require full, nonindexed scans through entire state stores, which does not scale for nontrivial amounts of data.

A full scan, also known as a table scan, is a query operation that involves examining and processing every record or row in a dataset, table, or database. While full scans can be useful in certain scenarios, they often introduce various issues and challenges when querying data. Full scans can be resource intensive and time consuming, especially when dealing with large datasets. Processing every record in a table can lead to slow query performance, particularly if the dataset is extensive.

The implementation of the persistence layer of a streaming database determines the range of queries that it can support efficiently. RisingWave, Materialize, and Timeplus make use of more database-like implementations of their persistence layers (Timeplus, for example, uses a version of the RTOLAP database ClickHouse) with flexible indexing schemes. This allows them to serve a large variety of pull queries efficiently.

Streaming Database Architecture

The materialized views (the change tables) in the streaming database are held in the state store. Conversely, the append tables are not. Either append tables pass through cleanly or they are placed into another topic-like construct in the streaming database.

To help better summarize the architecture of a streaming database, Figure 5-9 helps describe the path and steps that the click events and customer CDC data follow.

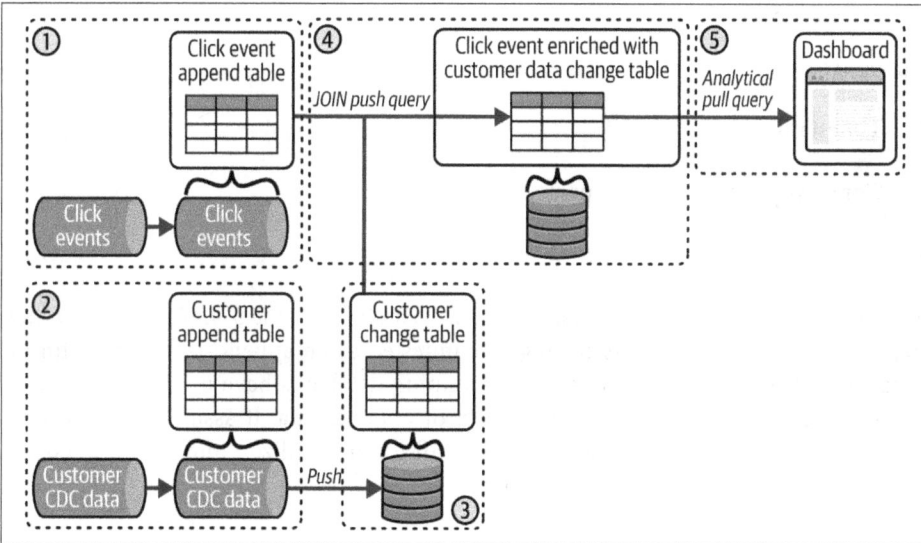

Figure 5-9. Path append and change streams in a streaming database

In the first step, the click events are in an append topic in a streaming platform like Kafka. To bring this data into the streaming database, we invoke a data definition language (DDL) to create the table. See Example 4-1.

> DDL is a subset of SQL that describes how to create, alter, and delete database objects like tables.

In Example 5-3, we create a source table in a streaming database. This is the same SQL example provided in Chapter 2.

Example 5-3. Create a source table from a Kafka topic for the click events

```
CREATE SOURCE click_events (
    id integer,
    ts long,  ❶
    url varchar,  ❷
    ipAddress varchar,  ❸
    sessionId varchar,
    referrer varchar,
    browser varchar
)
WITH (
    connector='kafka',
    topic='clicks',
    properties.bootstrap.server='kafka:9092',
    scan.startup.mode='earliest'
)
ROW FORMAT JSON;
```

❶ Timestamp

❷ Contains product ID to be parsed out

❸ The ipAddress that identifies a customer

Next, we do the same with the customer CDC data in Example 5-4. Notice that in this step, the data exists as a "pass-through" manifested as an append-only table with no state store. The stream processors and streaming databases have no way of knowing if the content of the topic has change data or append data. It assumes append data because all streaming data is append data until it's materialized into a view persisted in a state store. This is why we need step 3.

Example 5-4. Ingest and create a table for the customers. The table's schema uses a Debezium CDC format, which provides before, after, and op fields.

```
CREATE SOURCE customers (
    before ROW<id long, name varchar, email varchar, ipAddress varchar>, ❶
    after ROW<id long, name varchar, email varchar, ipAddress varchar>, ❷
    op varchar, ❸
    ts timestamp, ❹
    source <...>,
)
WITH (
    connector='kafka',
    topic='customers',
    properties.bootstrap.server='kafka:9092',
    scan.startup.mode='earliest'
)
ROW FORMAT JSON;
```

❶ The before field holds the state of the record before the change was made.

❷ The after field holds the state of the record after the change was made.

❸ The op identifies the type of change: insert, update, or delete.

❹ The ts is the timestamp for when the change occurred.

In step 3 of Figure 5-9, we tell the streaming database to materialize the values in the append table into a materialized view. Example 5-5 is one way of getting the latest state of each record.

Example 5-5. Create a materialized view of the latest records using a common table expression (CTE) and windowing

```
CREATE MATERIALIZED VIEW customers_mv AS
WITH ranked_customers AS (
  SELECT
    c.AFTER,
    c.op,
    c.ts,
    ROW_NUMBER() OVER (PARTITION BY c.AFTER.id ORDER BY c.ts DESC) AS rn ❶
  FROM customers AS c
)
SELECT * FROM ranked_customers WHERE rn = 1 AND op IS NOT 'D'; ❷
);
```

❶ This is a windowing statement that partitions the records by id and then places them in descending order by timestamp. The ROW_NUMBER() assigns each instance of an id a row number and guarantees record 1 is the latest record.

❷ We select only the latest record, which will have an rn value of 1. We also filter out all deleted records where op is not D.

The output of Example 5-5 should result in a materialized view that contains the latest state of customer data.

Some streaming databases have the ability to skip step 3 by having a custom connector that processes Debezium CDC-formatted data directly into a materialized view (see Example 5-6).

Example 5-6. Using a Debezium connector to directly create a materialized view

```
CREATE SOURCE customers (
    before ROW<id long, name varchar, email varchar, ipAddress varchar>,
    after ROW<id long, name varchar, email varchar, ipAddress varchar>,
    op varchar,
    ts timestamp,
    source <...>,
)
WITH (
    connector='kafka-debezium-cdc', ❶
    topic='customers',
    properties.bootstrap.server='kafka:9092',
    scan.startup.mode='earliest'
)
ROW FORMAT JSON;
```

❶ A custom connector named kafka-debezium-cdc is able to read data from a Kafka topic and build a materialized view that only shows the latest state of the customer's table.

CDC Connectors

Every streaming database will have different names for their custom CDC connectors. Do not expect the name to be kafka-debezium-cdc. You will need to refer to the documentation to get the actual name of the connector to use.

Some streaming databases will have their own CDC connectors that bypass the topic in the streaming platform and connect directly to the database. These connectors still will read the WAL and build a replica of tables in the streaming database. However, bypassing the streaming platform might be limiting if the CDC data needs to be replicated to other target databases in addition to the streaming database. We'll discuss architectural options for deploying streaming databases in more detail in Chapter 10.

In step 4 of Figure 5-9, another materialized view is created. Example 5-7 joins the CLICK_EVENTS table with the CUSTOMERS table, resulting in a materialized view of customer-enriched click events.

Example 5-7. Create another materialized view of enriched click events

```
CREATE MATERIALIZED VIEW CLICK_EVENTS_ENRICHED AS
SELECT e.*, c.*
FROM CLICK_EVENTS e
JOIN CUSTOMERS c on e.ipAddress = c.ipAddress
```

We can repeat the steps taken with the CUSTOMERS table and use the PRODUCTS table to enrich the CLICK_EVENTS with both customer and product information.

Example 5-8. Create another materialized view of enriched click events

```
CREATE MATERIALIZED VIEW CLICK_EVENTS_ENRICHED AS
SELECT e.*, c.*, p.*
FROM CLICK_EVENTS e
JOIN CUSTOMERS c on e.ipAddress = c.ipAddress
JOIN PRODUCTS p on e.productid = p.productid
```

At this point, we've arrived at step 5 of Figure 5-9. Now end users can invoke analytical pull queries against the CLICK_EVENTS_ENRICHED materialized view. The type of storage (row-based or columnar-based) of the streaming database will dictate the complexity of the analytical query you can invoke. Many use cases don't require a human to invoke the pull query. Instead, applications themselves can consume real-time materialized views.

In some cases, applications may want to use both row and columnar streaming databases to serve different low-latency analytical queries. This will require both streaming databases to build replicas of the tables. If you recall, streaming platforms enable the publishing and subscribing of CDC data to allow multiple systems to build replicas of its tables.

ELT with Streaming Databases

In Chapter 2, we said ELT (extract, load, transform) data pipelines do not support real-time use cases because the transformation occurs in the destination database. The database, in this case, places the streaming data at rest, which forces batch semantics for all downstream processing.

However, if the destination database using ELT is a streaming database, then the pipeline can be considered still in real time. This integration between the "loading" and "transformation" parts of ELT is mediated by a topic on a streaming platform from which the streaming database consumes the data.

There is a large ecosystem that supports ELT solutions, for example, *dbt*.[2] In combination with streaming databases, these tools can support real-time ELT for the first time. And because streaming databases behave, on the surface, like databases and not so much like a stream processor, ELT with streaming databases can actually be implemented by the same teams who have previously worked on ELT in a data warehouse. In this vein, a lot of ELT jobs that now run later in the pipeline (in the data warehouse or lakehouse) can be moved to the real-time streaming layer.

Summary

The term *streaming database* converges stream processing and databases. "Databases" is normally associated with batch processing of data. So marrying "streaming" and "databases" also converges streaming with batching and data in motion with data at rest.

Streaming databases bring the two constructs that Martin Kleppmann pulled out of the database, the WAL and the materialized view, back into the database.

Database SQL engines only supported data at rest so far. By allowing the materialized view to run asynchronously in the background, we can enable the existing SQL to process data at rest and in motion. This transforms the database into a streaming database.

Streaming databases differ with respect to the implementation of their persistence layer. ksqlDB makes use of RocksDB and primary key indexes. Newer streaming databases use a more database-like persistence layer for supporting a large set of queries efficiently.

We also know that streaming databases support both push and pull queries. Push is executed in the "streaming" half of a streaming database. The pull queries are executed on the "database" half of the streaming database. If the "streaming" half of the streaming database uses the "database" half for its state store, you have a true streaming database.

The type of storage of the streaming database determines what type of pull query can be served efficiently. For columnar-based databases, pull queries can be analytical, including fast aggregations. For row-based databases, pull queries are typically more simple lookups, like point queries.

---

2 Dbt (data build tool) is an open source software tool that enables data engineers and analysts to transform, test, and deploy data transformations using SQL and Python.

In Figure 5-10, we show a spectrum of streaming databases that range from row-based to column-based. On the left side, pull queries are normally invoked by an application, which are event driven and where no human is involved. On the right side, pull queries are usually invoked by a human or a dashboard.

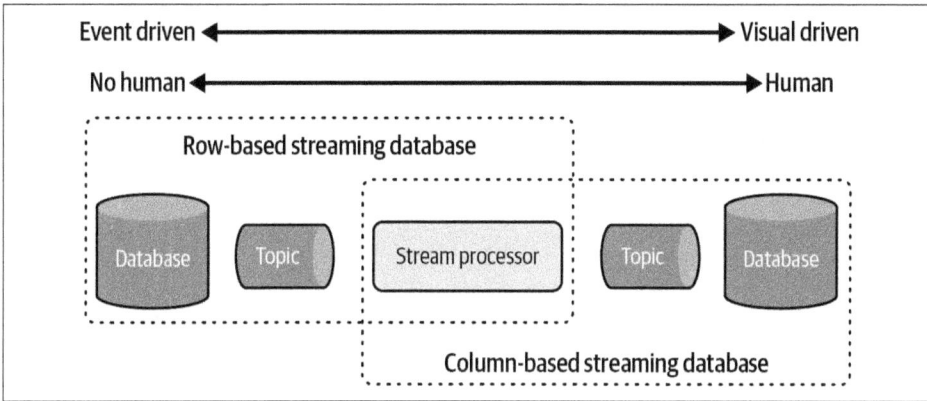

Figure 5-10. Spectrum of streaming databases

A crucial property of streaming databases is consistency. Consistency in a database refers to the state in which data is always valid and adheres to predefined rules and constraints. It ensures that any transaction, whether successful or not, brings the database from one consistent state to the next, without violating integrity rules. In a consistent database, all data modifications follow a set of predefined rules, ensuring the data remains accurate and reliable.

In the next chapter, we will go through the importance of consistency in streaming databases (and also stream processors).

## CHAPTER 6

Consistency

If you're familiar with databases, you take consistency for granted. You know that the results of your queries are going to be consistent with the input data. Now imagine you dare to cross the bridge from the database to the streaming world. Can you bank on similar consistency guarantees here, even with the additional complexity of data arriving late and out of order, as well as the emphasis on low latency and high throughput?

For classical stream processors, the answer is no. They guarantee a weaker form of consistency called *eventual consistency*. For classical stream processing use cases, often involving aggregations on *windowed data*, eventual consistency is a perfect fit, and it also enables data pipelines with ultra-low latency, with very high throughput, and at extremely large scale. The problem is, if you come from the database world, eventual consistency can turn out to be a confusing and counterintuitive experience—especially in combination with *nonwindowed data*.

In this chapter, we will use a toy example from the banking domain to demonstrate what can go wrong in eventually consistent stream processors like Flink, ksqlDB, and Proton if you just follow your intuitions from the database world.

Interestingly, some more recent stream processing systems support a stronger form of consistency, where every output is the correct output for a subset of the inputs: *internal consistency*.[1] Of these stream processing systems, we put RisingWave, Materialize, and Pathway on the same job to see whether *they* allow us to solve the toy example in a way that more closely mirrors the intuitions of a typical database engineer.

---

1 Jamie Brandon. "Internal Consistency in Streaming Systems," Blog, 2021 (*https://oreil.ly/mwuyl*).

The chapter continues by detailing what exactly can go wrong when following the path of eventual consistency and how the stream processing systems providing stronger consistency guarantees can actually fare better.

Finally, we turn to the question of whether it would make sense for classical stream processors such as Flink to support stronger consistency guarantees. In other words, how much of their low latency and high throughput would they actually have to give up—and could it be worth it?

A Toy Example

This chapter is brought to life by a toy example adapted from Jamie Brandon's blog about internal consistency. The example is intentionally not a classical stream processing use case. It is not windowed, and it requires a form of synchronization not fully available out of the box in classical stream processing systems. The rationale behind choosing this example is that in this book, we are interested in streaming *databases* in the convergence of the streaming and the database world. And we think that for this convergence to really take place, stream processing systems should be able to handle nontypical, nonwindowed use cases in a way comparable to the database world, especially with respect to consistency.

Imagine a bank with 10 accounts, where the accounts continuously transfer $1 to other bank accounts. This looks like Table 6-1, where each "Transaction" column is a transaction that performs a debit and a credit. The columns "Account" and "Starting value" on the left show three accounts, namely 1, 2, and 3, with starting values of $0. The next column, "Transaction 1," debits account 1 and credits account 2, etc. For every column representing a debit and credit transaction, all the rows should sum up to zero.

Table 6-1. Debit and credit transactions

Account	Starting value	Transaction 1	Transaction 2	Transaction 3	Transaction 4
1	$0	−$1	−$2	−$3	−$2
2	$0	$1	$1	$2	$2
3	$0	$0	$1	$1	$0
Sum	$0	$0	$0	$0	$0

The way we test consistency is to see if the stream processor can return zero when we sum up the balances of all the accounts. This is our *invariant*. Any moment the sum does not total zero would indicate an issue with consistency.

Transactions

We set up our toy bank example with the Python code in Example 6-1.

Example 6-1. The Python code to set up our toy bank example

```python
import datetime, json, random, time
from kafi.kafi import Cluster

c = Cluster("local")
c.create("transactions", partitions=1)
p = c.producer("transactions")
random.seed(42)
for id_int in range(0, 10000):
  row_str = json.dumps({
        "id": id_int,
        "from_account": random.randint(0, 9),
        "to_account": random.randint(0, 9),
        "amount": 1,
        "ts": datetime.datetime.now().isoformat(sep=" ", timespec="milliseconds")
    })
  print(row_str)
  p.produce(row_str, key=str(id_int))
  time.sleep(0.01)
p.close()
```

Ten thousand times, every 10 milliseconds, the code produces a new message to a (one-partition) Kafka topic called transactions, where one bank account, from_account, transfers $1 to another bank account, to_account. We exhibit an example message in Example 6-2.

Example 6-2. An example message/transaction

```json
{
    "id": 42,
    "from_account": 3,
    "to_account": 0,
    "amount": 1,
    "ts": "2023-10-24 23:27:57.603"
}
```

Analyzing the Transactions

We now put SQL on the job to analyze the transactions further. We first set up two views aggregating the credits and debits of the accounts: the credits are the sum of the money transferred *to* the account and, analogously, the debits are the sum of the money transferred *from* it (Example 6-3).

Example 6-3. Setting up the views for `credits` and `debits`

```
CREATE VIEW credits AS
    SELECT
        to_account as account,
        SUM(amount) as credits
    FROM transactions
    GROUP BY to_account;

CREATE VIEW debits(account, debits) AS
    SELECT
        from_account as account,
        SUM(amount) as debits
    FROM transactions
    GROUP BY from_account;
```

Next, we calculate the balance of an account, its credits minus its debits:

```
CREATE VIEW balance AS
    SELECT
        credits.account AS account,
        credits - debits AS balance
    FROM credits
    INNER JOIN debits ON credits.account = debits.account;
```

Finally, we create a view that sums up the balances of all accounts. Since no money can appear out of the blue, and no money can be lost, that sum should always be 0 and give us the invariant to test the behavior of stream processors and streaming databases with respect to consistency:

```
CREATE VIEW total(total) AS
    SELECT SUM(balance) FROM balance;
```

Comparing Consistency Across Stream Processing Systems

Now how do some of the existing stream processing systems fare when confronted with the toy bank example? We take a look at six of them:

- Flink SQL
- ksqlDB
- Proton (Timeplus)
- RisingWave
- Materialize
- Pathway

Flink SQL

We start out with Flink, one of the most popular stream processing systems. Because in this book, we are primarily interested in SQL-based streaming databases, we make use of Flink's SQL layer/API *Flink SQL* (we used version 1.19.0).

In Flink SQL, we first set up a connection to the source topic transactions:

```
CREATE TABLE transactions (
    id  BIGINT,
    from_account INT,
    to_account INT,
    amount DOUBLE,
    ts TIMESTAMP(3)
) WITH (
    'connector' = 'kafka',
    'topic' = 'transactions',
    'properties.bootstrap.servers' = 'localhost:9092',
    'properties.group.id' = 'transactions_flink',
    'scan.startup.mode' = 'earliest-offset',
    'format' = 'json',
    'json.fail-on-missing-field' = 'true',
    'json.ignore-parse-errors' = 'false'
);
```

In the next step, we create the views credits, debits, balance, and total:

```
CREATE VIEW credits(account, credits) AS
SELECT
  to_account as account,
  SUM(amount) as credits
FROM
  transactions
GROUP BY
  to_account;

CREATE VIEW debits(account, debits) AS
SELECT
  from_account as account,
  SUM(amount) as debits
FROM
  transactions
GROUP BY
  from_account;

CREATE VIEW balance(account, balance) AS
SELECT
  credits.account,
  credits - debits as balance
FROM
  credits,
  debits
WHERE
  credits.account = debits.account;

CREATE VIEW total(total) AS
SELECT
  SUM(balance)
```

```
FROM
    balance;
```

As our last step, we write back the results from the view `total` to a *sink* Kafka topic called `total_flinksql`:

```
CREATE TABLE total_sink (
    total DOUBLE,
    PRIMARY KEY (total) NOT ENFORCED
) WITH (
    'connector' = 'upsert-kafka',
    'property-version' = 'universal',
    'properties.bootstrap.servers' = 'localhost:9092',
    'topic' = 'total_flink',
    'key.format' = 'json',
    'value.format' = 'json',
    'properties.group.id' = 'total_flink'
);

INSERT INTO total_sink SELECT * FROM total;
```

Now let's have a look at the dataflow graph for our Flink SQL code in Figure 6-1. You see the `transactions` source table on the left, which is then split into the two aggregations for `credits` and `debits`. Then, these two aggregations are JOINed into `balance` before the sum of the balances of all accounts is calculated in `total`.

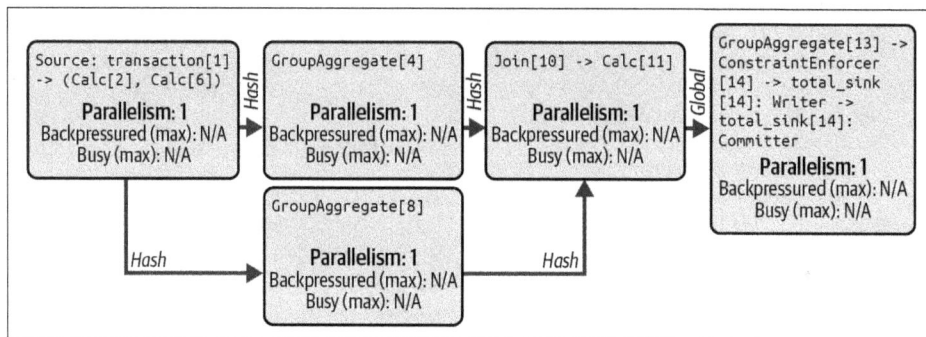

Figure 6-1. The dataflow graph of Flink SQL code for the toy example

> A dataflow graph/topology similar to Figure 6-1 is used inside all the compared stream processing systems here, including ksqlDB, Proton, RisingWave, Materialize, and Pathway.

To run the example in Flink SQL, we first set up the tables and views before we run the Python code to set up 10,000 transactions in our toy bank—and see what happens. If we came from the database world, we would expect nothing serious to happen—the result topic should, like the view `total`, always return the total sum 0.

Let's visualize the results calculated by Flink SQL from the Kafka topic `total_flinksql` in Figure 6-2.

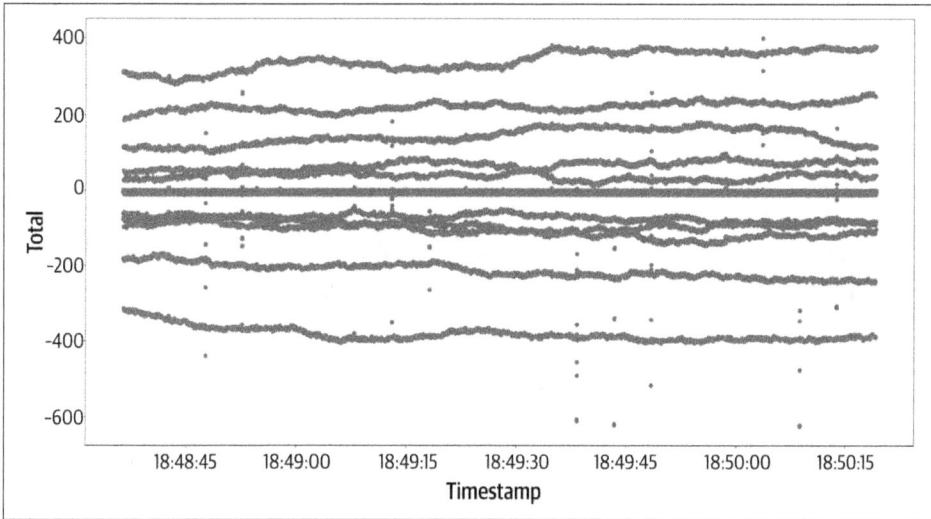

Figure 6-2. Visualization of the sink Kafka topic `total_flinksql`

In Figure 6-2, we see almost 80,000 messages (!), wildly oscillating between +400 and −600 as the total sum of balances of all accounts. When the input stream eventually stops after 10,000 messages, however, Flink SQL does converge on the correct, consistent sum, 0, as shown in Table 6-2.

Table 6-2. The last few messages in the `total_flinksql` sink Kafka topic

Offset	Total
79936	−3.0
79937	40.0
79938	40.0
79939	−2.0
79940	−2.0
79941	−103.0
79942	−103.0
79943	−1.0
79944	−1.0
79945	−83.0
79946	−83.0
79947	0.0

The reason for this behavior is a design choice for Flink SQL—namely, on a high level, to support eventual consistency over internal consistency, which goes hand in hand with the choice for low latency over consistency. In the eventual consistency model, it suffices if the result of the stream processing is not always consistent, but "consistent at some later time." In our case, "at some later time" is exactly the point in time when the Python code stops pushing new messages into the source topic transactions.

The eventual consistency model has the clear benefit of keeping latency as low as possible and is an ideal model for windowed stream processing, which is what Flink and Flink SQL are most commonly used for. However, in our case, it leads to a dilemma. We have an unbounded, nonwindowed use case here, and we can never be sure whether the intermediate result Flink SQL returns is correct unless we stop the input stream. But we *cannot* stop the input stream at any time, at least not in a productive setting, as we cannot forbid our imaginary customers to make transactions…

With version 1.19, Flink has introduced so-called MiniBatch for JOIN operators. MiniBatch, if configured correctly for the use case at hand, not only dramatically improves its performance but also helps in achieving a higher degree of consistency. We will go into this later in this chapter.

ksqlDB

Our next stream processor/streaming database is ksqlDB from Confluent (we used version 7.6.0). Many see ksqlDB as the first streaming database (its first version was released in 2017). This chapter focuses on SQL-based stream processing systems, so we include only ksqlDB in this chapter and not its underlying library, Kafka Streams.

Again, we first set up a connection to the source topic transactions in Example 6-4.

Example 6-4. Setting up the table transactions in ksqlDB

```
CREATE TABLE transactions (
  id VARCHAR PRIMARY KEY,
  from_account INT,
  to_account INT,
  amount DOUBLE,
  ts VARCHAR
) WITH (
  kafka_topic = 'transactions',
  value_format = 'json',
  partitions = 1,
  timestamp = 'ts',
  timestamp_format = 'yyyy-MM-dd HH:mm:ss.SSS'
);
```

In the next step, we create the views credits, debits, balance, and total, each corresponding to a ksqlDB TABLE:

```
CREATE TABLE credits WITH (
  kafka_topic = 'credits',
  value_format = 'json'
) AS
SELECT
  to_account AS account,
  SUM(amount) AS credits
FROM
  transactions
GROUP BY
  to_account EMIT CHANGES; ❶

CREATE TABLE debits WITH (
    kafka_topic = 'debits',
    value_format = 'json'
  ) AS
SELECT
  from_account AS account,
  SUM(amount) AS debits
FROM
  transactions
GROUP BY
  from_account EMIT CHANGES;

CREATE TABLE balance WITH (
    kafka_topic = 'balance',
    value_format = 'json'
  ) AS
SELECT
  credits.account AS account,
  credits - debits AS balance
FROM
  credits
  INNER JOIN debits ON credits.account = debits.account EMIT CHANGES;

CREATE TABLE total WITH (
    kafka_topic = 'total_ksqldb',
    value_format = 'json'
  ) AS
SELECT
  'foo',
  SUM(balance)
FROM
  balance
GROUP BY
  'foo' EMIT CHANGES;
```

❶ EMIT CHANGES informs ksqlDB that the query is a push query.

When we set up the table `total`, we sink the resulting total sums of the balances of all accounts into a sink Kafka topic `total_ksqldb`.

Now, as we did for Flink SQL, we first set up the tables in ksqlDB and then run the Python code to create 10,000 transactions. Then, we visualize the results calculated by ksqlDB from the Kafka topic `total_ksqldb` (see Figure 6-3).

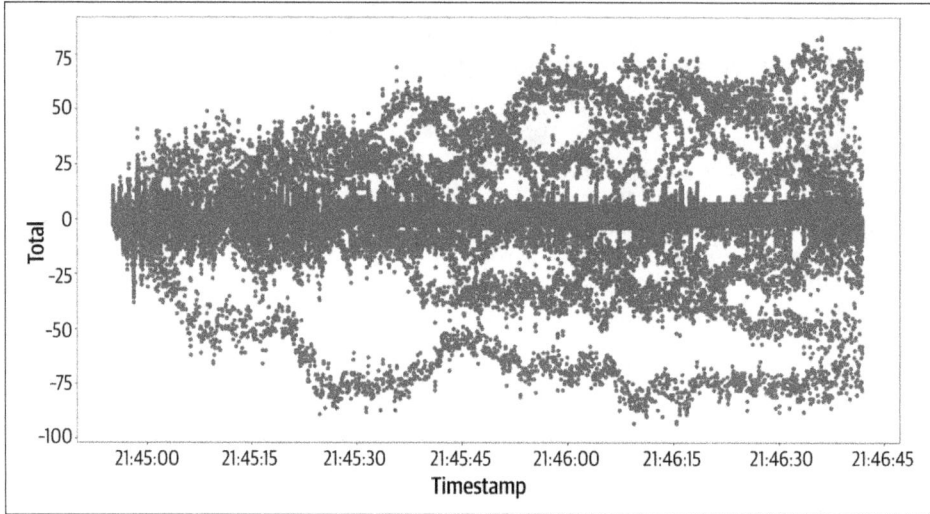

Figure 6-3. The sink Kafka topic `total_ksqldb`

Similar to Figure 6-2, we see a lot of messages (almost 40,000), still wildly oscillating around 0 (between +100 and −100). Again, when the input stream stops after 10,000 messages, ksqlDB does converge on the correct, consistent sum 0, as the last couple of Kafka messages in the sink Kafka topic `total_ksqldb` show:

Offset	Total
39905	−6.0
39906	−78.0
39907	−5.0
39908	68.0
39909	−4.0
39910	−3.0
39911	−3.0
39912	7.0
39913	−2.0
39914	−10.0
39915	−1.0

Offset	Total
39916	−26.0
39917	0.0

The reason for this behavior of ksqlDB is the same as for Flink SQL—ksqlDB has adopted the model of *eventual consistency* (or, as it is called in the context of Kafka Streams/ksqlDB, *continuous refinement*). In the case of our example, ksqlDB leads us into the same dilemma as Flink SQL: unless we stop the input stream, we never know which of the intermediate results is actually correct.

Proton (Timeplus)

In this section, we look at Proton, the open source streaming database underlying Timeplus. The setup for Proton starts by creating a STREAM to connect to the input Kafka topic transactions in Example 6-5.

Example 6-5. Setting up the input STREAM in Proton

```
CREATE EXTERNAL STREAM transactions(
    id int,
    from_account int,
    to_account int,
    amount int,
    ts datetime64
) SETTINGS
    type = 'kafka',
    brokers = 'broker:29092',
    topic = 'transactions',
    data_format = 'JSONEachRow';
```

In the next step, we set up the views credits, debits, and balance in Example 6-6.

Example 6-6. Setting up the views credits, debits, and balance in Proton

```
CREATE EXTERNAL STREAM transactions(
    id int,
    from_account int,
    to_account int,
    amount int,
    ts datetime64
) SETTINGS type = 'kafka',
brokers = 'broker:29092',
topic = 'transactions',
data_format = 'JSONEachRow';

CREATE VIEW credits AS
SELECT
```

```
    now64() as ts,
    to_account as account,
    sum(amount) as credits
FROM
    transactions
GROUP BY
    to_account EMIT PERIODIC 100ms;

CREATE VIEW debits AS
SELECT
    now64() as ts,
    from_account as account,
    sum(amount) as debits
FROM
    transactions
GROUP BY
    from_account EMIT PERIODIC 100ms;

CREATE VIEW balance AS
SELECT
    c.account,
    credits - debits as balance
FROM
    changelog(credits, account, ts, true) AS c
    JOIN changelog(debits, account, ts, true) AS d ON c.account = d.account;
```

Now that we have these views in place, all that remains to be done in Example 6-7 is creating the output STREAM sinking out the results to the sink Kafka topic total_pro ton and the materialized view total.

Example 6-7. Setting up the output STREAM and the MATERIALIZED VIEW total in Proton

```
CREATE EXTERNAL STREAM total_s(total int) SETTINGS type = 'kafka',
brokers = 'broker:29092',
topic = 'total_proton',
data_format = 'JSONEachRow';

CREATE MATERIALIZED VIEW total INTO total_s AS
SELECT
    sum(balance) as total
FROM
    balance;
```

We see only 56 messages in the result topic, moving around between −10 and 9. When the input stream stops after all 10,000 messages, Proton converges to the correct sum: 0. This can be observed when looking at the last few messages in the sink Kafka topic total_proton (Table 6-3).

Table 6-3. The last few messages in the total_proton sink Kafka topic

Offset	Total
48	9
49	9
50	9
51	9
52	9
53	−9
54	9
55	0

In Figure 6-4, we present the visualized results for Proton, where you easily spot the last, correct total sum, 0, on the right because the resulting sink topic is relatively small.

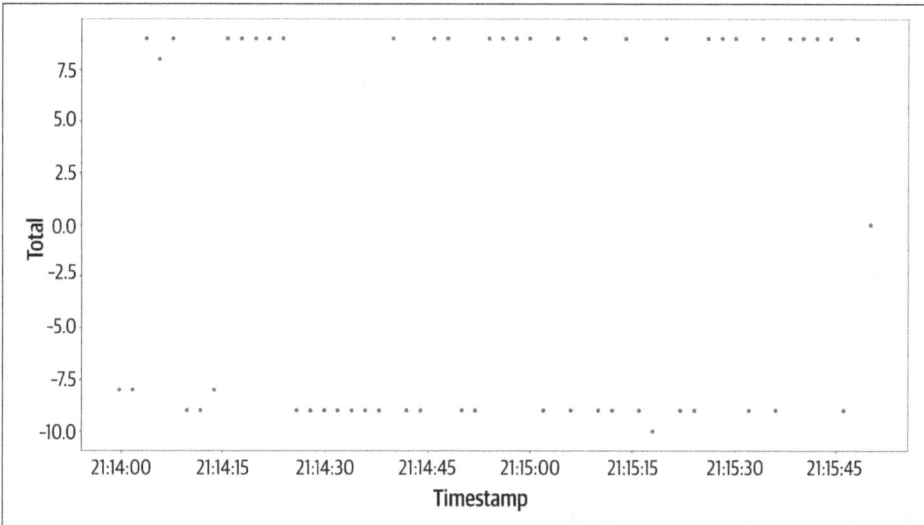

Figure 6-4. Visualization of the sink Kafka topic total_proton

Again, as with Flink and ksqlDB, the underlying model is eventual consistency, and the dilemma we end up in is similar—even though we get less extreme errors in the intermediate results, we still have to stop the input stream to make sure we end up with the correct result.

RisingWave

Next up is RisingWave, a streaming database with PostgreSQL wire protocol compatibility. We set up the example for RisingWave as follows. We first create a table fed by our input Kafka topic transactions:

```
CREATE TABLE IF NOT EXISTS transactions (
   id INT,
   from_account INT,
   to_account INT,
   amount INT,
   ts TIMESTAMP
) WITH (
   connector = 'kafka',
   topic = 'transactions',
   properties.bootstrap.server = 'broker:29092',
   scan.startup.mode = 'earliest',
   scan.startup.timestamp_millis = '140000000'
) ROW FORMAT JSON;
```

Secondly, we set up the views in Example 6-8.

Example 6-8. Setting up the views credits, debits, balance, and total in RisingWave

```
CREATE VIEW accounts AS
SELECT
  from_account AS account
FROM
  transactions
UNION
SELECT
  to_account
FROM
  transactions;

CREATE VIEW credits AS
SELECT
  transactions.to_account AS account,
  SUM(transactions.amount) AS credits
FROM
  transactions
  LEFT JOIN accounts ON transactions.to_account = accounts.account
GROUP BY
  to_account;
```

```
CREATE VIEW debits AS
SELECT
  transactions.from_account AS account,
  SUM(transactions.amount) AS debits
FROM
  transactions
  LEFT JOIN accounts ON transactions.from_account = accounts.account
GROUP BY
  from_account;

CREATE VIEW balance AS
SELECT
  credits.account AS account,
  credits - debits AS balance
FROM
  credits
  INNER JOIN debits ON credits.account = debits.account;

CREATE VIEW total AS
SELECT
  sum(balance)
FROM
  balance;
```

And finally, we sink the view total into the topic total_risingwave:

```
CREATE SINK total_sink
FROM
  total WITH (
    connector = 'kafka',
    properties.bootstrap.server = 'broker:29092',
    topic = 'total_risingwave',
    type = 'append-only',
    force_append_only = 'true'
  );
```

We then set up the tables and views in RisingWave and run the Python code to create 10,000 transactions. The visualized results for RisingWave are as shown in Figure 6-5.

We end up with 105 messages in the sink topic, which is a bit more than what we got with Proton, and much less than what Flink SQL and ksqlDB produced. But, more importantly, each of the messages gives us the correct result: 0.

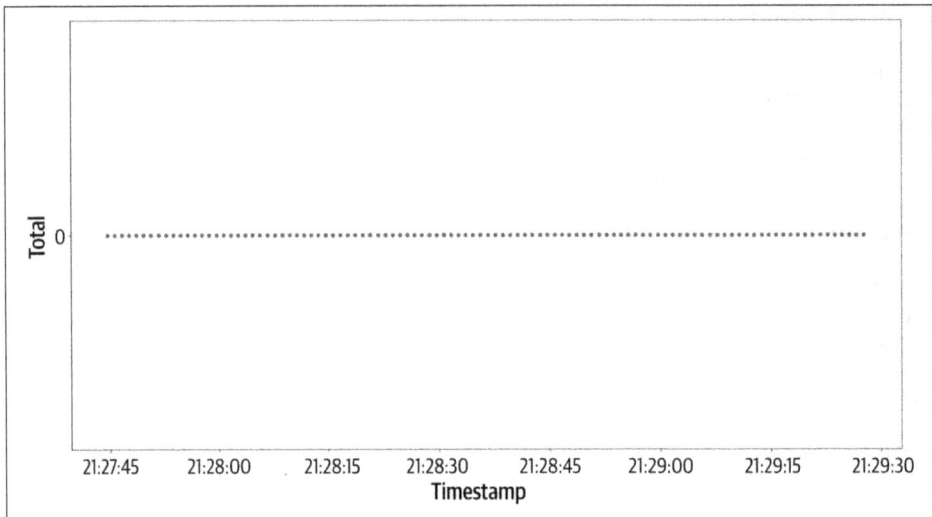

Figure 6-5. Visualization of the sink Kafka topic `total_risingwave`

Materialize

Our fifth stream processing system is Materialize, another streaming database offering a PostgreSQL-compatible API like RisingWave. We first create a table fed by our input Kafka topic `transactions`.

```
CREATE CONNECTION kafka_connection TO kafka (broker 'broker:29092');

CREATE SOURCE transactions_source
FROM
  kafka connection kafka_connection (TOPIC 'transactions', START OFFSET (0)) KEY FORMAT
  TEXT VALUE FORMAT TEXT INCLUDE KEY ENVELOPE UPSERT WITH (SIZE = '1');

CREATE VIEW transactions AS
SELECT
  ((text :: jsonb) ->> 'id') :: string AS id,
  ((text :: jsonb) ->> 'from_account') :: int AS from_account,
  ((text :: jsonb) ->> 'to_account') :: int AS to_account,
  ((text :: jsonb) ->> 'amount') :: int AS amount,
  ((text :: jsonb) ->> 'ts') :: timestamp AS ts,
  key
FROM
  transactions_source;
```

Then, we set up the views in Example 6-9.

Example 6-9. Setting up the views `credits`, `debits`, `balance`, *and* `total` *in Materialize*

```
CREATE VIEW accounts AS
SELECT
  from_account AS account
FROM
  transactions
UNION
SELECT
  to_account
FROM
  transactions;

CREATE VIEW credits AS
SELECT
  transactions.to_account AS account,
  SUM(transactions.amount) AS credits
FROM
  transactions
  LEFT JOIN accounts ON transactions.to_account = accounts.account
GROUP BY
  to_account;

CREATE VIEW debits AS
SELECT
  transactions.from_account AS account,
  SUM(transactions.amount) AS debits
FROM
  transactions
  LEFT JOIN accounts ON transactions.from_account = accounts.account
GROUP BY
  from_account;

CREATE VIEW balance AS
SELECT
  credits.account AS account,
  credits - debits AS balance
FROM
  credits
  INNER JOIN debits ON credits.account = debits.account;

CREATE VIEW total AS
SELECT
  SUM(balance)
FROM
  balance;
```

And finally, we sink the view `total` into the topic `total_materialize`:

```
CREATE SINK total_sink
FROM
    total INTO kafka connection kafka_connection (TOPIC 'total_materialize')
    FORMAT JSON ENVELOPE DEBEZIUM WITH (SIZE = '1');
```

We can now run the toy example by first setting up the sources and views in Materialize and then executing the Python code to create 10,000 transactions. The visualized results for Materialize are shown in Figure 6-6.

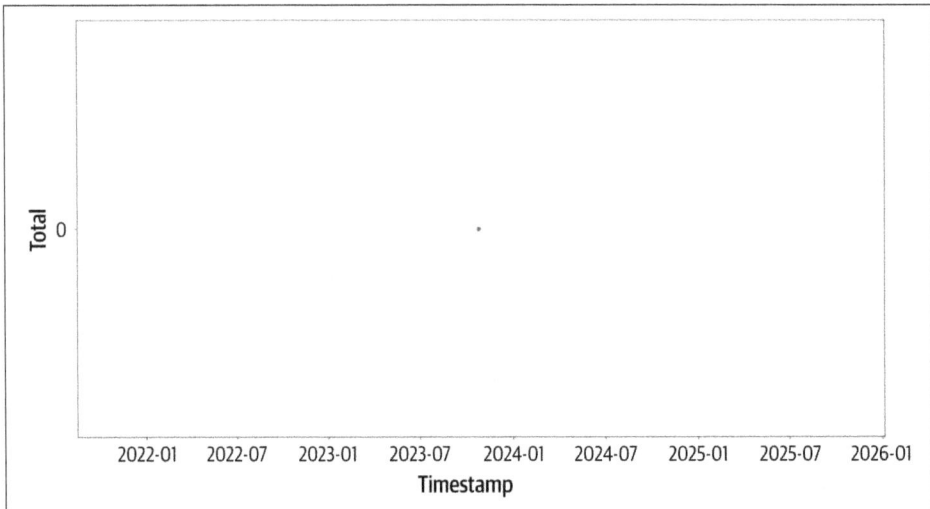

Figure 6-6. The Kafka topic `total_materialize`

Materialize only outputs one message to the sink Kafka topic, and this message contains the correct result, 0, whenever we run it. We will go into more detail about how Materialize achieves this below.

Pathway

Pathway is actually more of a stream processing library for Python and not a full-fledged streaming database. We still added it to this chapter to show that consistency can be achieved using a stream processor as well and that a streaming database is not a requirement.

What's more, it's a stream processor that uses Python as the imperative language to author streaming pipelines. The Python code in Example 6-10 contains SQL statements similar to those used for Flink SQL, ksqlDB, Proton, RisingWave, and Materialize, except the source and destination of the results are defined in Python + SQL instead of just SQL.

Example 6-10. Setting up the example in Python with Pathway

```python
#!/bin/python

import pathway as pw

rdkafka_settings = {  ❶
    "bootstrap.servers": "localhost:56512",
    "group.id": "pw",
    "session.timeout.ms": "6000"
}

class InputSchema(pw.Schema):  ❷
  id: int
  from_account: int
  to_account: int
  amount: int
  ts: str


t = pw.io.kafka.read(  ❸
    rdkafka_settings,
    topic="transactions",
    schema=InputSchema,
    format="json",
    autocommit_duration_ms=1000
)

credits = pw.sql(  ❹
  """
  SELECT to_account, sum(amount) as credits
  FROM T GROUP BY to_account
  """, T=t)

debits = pw.sql(  ❺
  """
    SELECT from_account, sum(amount) as debits
    FROM T GROUP BY from_account
    """, T=t)

balance = pw.sql(  ❻
    """
    SELECT CC.to_account, credits - debits as balance
    FROM CC
    join DD on CC.to_account = DD.from_account
    """, CC=credits, DD=debits)

total = pw.sql(  ❼
    """
    SELECT sum(balance) as total FROM BB
    """, BB=balance)
```

```
pw.io.kafka.write( ❽
    total,
    rdkafka_settings=rdkafka_settings,
    topic_name='total_pathway',
    format='json')

pw.run() ❾
```

❶   The connection information to Kafka.

❷   The schema of the transactions being consumed.

❸   t represents the streaming transactions coming from Kafka.

❹   The credits table.

❺   The debits table.

❻   The balance after the debits are subtracted from credits.

❼   The total that will be used to emit to Kafka.

❽   The result in a Kafka topic named total_pathway.

❾   Run the dataflow asynchronously.

The result of running this application is a single record written to the total_pathway topic in Kafka (see Example 6-11).

Example 6-11. The single record written to the result topic total_pathway

```
{
    "total": 0, ❶
    "diff": 1,
    "time": 1698960910176
}
```

❶   This is the value of the record with a total of 0.

The visualization of the sink topic in Figure 6-7 shows exactly the same behavior as Materialize.

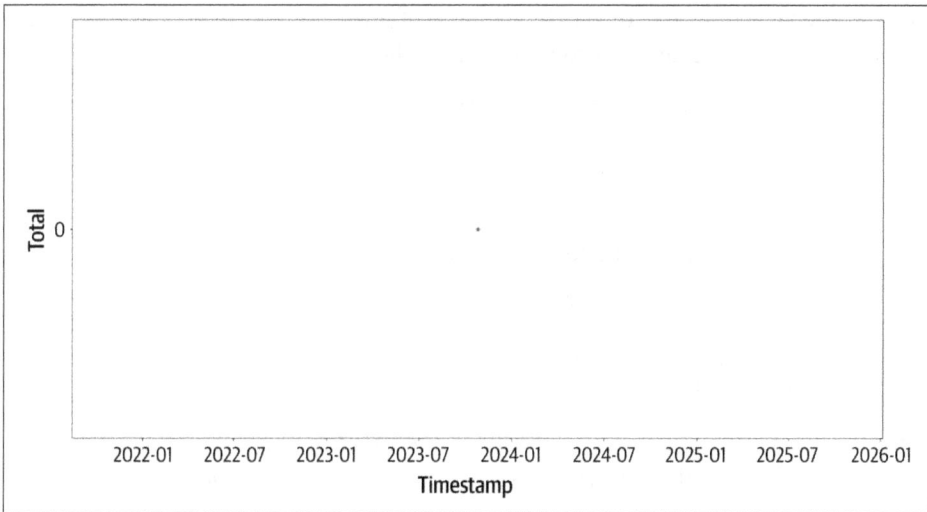

Figure 6-7. The Kafka topic `balance`

Out-of-Order Messages

To model more realistic conditions, we modified the Python code from Example 6-1 to produce about 1/10 of the messages out of order. From the 10,000 messages, about 1,000 were out-of-order. We obtained almost the same results as in the trivial case without any late-arriving/out of order messages for Flink SQL, ksqlDB, and Proton, and *exactly* the same results for RisingWave, Materialize, and Pathway.

Going Beyond Eventual Consistency

After you have seen how the five stream processing systems have fared, there are a number of unanswered questions:

- Why do the eventually consistent Flink SQL, ksqlDB, and Proton fail our toy example?

- How do the internally consistent RisingWave, Materialize, and Pathway pass it?

- And what can we learn from that—can we even derive a workaround for Flink SQL, ksqlDB, and Proton?

Why Do Eventually Consistent Stream Processors Fail the Toy Example?

Let's trace back to what we did in our toy example. We first created the two views `credits` and `debits`. Up until this point, all was still fine. But once we joined the two views in the view `balance`, the `JOIN` operators of Flink SQL, ksqlDB, and Proton did not correctly match up the data coming in from the views `credits` and `debits`.

To understand how this happened, we restrict ourselves to four transactions:

1. Transfer $1 from account 0 to account 1.
2. Transfer $1 from account 0 to account 2.
3. Transfer $1 from account 1 to account 2.
4. Transfer $1 from account 2 to account 0.

Now let's see what can happen in an eventually consistent stream processing system like Flink SQL, ksqlDB, and Proton.

Since the two inputs of the `JOIN` operator in the `balance` view are not synchronized, a possible scenario is that the `credits` view emits its results earlier than the `debits` view, which results in the `balance` view combining its inputs as follows:

1. `balance` combines the first result of the `credits` view with the first result of the `debits` view.
2. `balance` combines the second result of `credits` with the first result of `debits`.
3. `balance` combines the third result of `credits` with the first result of `debits`.
4. `balance` combines the fourth result of `credits` with the first result of `debits`.

What happens here can be likened to a *race condition* illustrated in Figure 6-8, where the four transactions can be seen on the left and the results in the `credits` and `debits` views are shown in the middle. On the right, you can see the results in the `balance` view and corresponding sums in the `total` view. In the `credits`, `debits`, and `balance` parts of the diagram, "`0:1`" stands for "account 0, value 1," "`2:1`" stands for "account 2, value 1," and so on (where "value" is either `credits`, `debits`, or `balance`, depending on the position in the diagram).

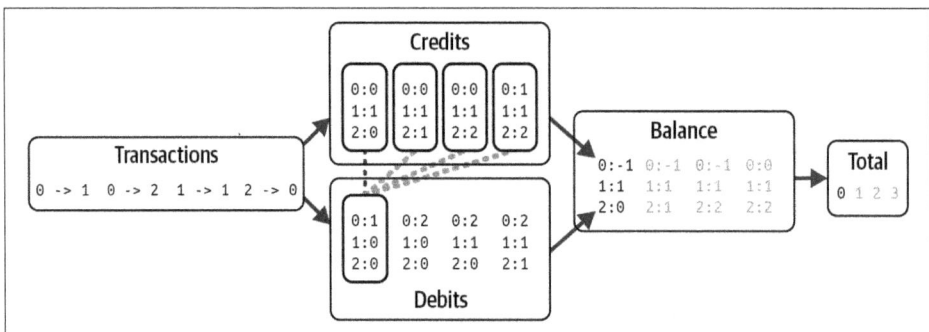

Figure 6-8. Incorrect intermediate results: `credits` emits faster than `debits`

The four combinations of results from `credits` and `debits` into `balance` are indicated by the dotted lines. The three rightmost dotted lines indicate incorrect combinations, and the three rightmost results indicate incorrect results in `balance` and `total`. As you can see, while the first result (in boldface) of the `balance` view (where the first result of `credits` is correctly joined with the first result of `debits`) is correct, the next three results are incorrect and break our invariant of the total sum of the balances having to be 0. Since the `credits` view has emitted its results earlier than the `debits` view, the resulting wrong total calculations yield positive results (1, 2, and 3).

For further illustration, let's look at another possible scenario. Here, the `debits` view emits its results faster than the `credits` view:

1. `balance` combines the first result of the `credits` view with the first result of the `debits` view.

2. `balance` combines the first result of `credits` with the second result of `debits`.

3. `balance` combines the first result of `credits` with the third result of `debits`.

4. `balance` combines the first result of `credits` with the fourth result of `debits`.

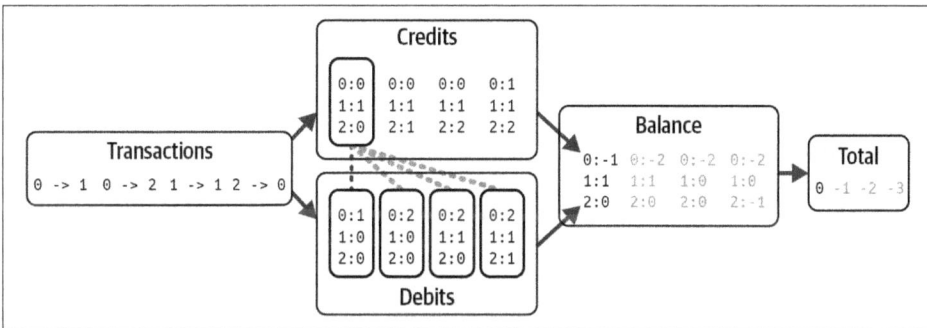

Figure 6-9. Incorrect intermediate results: `debits` emits faster than `credits`

Here, the `debits` view has emitted its results earlier than the `credits` view, and consequently, the resulting wrong total calculations yield negative results (−1, −2, and −3). Let's delve deeper into what could have caused this.

Early emission from nonmonotonic operators

The main goal of eventually consistent stream processing systems is low latency. To achieve this goal, one of the design decisions made by Flink SQL and ksqlDB is to emit results as early as possible. As a side note, this also caused these systems to emit so many messages into the sink Kafka topic (almost 80,000 for Flink SQL and almost 40,000 for ksqlDB).[2]

Proton, though also eventually consistent, emitted many fewer messages (56). For most classical stream processing use cases, this behavior is fine, but for nonwindowed data, this can become a *failure mode*, called *early emission from nonmonotonic operators* in Brandon's blog.

Early emission of results doesn't pose a problem for monotonic operators such as filters. But it *can be* problematic for nonmonotonic operators, as we see in the example. Here, nonmonotonic operators such as JOINs and UNIONs cannot just "combine what they get as early as they get it" from both of their inputs and then emit these intermediate results. They have to make sure that they only combine aligned, synchronized inputs.

MiniBatch, as used in Proton and also optionally in Flink 1.19+, can be a cure for this failure pattern, as we will discuss later, as can be caching for ksqlDB.

Combining streams without synchronization

In fact, what leads to the eventually consistent stream processing systems breaking our toy example is a combination of "early emission from nonmonotonic operators" and these operators not synchronizing their inputs (*combining streams without synchronization* in Brandon's blog).

What goes wrong is that the transactions of our toy bank, which actually correspond to database transactions here, are lost as soon as we JOIN the credits and debits views in the balance view. Essentially, the JOIN operators in Flink SQL, ksqlDB, and, to an extent, Proton just JOIN whatever comes in from both input views—and if it falls foul to the race condition and any of the two input views provides its inputs faster than the other, we get incorrect/inconsistent results (as shown in Figures 6-8 and 6-9).

A common response to the need for synchronization is that this form of synchronization implies requiring a global lock, just like in a database, and such a global lock would not scale. In fact, using a global lock for synchronization is only one option (the simplest and least scalable). There are ways for achieving synchronization in a concurrent and scalable way, as we will see in the following sections.

---

2 These numbers of intermediate results can be significantly reduced by optimizing the Flink SQL and ksqlDB configurations (e.g., MiniBatch for Flink SQL, KTable caches, and/or commit interval for ksqlDB) for this particular use case. We simply used the defaults.

How Do Internally Consistent Stream Processing Systems Pass the Toy Example?

As we have seen, the key to getting our toy example right is to be able to combine streams *with* synchronization. Intuitively, we have to make sure that only those results from credits and debits that *belong together*—or, in other words, correspond to the same transaction in the transactions source Kafka topic—are combined.

The graphs showing the results in the total topics indicated that RisingWave (Figure 6-5), Materialize (Figure 6-6), and Pathway (Figure 6-7) might have found a way to implement this. But how?

RisingWave

RisingWave makes use of the concept of *barriers*, inspired by the *checkpoint barriers* of Flink. Essentially, barriers are control records containing *epochs* (timestamps), which are automatically injected periodically (e.g., every second) into all sources. In RisingWave, barriers are used as version numbers for data. Operators are only allowed to emit the result associated with a specific version once the same version/barrier has been received from all inputs.

Flink uses barriers for consistent checkpointing. RisingWave, on the other hand, also fully exploits the fact that it is a streaming database and not just a stream processor, and thus has full control over its persistence layer, including the checkpoints. RisingWave can thus go beyond Flink in this regard and can use the checkpointing barriers not only for checkpointing itself but also for versioning in an adaptation of the concept of *snapshot isolation* from the database world.

Let's visualize what happens with our four transactions and how RisingWave would process them. In Figure 6-10, we inject barriers after each of the transactions, signified by the vertical lines. Each of the barriers has its own version indicated by the subscripts (1, 2, 3, 4). During processing in RisingWave, the transaction barriers are forwarded to the next operators. Now when the balance view is calculated, the barriers are used to ensure that inputs from the credits and debits views are only combined if both of them precede the same barrier (i.e., have the same version).

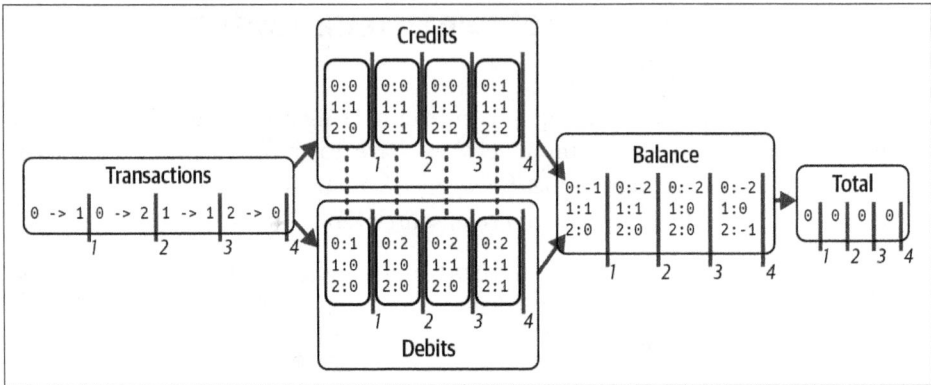

Figure 6-10. Using transaction barriers to ensure consistency

In principle, barriers can also be injected less frequently. Consider the diagram in Figure 6-11, where we only inject one for every two messages in the transactions.

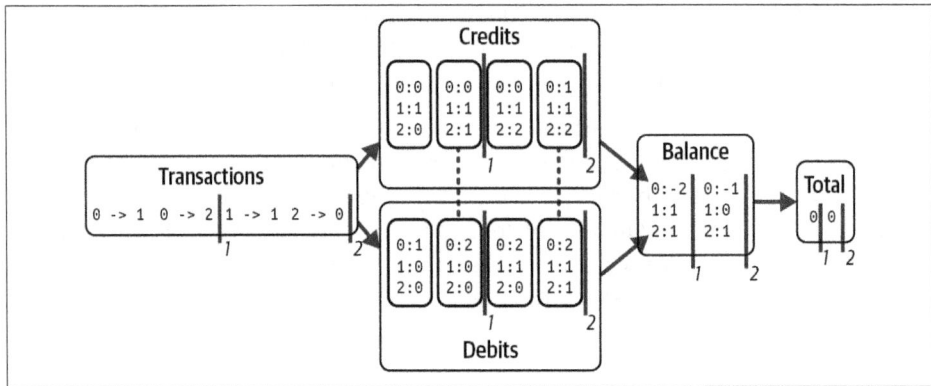

Figure 6-11. Using (less frequent) transaction barriers to ensure consistency

The frequency of injection of these *epoch barriers* in RisingWave has direct consequences with respect to latency and memory consumption. Increased frequency of injection reduces end-to-end latency, but at the cost of more memory consumption because maintaining more versions of the data consumes more memory.

> At first glance, barriers resemble *watermarks* known from stream processors like Flink by also being *control records* in the dataflow graph. However, barriers and watermarks have slightly different semantics. With barriers, operators can only emit results once they have reached the same barrier for all inputs. With watermarks, operators can only proceed once they encounter a watermark. A watermark signals that all events up to a certain timestamp should have arrived.

Materialize

Materialize is based on Differential Dataflow (DD).[3] Data in DD is always versioned and all of DD's operators respect these versions. Hence, the diagram in Figure 6-12 for Materialize is very similar to Figure 6-10, with the only difference being that the data is versioned out of the box—DD doesn't need any additional concepts like barriers.

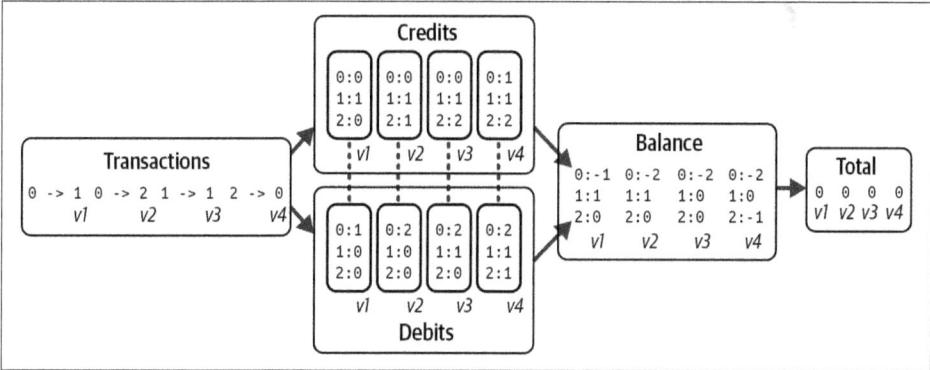

Figure 6-12. How DD/Materialize ensures consistency through versions of data

Operator synchronization in DD is thus achieved as follows:

1. Each datum is accompanied with a version (in Figure 6-12, they are called "v1," "v2," "v3," and "v4").

2. Operators can only combine data of the same version.

In this way, DD also implements a form of snapshot isolation and can pass our toy example.

Pathway

Like Materialize, Pathway is also based on DD and thus also uses versioning to achieve the operator input synchronization required for passing our toy example challenge. We included Pathway to show that this form of consistency can be achieved not only by a streaming database but also by a stream processing library with an internally consistent underlying engine like DD.

---

3 Derek G. Murray et al., "Naiad: A Timely Dataflow System," Proceedings of SOSP'13: The 24th ACM Symposium on Operating Systems Principles (*https://oreil.ly/-dBrD*).

How Can We Fix Eventually Consistent Stream Processing Systems to Pass the Toy Example?

We have seen that one of the key features of internally consistent stream processing systems is their ability to synchronize the inputs of their binary, nonmonotonic operators such as UNIONs and JOINs, either by barriers (RisingWave) or versions (DD, Materialize, Pathway). More abstractly, the keys to the "global-lock-free synchronization kingdom" are efficient systems of semantically meaningful timestamps allowing for decoupled progress to happen across the stream processing topology.

Can we use this insight to derive a fix to make Flink SQL also pass our toy example?[4]

How Flink SQL can pass the toy example

For Flink SQL, there are indeed ways to pass our toy example. One is to make explicit use of the timestamp field ts in the WHERE clause of the balance view to JOIN the credits and debits only if the ts field of credits and debits matches.[5] We display the changes to the Flink SQL code in Example 6-12.

Example 6-12. Setting up the views balance and total in Flink SQL using an explicit ts field for operator input synchronization

```
CREATE VIEW credits(account, credits, ts) AS
SELECT
  to_account as account,
  sum(amount) as credits,
  ts
FROM
  transactions
GROUP BY
  to_account,
  ts;

CREATE VIEW debits(account, debits, ts) AS
SELECT
  from_account as account,
  sum(amount) as debits,
  ts
FROM
  transactions
GROUP BY
  from_account,
```

---

4 We have tried to implement a similar fix for ksqlDB but failed because of ksqlDB's limited SQL syntax. It's probably possible to implement the fix with Kafka Streams using its lower-level ProcessorAPI.

5 In the real world, however, it's very hard to keep timestamps in different records exactly the same; hence synchronizing on the ts field could be a brittle fix.

```
  ts;

CREATE VIEW balance(account, balance) AS
SELECT
  credits.account,
  credits - debits as balance
FROM
  credits,
  debits
WHERE
  credits.account = debits.account
  AND credits.ts = debits.ts;
```

With this fix, the size of the Flink SQL sink topic `total_flinksql_ts` goes down from about 80,000 to 1, without any intermediate results. Now, it only includes one message with the correct sum, 0, just like Materialize and Pathway, as you can see in Figure 6-13.

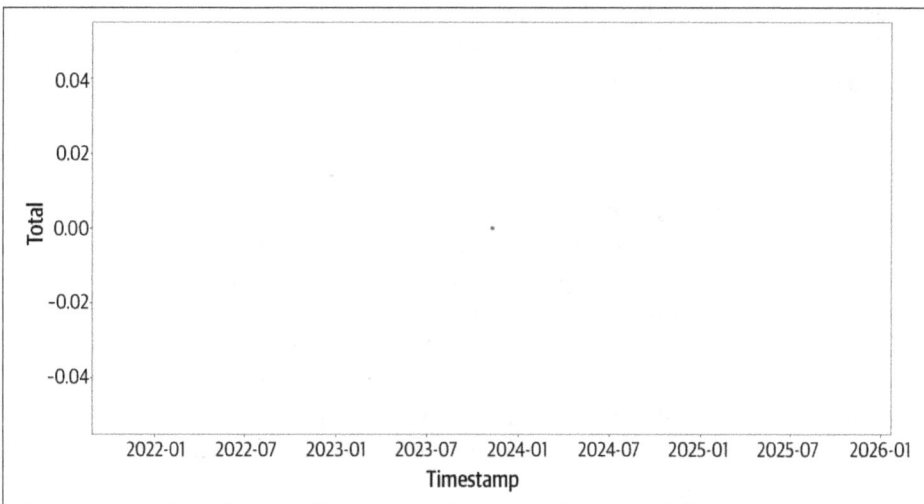

Figure 6-13. The Kafka topic `total_flinksql_ts`

Why this fix can be problematic

By having identified the key feature of internally consistent stream processing systems that helped them solve our toy example, we could also solve it with Flink SQL by adding explicit operator input synchronization via timestamps. So is eventual consistency strong enough for stream processing after all? Why would we need a stronger form of consistency at all?

The fix for Flink SQL to pass our toy example can be problematic in a number of ways that are not immediately obvious. It does work perfectly for a toy example, but:

- By adding the timestamp (`ts`) to the `GROUP BY` in Example 6-12, we create an unboundedly growing internal state store for the aggregation, which would lead to Flink exhausting its memory at a later stage.

- As we stated in the introduction to this chapter, an engineer coming over from the database world would have a hard time understanding why their intuitive solution creates 80,000 mostly incorrect results in Flink SQL and why they would have to fix any of their perfectly fine-looking, intuitive SQL code at all.

- Explicitly "bolting on" consistency on an eventually consistent system can only be done on a case-by-case basis. Each new use case can require a different fix.

- Fixes like this can still lead to subtle inconsistencies. Assume you have not one but two input topics, `transactions1` and `transactions2`—one holding bank accounts 0 to 4, and the other bank accounts 5 to 9. Now, what if a transaction from `transactions1` has the same timestamp as a transaction from `transactions2`? Then you couldn't stop Flink SQL from combining wrong inputs any longer. Once again, you would have to search for a fix of your fix (e.g., include the transaction ID in the `JOIN` clause, etc.).

Taken together, it seems that eventually consistent stream processing systems *can* often be fixed to behave more consistently, but the level of consistency that you can reach is entirely up to you, the engineer—and can change with the next `JOIN` that you have to implement on top of your existing SQL code. Consistent stream processing on nonwindowed data *can* be done in eventually consistent stream processors, but it's almost guaranteed to be more time consuming and error prone and, on top, hardly accessible to anybody outside the small circle of stream processing experts. It's far too easy to get inconsistent results even though the SQL code looks perfectly fine at first glance.

MiniBatch in Flink 1.19+

Flink 1.19 introduced MiniBatch semantics for `JOIN`s. If activated and configured in a way that fits the use case at hand, MiniBatch can not only significantly improve the performance of Flink but also lead up to a much higher level of consistency.

MiniBatch is an optimization to buffer input records to reduce state access. We have experimented with various configurations for MiniBatch and found out that for the toy example of this chapter, it's a very effective cure for the "inconsistency" that we experienced before.

To activate MiniBatch, three parameters have to be configured:

```
SET 'table.exec.mini-batch.enabled' = 'true';

SET 'table.exec.mini-batch.allow-latency' = '5S';

SET 'table.exec.mini-batch.size' = '5000';
```

The configuration item `table.exec.mini-batch.allow-latency` sets the maximum latency for the MiniBatch optimization to buffer input records to the `JOIN` operators. `table.exec.mini-batch.size` sets the maximum number of input records to be buffered. MiniBatch is then triggered with the allowed latency interval and when the maximum number of records is reached.

We found out that if `table.exec.mini-batch.size` is set to 1, Flink still outputs the same number of records (almost 80,000), most of them incorrect, to the sink topic. This is not surprising, since that setting essentially disables MiniBatch, and Flink returns to its default behavior. If we increase the batch size to 10, we already get a massive reduction of output messages (403), and when we go up to 50 or more, only one message is written out to the sink topic—giving us the correct result, 0. This consistent result still holds when we send out the transactions out of order.

Hence, it seems that MiniBatch not only is a performance optimization but also impacts the level of consistency of Flink. Keep in mind, however, that it doesn't turn Flink from an eventually consistent into an internally consistent stream processor. And to be fair, in the Flink documentation, MiniBatch is described as a performance optimization only. To get advantages in terms of consistency, MiniBatch needs to be tuned to the right configuration, and even then, it doesn't guarantee a truly higher level of consistency in all circumstances.

Consistency Versus Latency

The elephant in the room—the question you as a reader have probably asked yourself already—is about latency. How much of the low latency of an eventually consistent stream processing system do we have to sacrifice to achieve the stronger level of internal consistency?

Before we answer that question, let's distinguish two different kinds of "latency":

Processing time latency
> The time required for a stream processing system to come up with *any* answer to a query.

End-to-end latency
> The time required for a stream processing system to come up with a *consistent* answer to a query.

Internally consistent stream processing systems have higher latencies than eventually consistent ones when it comes to pure processing time. For most nonclassic stream processing use cases, like those involving JOINs on nonwindowed data, however, users are more interested in end-to-end latency. In the extreme case of our toy example, we observed that all three internally consistent stream processing systems were able to come up with a consistent result after much less than a second—compared to *never* for the eventually consistent systems (unless you stop the input stream or fix your SQL in some way)…

To conclude, in an ideal world, newer versions of Flink SQL, ksqlDB, and Proton would include a switch to turn internal consistency on and off—so that users could easily choose their desired trade-off:

- Switch on internal consistency for use cases involving nonwindowed/unbounded data and where ultra-low latency is not required.

- Switch off internal consistency and revert to eventual consistency for classical stream processing use cases involving windowed data and where ultra-low latency is required.

This would allow them to keep their current processing model for ultra-low latency use cases, and, at the same time, enable them to treat nonwindowed data in a more consistent way, allowing practitioners to seamlessly move from and to the database and the streaming worlds without having to explicitly bolt on consistency as an afterthought.

Summary

You have seen that while being perfectly suited for classical low-latency, high-throughput use cases at scale involving windowed data, classical eventually consistent stream processing systems have their drawbacks:

- They can be hard to apply for use cases involving nonwindowed data.

- Engineers coming from the database world cannot stick to their tried and tested SQL intuitions and formulas.

We think that these are two of the biggest roadblocks for the broader adoption not only of stream processing systems, but also of streaming in general. If you are coming from the database world, would you bother to work with a system that can turn perfectly fine-looking SQL into such inconsistent chaos as we observed for our toy example? Of course, consistency can be bolted on, for example, by complicating the SQL code with additional conditions, watermark definitions, etc., but this can usually only be done reliably by a small minority of expensive and hard-to-find stream processing experts.

Internally consistent stream processing systems such as RisingWave, Materialize, and Pathway provide stronger consistency guarantees. They could solve our toy example out of the box by offering a higher level of abstraction (and a less leaky abstraction) on the difficult concepts dealing with time that are behind stream processing. Thus, these systems have the potential to *democratize* stream processing for those who dare to come over from the database to the streaming world and to significantly extend the streaming market as a whole.

As for latency with respect to processing time, internally consistent stream processing systems cannot outperform eventually consistent ones. When you look at the often more important metric of end-to-end latency though, they can.

In the next chapter, we move into the space of hybrid data systems that is highly related to streaming databases.

## CHAPTER 7

Emergence of Other Hybrid Data Systems

In this chapter, we broaden our focus to include the greater landscape of hybrid systems that have surfaced in response to the growing demands of modern real-time event-driven applications. While these systems are not streaming databases as we defined them in this book, they share qualities and features that bridge between relational, analytical, and streaming workloads. We will explore the motivations behind their development, the innovative techniques they employ, and the specific use cases that make them relevant. More importantly, we will discuss the niches these other hybrid databases cover. This understanding will allow us to uncover the trends that databases are following to provide real-time analytics.

It's important to acknowledge that a streaming database is also an example of a hybrid system. Hybrid systems take at least two perspectives, and in the streaming database case, the two perspectives are stream processing and the database.

Appreciating the perspectives of hybrid systems will reveal the problems that they try to solve and how. In this book, we define streaming databases from the stream processing perspective as follows: a streaming database is a stream processor that exposes its state store for clients to issue pull queries.

An alternative definition created from the database perspective is as follows: a streaming database is a database that can consume and emit streams as well as execute materialized views asynchronously.

By defining the hybrid system from both perspectives, you will expand the hybrid system's accessibility to other engineers and use cases. Consistency in stream processing is an example of this. Streaming database engineers were forced to see the database perspective, through which the lack of consistency in some established stream processors was then identified.

State stores can be implemented in many ways: key-value, row-based, and column-based. The implementation of the state store determines the supportable use cases that can range from high consistency requirements to low-latency analytical queries.

Interestingly, streaming databases are just one example of emerging hybrid and converging systems, reducing infrastructure complexity and increasing developer accessibility.

Data Planes

Let's better understand these emerging systems by creating a Venn diagram (Figure 7-1) of where real-time systems live today. This will help in discerning the different use cases (we'll cover these use cases in more detail in Chapter 11) and deployment models in real-time analytical scenarios.

The diagram will make us see not only the streaming but also the database perspective. For example, our definition of a streaming database at the beginning of this chapter was from a stream processing perspective. We can change this definition to a database perspective: a streaming database is a database that can consume and emit streams as well as execute materialized views asynchronously.

Respecting all perspectives will also provide hints as to what the next-generation databases might look like.

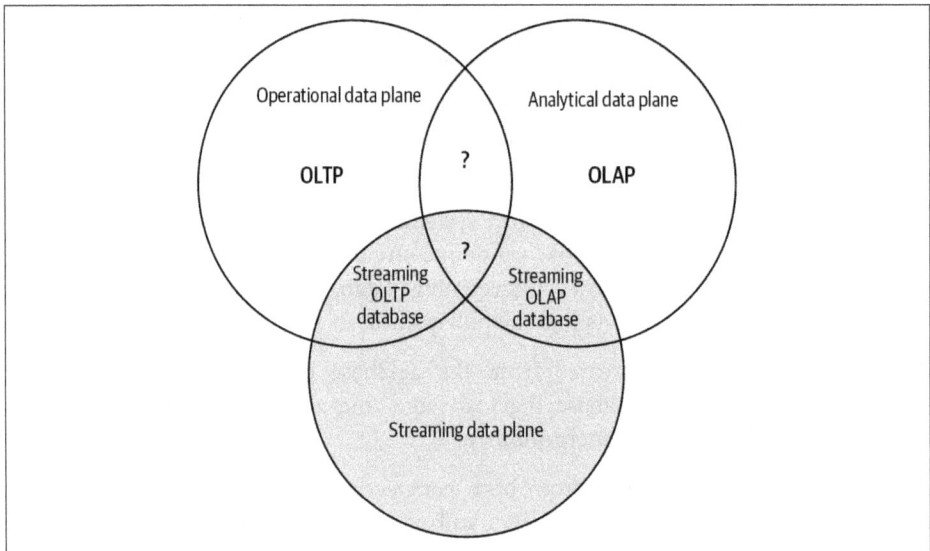

Figure 7-1. The streaming plane

The Venn diagram also helps us to improve our understanding of the role of streaming systems in the analytical ecosystem. Figure 7-1 presents a diagram of the two data planes that we already know: the operational plane and the analytical data plane.

The diagram adds a third plane: the streaming data plane. This data plane has always existed but was never acknowledged. It is the only data plane where data is mostly in motion. The other planes hold data at rest. Where the operational and analytical planes overlap with the streaming planes is where we have both data at rest and data in motion. This is where the streaming databases lie. We will address the other areas of overlap later in this chapter.

The streaming data plane connects the operational and analytical aspects of data processing. It captures and processes real-time data, allowing it to flow seamlessly into the analytical plane, storing, analyzing, and using it for insights and decision-making. Hence, it acts as a bridge to enable organizations to make quicker, data-driven decisions based on the combination of real-time and historical data.

To review, the operational plane holds OLTP databases, which are consistent and use row-based storage. This plane also contains the applications that use the OLTP database. The analytical plane includes OLAP databases, which are columnar based and eventually consistent storage. These OLAP databases are optimized to serve analytical queries.

The streaming plane holds source connectors that bring data at rest into data in motion. They also have sink connectors that write streaming data into RTOLAP databases for low-latency serving. The streaming plane leverages platforms like Kafka and Kafka Connect to replicate and serve streaming data. Stateful stream processors and streaming databases are also contained in the streaming plane.

Let's take a closer look at just the streaming plane in Figure 7-2. In Chapter 6, you learned about the consistency spectrum of stream processors. Figure 7-2 shows a detailed version of just the streaming plane circle from Figure 7-1. Figure 7-2 divides strictly consistent stream processors from those that would be eventually consistent, starting from the left to the right, as well as the storage types from top to bottom.

Streaming data travels from the left to the right in Figure 7-2, as it makes its way from the operational plane to the analytical plane. Keep in mind that connectors and streaming platforms like Kafka also live in the streaming plane.

As always with Venn diagrams, the interesting parts are where the circles overlap. Let's look at the overlap between the operational and analytical data planes next.

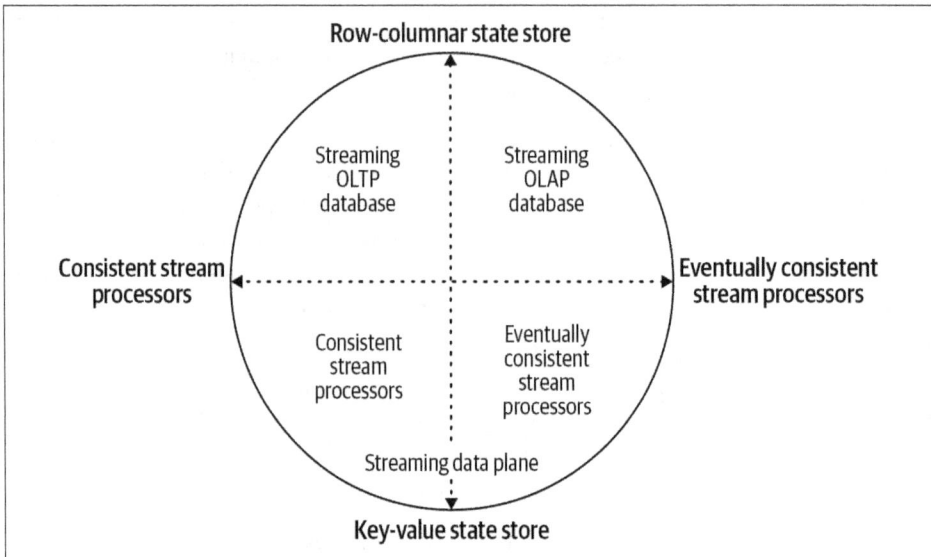

Figure 7-2. The streaming plane

Hybrid Transactional/Analytical Database

Streaming OLTP databases (row-based storage) converge the stream processing in the streaming plane with the OLTP database in the operational plane. This is where the row-based, consistent streaming databases reside (e.g., RisingWave and Materialize).

Streaming OLAP databases (column-based storage) converge the characteristics of an OLAP database in the analytical plane with the stream processing characteristics of the streaming plane. These databases are optimized for complex analytical queries using indexing and columnar storage and have eventual consistency characteristics. Proton resides in this area.

The overlap between operational and analytical (without streaming) represents hybrid transactional/analytical processing (HTAP) databases (see Figure 7-3). These databases can handle both OLTP and OLAP workloads. This idea was conceived by Gartner in 2014 (*https://oreil.ly/75RaD*).

HTAP is an emerging application architecture that "breaks the wall" between transaction processing and analytics. It enables more informed and "in business real-time" decision-making.

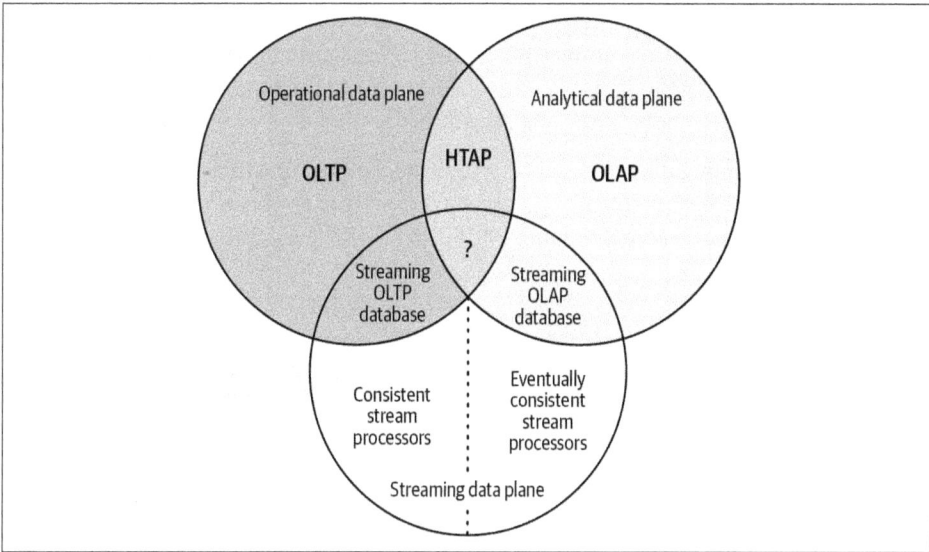

Figure 7-3. HTAP database is a hybrid OLTP/OLAP database without stream processing

You may be asking, "Wasn't there a reason why OLTP and OLAP workloads were separated to begin with? Wasn't this *wall* placed there intentionally?"

There are two storage types in an HTAP database: in-memory and persistent. Gartner's HTAP database design can execute analytical queries on "in-flight" transactions that are performing writes. What enables HTAP databases to do both workloads is leveraging an in-memory database. For OLTP workloads, HTAP databases satisfy ACID properties with transactions and persistent writes. See Figure 7-4.

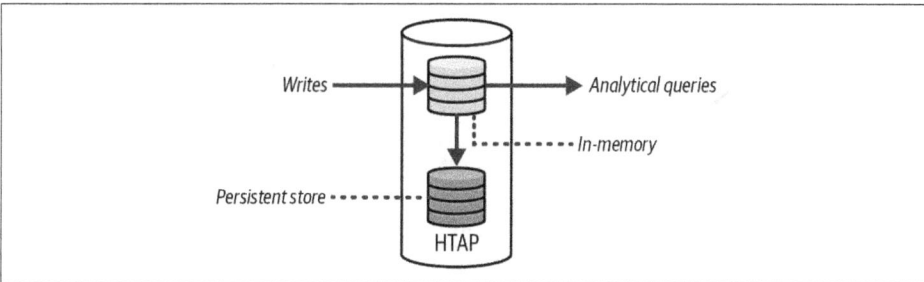

Figure 7-4. HTAP internal architecture defined by Gartner

Exposing the in-memory storage to serve analytical queries is very similar to what streaming databases do. The difference with HTAP is that it doesn't support stream processing. Some HTAP databases also do not support materialized views that run asynchronously, which takes away any stream processing-like features.

HTAP databases can effectively serve simple real-time analytics because they can serve queries from their in-memory store directly to the application, which performs writes. Table 7-1 shows some existing HTAP databases available in the market as of this writing.

Table 7-1. HTAP databases in the market as of writing

Name	Vendor	Storage implementation
Unistore	Snowflake	All data in a hybrid table is put in both row store and columnar store. Data, when changed, is synchronously changed in the row store and asynchronously flushed to columnar store.
SingleStoreDB	SingleStore	SingleStoreDB supports two types of tables: on-disk column-based (which they call Columnstore; this is the default table type for SingleStoreDB Cloud) and in-memory row-based. Columnstore is also known as Universal Storage.
TiDB	PingCAP	TiDB supports transactional key-value store and columnar store. TiKV is a distributed and transactional key-value database, which provides transactional APIs with ACID compliance. TiFlash is the analytical extension in the TiDB family that powers TiDB via columnar storage and a massively parallel processing (MPP) query engine.
HydraDB	Hydra	Open source database that supports transactional row-based store called *heap tables* and column-based storage layouts, which is the default layout.

The HTAP databases in Figure 7-4 do not follow the HTAP design proposed by Gartner. Under the storage implementation of Figure 7-4, every HTAP database incorporates both row-based and column-based storage. No in-flight, in-memory transactions are used to serve analytical queries.

Using HTAP databases effectively defeats the need for a streaming plane—this suggests that you can do all real-time data work within an HTAP database.

HTAP databases do have some limitations that prevent them from taking over real-time analytics. They are monolithic solutions that cannot hold historical data like the pure OLAP systems can. Historical data can be terabytes or even petabytes of data. It's a better solution to use when you don't need to keep historical data. Alternatively, you can keep both an OLAP and HTAP database in your infrastructure, which brings you back to the data divide we spoke of earlier in this book.

HTAP databases can better serve analytics to applications in the operational plane rather than running complex ad hoc analytical queries for data analysts. You will need to extract an aggregated history from the OLAP system, which reduces the size of history to one that the HTAP can accommodate. Again, you still have the data divide that the HTAP attempts to remove.

Figure 7-5 just shows the overlaps in the middle of the Venn diagram. As you can see, the overlaps form a flower with three petals: HTAP, streaming OLTP, and streaming OLAP databases.

Hybrid databases emerged to solve real-time analytical problems involving scalability and optimization that tend to require more or different infrastructure. More infrastructure leads to more data integration and movement of data before real-time analytics can be served to applications.

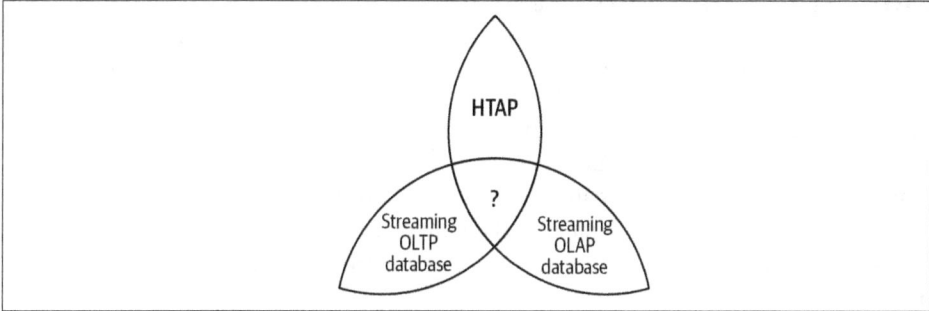

Figure 7-5. The triad of hybrid databases

The center of the flower (or the pistil) is still undefined at this point in the chapter, but we can start to infer what it means to implement a database that exists in the pistil. Before we do, other hybrid databases found on the operational plane need to be discussed because they don't fall nicely into our Venn model as easily.

Other Hybrid Databases

During our research for this book, we encountered many streaming-like databases that did not fit cleanly into our streaming or HTAP database definitions. These other hybrid databases combine unique features that solve problems that normally are solved with streaming systems you would find in the streaming plane.

Table 7-2. Other hybrid databases

Name	Hybrid systems	Description
PeerDB	Postgres OLTP database + stream processor	PeerDB is a Postgres-first data-movement platform that makes moving data in and out of Postgres fast and simple. It enables you to sync, transform, and load it into an OLAP system. Materialized views would have to be created in the OLTP database, so it doesn't meet our definition of a streaming database but still falls within the streaming OLTP database category.
Epsio	Postgres OLTP database + external asynchronous materialized view	Epsio plugs into existing databases and constantly updates results for queries you define whenever the underlying data changes, without ever recalculating the entire dataset. This approach allows Epsio to provide instant and always up-to-date results for complex queries while significantly reducing costs.

Name	Hybrid systems	Description
Turso	SQLite OLTP database + streaming platform	Turso allows you to develop locally and replicate globally to many locations around the world, exposing synchronous access to data instead of asynchronous access like Kafka.
Redpanda	Streaming Platform + Apache Iceberg (database)	Developers can bring their own query engines to query the data in Redpanda's tiered storage without moving them across different systems, reducing their infrastructure footprint on analytics.

Motivations for Hybrid Systems

Stream processing systems/vendors want to bring the database experience to streaming to help negate its stigma of being too hard and complex to adopt. Stream processing has often been associated with complexity, especially for those not well versed in the intricacies of real-time data processing. Stream processing systems and vendors aim to bridge this knowledge gap by providing a more user-friendly experience, akin to working with traditional databases. This involves simplifying the APIs, providing user-friendly interfaces, and offering tools that are more intuitive for a broader range of users.

The stigma of stream processing being too hard to adopt has discouraged many organizations from fully embracing real-time data analytics. By bringing the database experience to stream processing, vendors are attempting to reduce the barriers to entry, making it more accessible and approachable for businesses across various industries.

The scarcity of skilled data engineers who can effectively work with stream processing systems has also been a significant hurdle. Simplifying the adoption of stream processing by providing a familiar database-like environment can help organizations leverage real-time data analytics without extensive, specialized expertise.

Conversely, OLTP databases are trying to adopt features specific to OLAP databases so that they can better serve analytical queries at the operational plane. OLTP databases are also being pushed to adopt streaming features to meet the growing demand for real-time data analytics. These features avoid the round trip to the analytical plane, which, to many, is full of complex and unfamiliar infrastructure.

Many organizations operate in a distributed environment, and ensuring data consistency across multiple databases and systems can be challenging. OLTP databases are incorporating streaming features to make data replication and synchronization simpler. By leveraging streaming, they can propagate changes in real time, reducing the likelihood of data inconsistencies.

From the database perspective, database technologies recognize these needs but do not recognize they are characteristics of streaming.

The common goal every hybrid system has in the Venn diagram in Figure 7-1 is *providing real-time analytics with less infrastructure and greater accessibility to engineers.*

Many of these hybrid systems are based on an OLTP database partially because they are closer to the application facing the user and, in turn, more real time. It's becoming more so that delivering real-time analytics requires bringing data analytics closer to the operational plane, if not completely within it. Streaming systems need to recognize this to better understand their needs and to improve the reputation of being too difficult to implement.

The Influence of PostgreSQL on Hybrid Databases

Many of the hybrid databases are based on PostgreSQL (or Postgres), which is a very popular OLTP database. Postgres and its protocol are used by many of the more popular hybrid databases today: RisingWave, Materialize, Hydra, PeerDB, and Epsio.

Postgres' popularity and its community can be attributed to several additional factors listed in Table 7-3.

Table 7-3. Postgres popularity factors

Factor	Description
Extensibility	Postgres' extensible architecture allows developers to create custom data types, operators, and functions, making it suitable for a wide range of applications and industries.
Performance optimization	The community invests in optimizing the database engine, resulting in competitive performance and efficient query processing.
Third-party ecosystem	A rich ecosystem of third-party tools, libraries, and extensions has developed around Postgres, further enhancing its capabilities and flexibility.
Enterprise adoption	Many large organizations and enterprises have adopted Postgres for their critical applications, which contributes to its credibility and popularity.
Global reach	Postgres is not tied to a specific region or industry, making it appealing to a wide and diverse user base around the world.

The combination of open source principles, a welcoming and engaged community, robust development practices, and a feature-rich database engine has made Postgres a popular and enduring project in the world of relational databases. As its popularity continues to grow, expect more hybrid databases to provide a database experience that looks and feels like Postgres.

Near-Edge Analytics

Bringing analytics to the operational plane is a move to make data insights more accessible and responsive to end users. This approach is primarily driven by the goal of reducing latency, thereby enabling quicker decision-making in real-time scenarios. Hybrid databases play a pivotal role in this effort, as they aim to provide analytical capabilities without the need to replicate the entire analytical plane. Users, in many cases, do not require access to the entirety of the data repository. Instead, they demand only the specific and relevant subset of data necessary to inform their immediate, real-time decisions. This optimized data delivery ensures that valuable insights can be obtained swiftly.

Some analytical workloads will never make it to the operational plane because the analytical workloads often:

- Aggregate large amounts of historical data that is stored in the OLAP databases. These can be petabytes of data not suitable for operational infrastructure.
- Train machine learning models that require specialized systems, which do not exist on the operational plane.
- Require highly distributed systems that can partition the data for massively parallel processing, which, again, the operational plane does not fully support.
- Need the flexibility to execute ad hoc queries that serve data to users internally. Externally user-facing analytics do not possess this flexibility and often have to request additional metrics to show in their applications.

The goal of every real-time system is to find the easiest and optimal approach to get real-time analytics to end users without ballooning costs in infrastructure and resources. It's the hybrid databases that have the features to do this. Real-time is defining the next generation of hybrid databases. As more databases support real-time features, they become more hybrid by nature.

Next-Generation Hybrid Databases

Figure 7-6 provides a visual representation of the current landscape of real-time systems. It serves as a snapshot of the technologies and solutions that organizations are using today to meet their real-time data processing needs. These overlap zones that form petals are where the latest trends and innovations in real-time analytics are most pronounced. They include HTAP, streaming OLTP databases, and streaming OLAP databases.

The center of Figure 7-6 identifies the next generation of real-time databases. Next-generation databases will have features of all three data planes, including:

- Stateful stream processing
- Columnar storage for analytical workloads
- Consistency for operational workloads

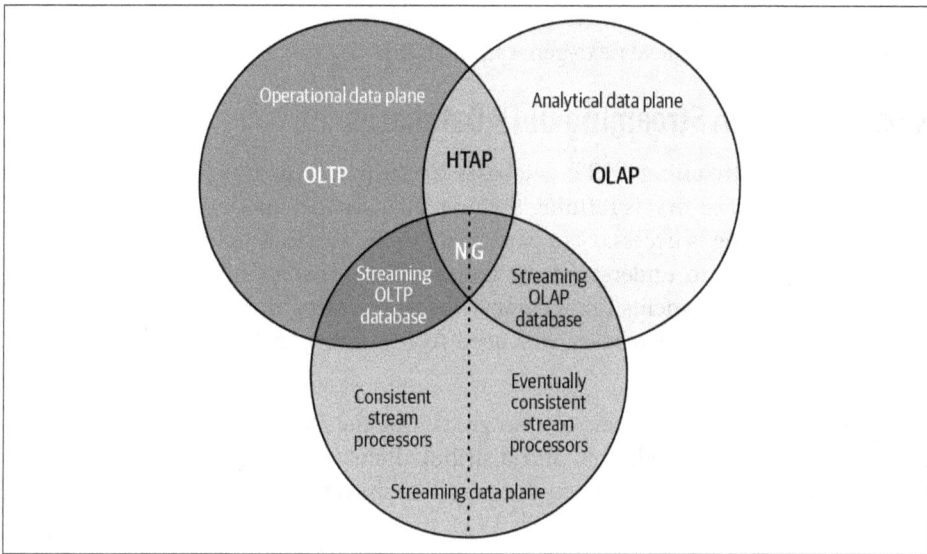

Figure 7-6. Next-generation databases

As of the publishing of this book, no databases exist within the next-generation area of Figure 7-6. Databases that fall within the petals would need to add the respective missing features to qualify for next-generation status. For example:

- HTAP databases can add Incremental View Maintenance (IVM), acting like a stateful stream processor. They also would need to integrate with streaming platforms like Kafka. We will cover IVM in Chapter 11.

- Streaming OLTP databases only need to provide column-based storage. They can achieve this by incorporating an embedded OLAP database like DuckDB. We will cover embedded OLAP databases in Chapter 8.

- Streaming OLAP databases can add consistency to their stream processors so that they can better participate in the actual logic of the application.

Existing hybrid systems are at the forefront of real-time analytics, offering organizations a versatile and more holistic means of handling their data needs in a dynamic and data-driven environment. The innovative spirit of these hybrid systems is propelling real-time analytics into new territories, where the lines between relational, analytical, and streaming workloads start to blur, and organizations can extract even more value from their data assets.

As further innovation leads to further evolution of these hybrid systems, we believe that each system will continue on the same path of adding features to reduce infrastructure, latency, and overall complexity.

Next, we'll delve deeper into the additional features that existing real-time hybrid databases can use to achieve next-generation status.

Next-Generation Streaming OLTP Databases

Next-generation streaming OLTP databases have three areas in which they can continue to improve. The first is refining their data consistency models. Data consistency in stream processing is necessary to participate in the application logic. As more engineers are beginning to understand the issues with consistency in stream processing and the higher requirements for accuracy when presenting the analytics to users, the more streaming OLTP databases will need to improve consistency in the analytics they output.

The second is improving access to change data or the WAL. CDC use cases require connectors running in dedicated and distributed clusters. This increases complexity and the amount of maintenance to the overall architecture. To simplify this process, emitting CDC transactions from their WAL to a streaming platform like Kafka is a feature already leveraged by databases like PeerDB and CockroachDB.

By emitting changes, database systems negate the need to build connectors for every possible integration point to ingest and egress data. Development of these connectors is time- and cost-consuming. It also limits the system to a few use cases at a time or until it becomes financially beneficial to develop one. In addition, some CDC connectors are often hard to manage, causing issues like out-of-memory or out-of-disk-space exceptions. Self-emitting CDC events natively can prevent issues encountered when using external CDC solutions. See Figure 7-7.

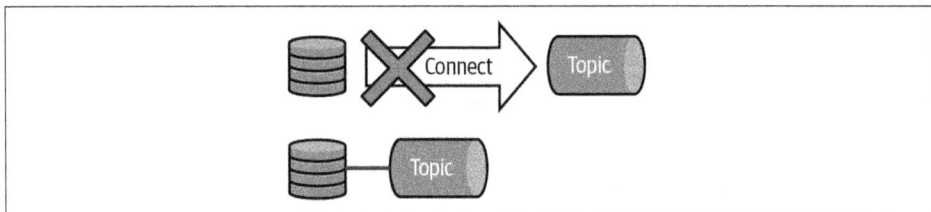

Figure 7-7. Next-generation streaming OLTP will push CDC data directly into a Kafka-compliant topic

Thirdly, streaming OLTP databases will start incorporating columnar storage formats for analytical workloads to provide analytical data to applications. This doesn't mean streaming OLTP databases will begin to hold all historical data. OLTP databases cannot store such large volumes of data. Streaming OLTP databases will need to provide a subset of the historical data from the OLAP system, either by streaming or batching (batching is allowed since the data is not real time). The subset of historical data will be limited to only the data within the application's domain context. This approach ensures that streaming OLTP databases can support analytical workloads without becoming overwhelmed by historical data storage requirements.

Next-Generation Streaming RTOLAP Databases

Existing RTOLAP databases currently do not have stream processing capabilities. Proton is the only solution that converges stream processing and an OLAP system. Its stream processor provides more advanced ingestion features and can balance push and pull queries.

Most existing RTOLAPs rely heavily on external stream processors, increasing the complexity and maintenance work for the entire real-time architecture.

In Chapter 4, we stated that data engineers often author the push queries, while data analysts write the pull queries. These two roles do not coordinate well because both are usually located in separate teams. Adding stream processing at ingestion will make RTOLAPs less dependent on external stream processors.

Moreover, external stream processors like Flink often publish data such that multiple consumers can subscribe. Usually, the data format requires additional transformations to meet the specific needs of the data analysts downstream. Putting these particular transformations into the push query will allow the stream processor system to also publish data for one particular subscriber.

Expect existing RTOLAP databases to adopt better ingestion by incorporating stream processing and providing push-query capabilities to the data analysts.

Next-Generation HTAP Databases

The next generation of HTAP databases will leverage their hybrid storage capabilities by incorporating IVM. IVM is a method for sustaining materialized views, where it asynchronously calculates and applies only incremental modifications to the views instead of reevaluating its entire contents. As we described in the earlier chapters, a materialized view that runs asynchronously is very much akin to stream processing.

By implementing IVM, HTAP databases can transform transactions from row-based to column-based form for low-latency analytical queries without the need to egress data.

Expect HTAP databases also to gain the ability to ingress limited historical data from the analytical plane. This will provide limited historical context to the real-time analytical data that they are serving.

Summary

We comprehensively discussed the diverse array of hybrid databases that exhibit real-time features, allowing you to make informed decisions when selecting the correct database for your specific real-time data processing needs. The data planes Venn diagram that we examined throughout the chapter helped illustrate the unique qualities of existing systems and how they converge to the right solution.

By definition, you may assume the convergence of systems is going to make data architectures less distributed and more monolithic. Monolithic systems tend to be inflexible and less scalable. In the following chapters, we'll discuss how systems are distributed today and how hybrid systems can avoid becoming too monolithic.

## CHAPTER 8

Zero-ETL or Near-Zero-ETL

In Chapter 7, we introduced emerging hybrid databases that provide alternative solutions to supporting real-time analytics. These systems reduce infrastructure and make data more accessible to analytical workloads. Since hybrid systems converge systems that are traditionally distributed, there is a supposition that hybrid systems lean toward a monolithic system. Monolithic systems are usually known for lacking modularity and scalability when performing data workloads.

Ironically, breaking up a monolithic data system will return us to decomposing a database and turning it inside out to scale the individual components specifically. This isn't necessarily a negative solution. In this book, we have been proposing putting these systems back into the database to reduce complexity and cost, which are traditionally associated with large distributed systems.

ETL is how we move data around from system to system, transforming it along the way. So far, we have used a form of ETL called streaming SQL. In this chapter, we will talk about how to balance complexity and scalability in the implementation of ETL by taking a look at existing systems and patterns used today to distribute and scale data workloads.

ETL Model

Figure 8-1 shows existing ETL solutions from no ETL in HTAP databases at the top to the turn-the-database-inside-out distributed solution at the bottom. The lower the solution is on the triangle, the more distributed and complex it becomes. Likewise, at the top, solutions are more centralized and monolithic, and they become more decentralized and modular as you move to the bottom.

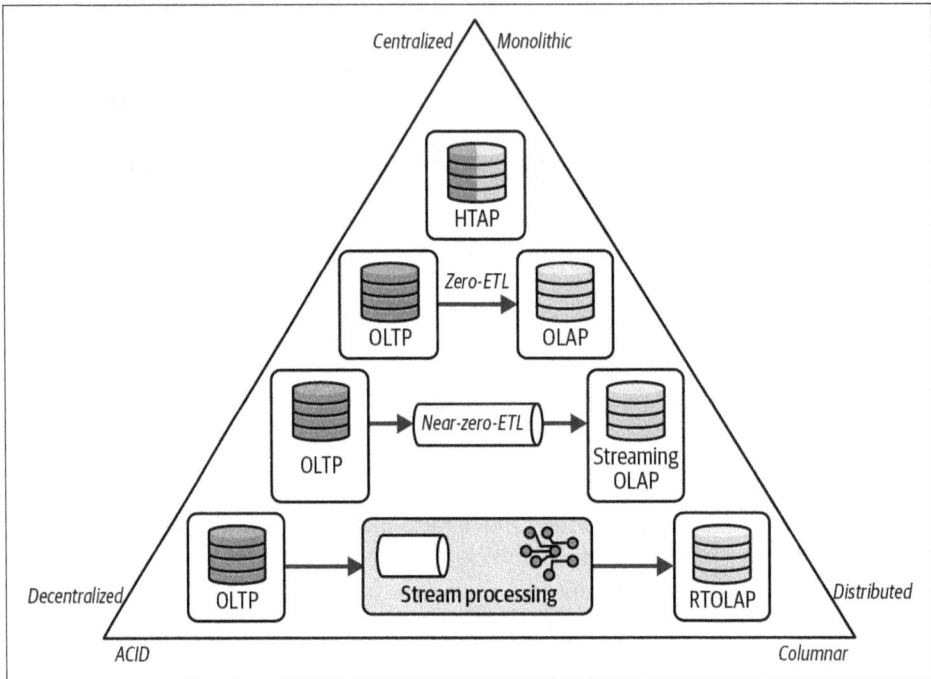

Figure 8-1. The increasing ETL model

On the left side of the triangle are transactional databases, while on the right are columnar databases. Midway down the triangle, you'll find zero-ETL.

Zero-ETL

Zero-ETL is a pattern first defined by Amazon Web Services (AWS) to simplify data integration from an OLTP database to an OLAP database. In its proposal, zero-ETL is defined as follows:

> [A] set of integrations that eliminates or minimizes the need to build ETL data pipelines. Extract, transform, and load (ETL) is the process of combining, cleaning, and normalizing data from different sources to get it ready for analytics, artificial intelligence (AI) and machine learning (ML) workloads.
>
> —AWS, "What Is Zero ETL?" (*https://oreil.ly/9-5CD*)

Zero-ETL refers to an approach or concept in data integration and analytics that aims to minimize or even eliminate the need for traditional ETL processes. The traditional ETL process involves extracting data from source systems, transforming it to meet the requirements of the target system, and then loading it into the destination. See Figure 8-2 for an architecture summary.

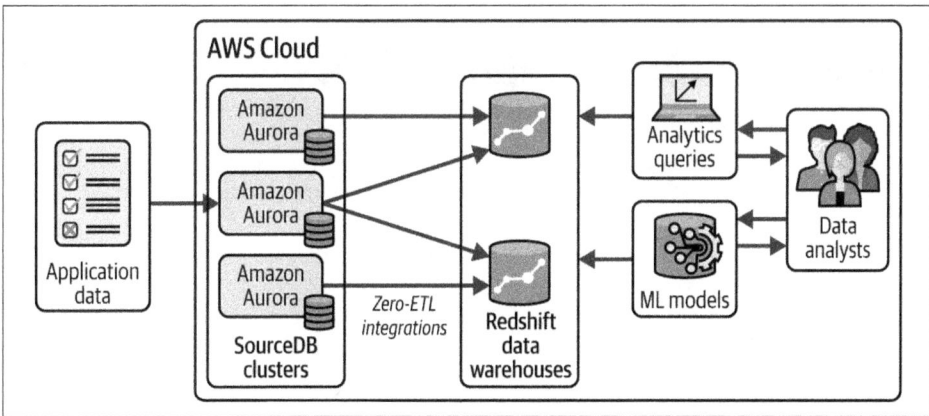

Figure 8-2. AWS's zero-ETL architecture for Amazon Aurora and Redshift

AWS's zero-ETL solution amounts to a managed integration between Amazon's OLTP database called Aurora and Amazon's data warehouse called Redshift. Near-real-time analytics can be implemented within minutes. It's a fully managed solution for making transactional data available in Redshift after it's written to Aurora.

AWS can tightly integrate Aurora and Redshift because it owns both database products, and they only exist on its cloud platform. AWS is free to build native integrations between any two systems they provide. The downside is that these solutions are not available outside of AWS.

While the zero-ETL concept can offer benefits in terms of agility, reduced latency, and cost savings, it may not be suitable for all scenarios. Most organizations, especially those with complex data integration requirements or regulatory constraints, may still need elements of traditional ETL processes.

In Chapter 2, we stated that transforming data in the data warehouse (also called ELT) forces batch processing semantics, which will add latency to any real-time analytical use case. In Figure 8-2, the integration points between Aurora and Redshift do not transform data. This implies the transformations are done in Redshift. Both HTAP databases and zero-ETL solutions have this problem. They both need to trigger a batch transformation process once the data reaches the data warehouse.

Alternatively, analytical queries submitted by the data analysts can include the transformation required, but this will make them very slow. Ultimately, without a stream processing component, you cannot create a materialized view to divide the analytical workload between push and pull queries.

Zero-ETL challenges the traditional integration approach and seeks to reduce the complexity, latency, and resource requirements associated with ETL at a cost. Table 8-1 lists some key aspects of zero-ETL.

Table 8-1. Zero-ETL

Key aspect	Description
Real-time data integration	Minimizing or eliminating batch processing to enable real-time or near-real-time data integration. This is particularly relevant for scenarios where timely insights are crucial.
Schema-on-read	Adopting a schema-on-read approach, where the data is not transformed into a predefined schema during the ETL process but is instead interpreted at the time of analysis. This allows for more flexibility in handling diverse and changing data.
Data virtualization	Leveraging data virtualization technologies that provide a unified and virtual view of data across multiple sources without physically moving or transforming the data. This can reduce the need for creating and maintaining a separate data warehouse.
In-database processing	Performing transformations and analytics directly within the database systems, where the data resides, avoiding the need to extract and move large datasets for processing.
Event-driven architecture	Adopting event-driven architectures, where data changes trigger immediate updates, reducing the reliance on periodic batch processes.
Modern data architectures	Embracing modern data architectures, such as data lakes and cloud-based solutions, that provide scalable and cost-effective options for managing and analyzing data without the traditional ETL bottlenecks.

Ultimately, the decision to adopt a zero-ETL approach depends on factors such as the nature of the data, business requirements, and the available technology landscape. It's important to carefully evaluate the trade-offs and choose an approach that aligns with the organization's goals and priorities.

If you need more of the flexibility provided by a traditional ETL pipeline, an alternative solution is to use near-zero-ETL.

Near-Zero-ETL

Near-zero-ETL still tries to limit infrastructure for ETL components without losing the flexibility needed to support complex data integration requirements. This involves using data systems that adopt hybrid approaches.

One solution is to leverage an OLTP database that has embedded features to send data to other systems, without the need for self-managing connectors running on a separate infrastructure.

Figure 8-3 shows two databases that have embedded features enabling the flexibility needed for complex data integration. It has an OLTP database and an OLAP database. PeerDB enables Postgres to send a stream of data to a topic on a streaming platform. Timeplus/Proton provides the transformation needed at ingestion before it can be served. Timeplus/Proton provides the materialized view that allows the differentiation of push and pull queries. This approach provides much more flexibility for fast real-time analytical queries.

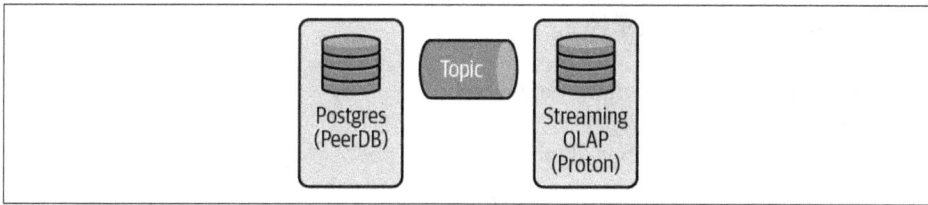

Figure 8-3. Near-zero-ETL using PeerDB and Timeplus/Proton

PeerDB

PeerDB is an open source solution to stream data from Postgres to data warehouses, queues/topics, and other storage engines. Its goal is to simplify ETL by providing a database experience when building integration to analytical systems.

In PeerDB, a PEER is a connection to a database that PeerDB can query. Peers are created using the CREATE PEER command. See Example 8-1.

Example 8-1. Setting up a peer from another Postgres database in PeerDB

```
CREATE PEER source FROM POSTGRES WITH ❶
(
  host = 'catalog',
  port = '5432',
  user = 'postgres',
  password = 'postgres',
  database = 'source'
);


CREATE PEER sf_peer FROM SNOWFLAKE WITH ❷
(
  account_id = '<snowflake_account_identifier>',
  username = '<user_name>',
  private_key ='<private_key>',
  password = '<password>' -- only provide when the private key is encrypted
  database = '<database_name>',
  schema = '<schema>',
  warehouse = '<ware_house>',
  role = '<role>',
  query_timeout = '<query_timeout_in_seconds>'
);

-- Query away tables in Snowflake
SELECT * FROM sf_peer.MY_SCHEMA.MY_TABLE; ❸
```

❶ Creates a peer to another Postgres database.

❷ Creates a peer to a Snowflake data warehouse.

❸ You can select any number of tables from the peer.

The peer allows you to query any table in the peered database and join it with transactional data. Effortless integrations between systems are effective but get complicated when peered databases exist in remote regions. PEERs act as pull queries that pull data synchronously from an analytical system. This requires both systems to exist in the same region or data center.

In other databases, including streaming OLTP databases, you have to build data pipelines to source data from a data warehouse or OLAP database and transfer it into the OLTP database. Building peers with PeerDB in Postgres makes sourcing data from the analytical plane much easier. But there are limitations.

Postgres cannot hold large amounts of data and isn't optimized for analytical queries. Therefore, it would not be optimal to build a materialized view using PeerDB on Postgres. The analytical data will need to be reduced to a size that fits within the capacity of the OLTP database. This implies that the push query performing the heavy transformation needs to be executed externally on a stream processor. We'll cover this later in this chapter.

Example 8-2 shows how PeerDB mirrors the data from one peer to another. The mirror asynchronously copies data from source peer to sink peer.

Example 8-2. Creating an ETL with a PeerDB MIRROR to an analytical system

```
CREATE MIRROR <mirror_name> [IF NOT EXISTS] FROM
        <source_peer> TO <target_peer> FOR
$$
  SELECT * FROM <source_table_name> WHERE
  <watermark_column> BETWEEN {{.start}} AND {{.end}}
$$
WITH (
        destination_table_name = '<schema_qualified_destination_table_name>',
        watermark_column = '<watermark_column>',
        watermark_table_name =
  '<table_on_source_on_which_watermark_filter_should_be_applied>',
        mode = '<mode>',
        unique_key_columns = '<unique_key_columns>',
        parallelism = <parallelism>,
        refresh_interval = <refresh_interval_in_seconds>,
        sync_data_format = '<sync_data_format>'
  num_rows_per_partition = 100000,
  initial_copy_onle = <true|false>,
```

```
  setup_watermark_table_on_destination = <true|false>,
);
```

Unfortunately, the mirrors do not support transformations. Transformations will need to be executed before or after the mirroring. Performing transformations before the mirroring can cause extensive resource utilization for an OLTP database whose purpose is to handle operational workloads. Moreover, this process will be executed as a batch process, not in real time. Performing transformations after the mirroring will also require batching semantics unless a streaming OLAP database like Proton is used.

Proton

The Venn diagram in Chapter 7 exhibits overlapping hybrid systems. One of these hybrid systems was a streaming OLAP database. Proton is a next-generation RTO-LAP database that allows stateful streaming ingestion and two APIs for consuming real-time analytics: asynchronous change stream and synchronous pull queries. Complex transformations can be implemented at ingestion time to build materialized views.

In Figure 8-3 in the previous section, PeerDB writes to a topic in a streaming platform that is subscribed to by Proton. Proton can execute complex push queries before the data is materialized for pull queries.

First, we create a PEER for a streaming platform—in this case, Kafka. See Example 8-3.

Example 8-3. Setting up a peer to another Postgres database in PeerDB

```
CREATE PEER <eh_peer_name> FROM KAFKA WITH (
  bootstrap_server = '<bootstrap-servers>'
);

CREATE MIRROR <mirror_name> [IF NOT EXISTS] FROM
        <source_peer> TO <target_peer> FOR
$$
  SELECT * FROM <source_table_name> WHERE
  <watermark_column> BETWEEN {{.start}} AND {{.end}}
$$
WITH (
        destination_table_name = '<topic>'
);
```

In Proton, create a stream to read from Kafka. See Example 8-4.

Example 8-4. Creating a stream from Kafka to Proton

```
CREATE EXTERNAL STREAM frontend_events(raw string)
SETTINGS type='kafka',
        brokers='<bootstrap-servers>',
        topic='<topic>'
```

All streaming databases provide two modes of output, synchronous pull queries and asynchronous push to a topic. This gives developers two ways of bringing real-time analytics back to the operational plane by using OLAP databases embedded in their applications.

Embedded OLAP

There is a trend to bring smaller analytical workloads closer to the operational plane. HTAP databases like Hydra and SingleStore provide columnar databases for analytical workloads, for example. However, due to their limited capacity, these databases cannot hold the amount of data analytical systems like Snowflake, Databricks, ClickHouse, and Pinot can.

Conversely, bringing bulky analytical systems to the operational plane for faster serving of real-time analytics makes it harder for analytical systems to source historical data. These are the limitations that created the data divide between operational and analytical data planes.

Alternatively, reducing the analytical data to a size fitting to the scope of the business domain and the capacity in the operational plane could provide a better solution.

In Figure 8-4, real-time operational data can be sent to a topic using PeerDB. Proton can ingest and transform the data in flight with a push query leading up to a materialized view.

The changes in the materialized view in Proton can be written to a topic for the original application to consume and to build a local replica in an embedded OLAP database like DuckDB or chDB.

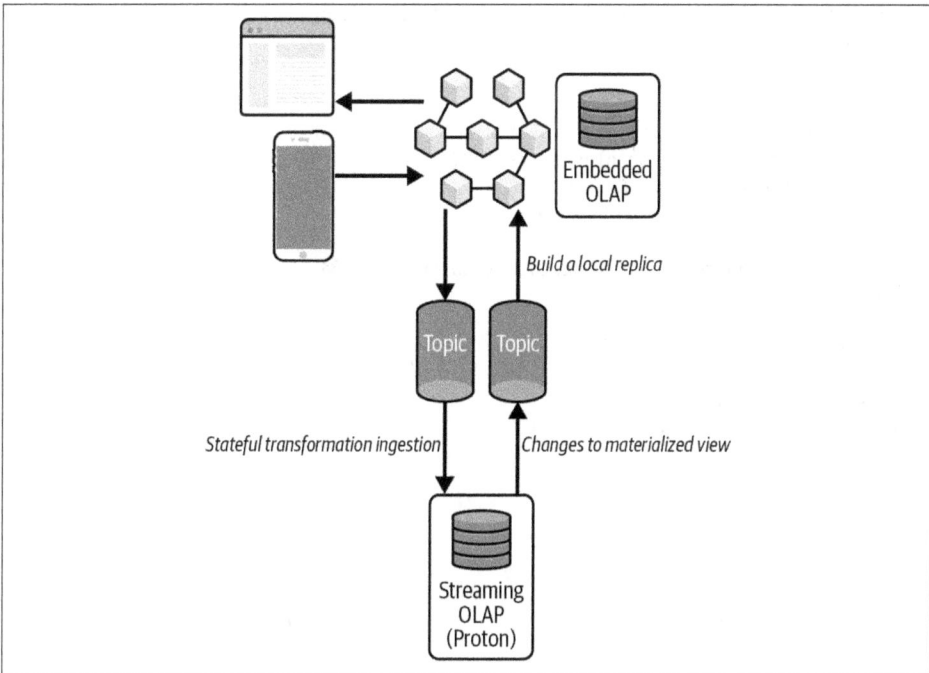

Figure 8-4. Streaming OLAP database reducing analytical data to be served in the operational plane

DuckDB

DuckDB is an embedded OLAP database designed to support analytical query workloads. Embedded means running inside an application, for example, a microservice. DuckDB provides the ability for users of the application to slice and dice data.

With change data coming from Proton and consumed by the microservice, a local replica of the materialized view can be made in DuckDB, shown in Example 8-5.

Example 8-5. Installing DuckDB for use in a Python microservice

```
pip install duckdb
```

Example 8-6 is a microservice skeleton that can subscribe to a Kafka topic and UPSERT the records into a DuckDB table. That table can then serve analytical queries via REST API using the FastAPI Python library.

Example 8-6. Pseudocode of a microservice that reads from Kafka and writes to DuckDB

```
import duckdb
from threading import Thread, current_thread
from fastapi import BackgroundTasks, FastAPI
from confluent_kafka import Consumer

app = FastAPI()
duckdb_con = duckdb.connect('my_peristent_db.duckdb')  ❶

def upsert(msg):  ❷
  # IMPLEMENT UPSERT LOGIC

def kafka2olap(conf):  ❸
  consumer = Consumer(conf)
  try:
    consumer.subscribe("my_data")
    while running:
      msg = consumer.poll(timeout=1.0)
      if msg is None: continue
      if msg.error():
        # handle error
      else:
        upsert(msg)
  finally:
    # Close down consumer to commit final offsets.
    consumer.close()


@app.on_event("startup")
async def initialize():  ❹
  conf = # Kafka configuration
  thread = Thread(
    target = kafka2olap,
    args = (conf,)
  )
  thread.start()

@app.get("/my_data/")
async def read_item(id:int):  ❺
    results = local_con.execute("""
        SELECT
            id,
            count(*) AS row_counter,
            current_timestamp
        FROM my_data
        where id = ?
    """, (id,)).fetchall()
```

❶   Create a connection to DuckDB.

❷ Define an `upsert` function to insert/update to DuckDB.

❸ Define a function to read from Kafka and write to DuckDB.

❹ Create an asynchronous thread to read from Kafka and write to DuckDB.

❺ FastAPI function for reading DuckDB via REST API.

DuckDB has a feature that can check if there is a conflict upon insertion of a record into a table. You can use the statement INSERT OR REPLACE, which will perform an update if the record exists.

Example 8-7. Installing UPSERT for DuckDB in Python

```python
def upsert(msg):
  # Deserialize the msg to get the column values
  primary_key, col1_value, col2_value = deserialize_message(msg)

  duckdb_con.execute("""
    INSERT OR REPLACE INTO t1(id, col1, col2) VALUES(1, ?, ?) ❶
    """,
    [primary_key, col1_value, col2_value]
  );
```

❶ INSERT OR REPLACE is how you can handle UPSERT in DuckDB.

chDB

Similar to DuckDB, chDB is also an embeddable OLAP database. chDB is based on ClickHouse. ClickHouse supports UPSERTs by leveraging *engines*. One particular engine is the *ReplacingMergeTree* table engine. This engine removes duplicate records during merges. *ReplacingMergeTree* is a good option for emulating upsert behavior (where you want queries to return the last row inserted). See Example 8-8 for details.

Example 8-8. ClickHouse ENGINE that supports UPSERT

```sql
CREATE TABLE hackernews_rmt (
    id UInt32,
    author String,
    comment String,
    views UInt64
)
ENGINE = ReplacingMergeTree ❶
PRIMARY KEY (author, id);

SELECT *
```

```
FROM hackernews_rmt
FINAL ❷
```

❶ The `ReplacingMergeTree` engine that mimics upsert behavior

❷ `FINAL` keyword that returns the latest record

Example 8-9 is an example of how to create a microservice using Flask and chDB. Flask is an alternative to the FastAPI Python model for building microservices.

Example 8-9. chDB microservice wrapper

```python
from flask import Flask, request
import chdb
import os

# chdb API server example with GET/POST support, compatible with play app
# for a full server example see https://github.com/metrico/chdb-server

app = Flask(__name__, static_folder="", static_url_path="")

@app.route('/', methods=["GET"])
def clickhouse():
    query = request.args.get('query', default="", type=str)
    format = request.args.get('default_format', default="JSONCompact", type=str)
    if not query:
        return "Query not found", 400

    res = chdb.query(query, format)
    return res.bytes()

@app.route('/', methods=["POST"])
def play():
    query = request.data
    format = request.args.get('default_format', default="JSONCompact", type=str)
    if not query:
        return "Query not found", 400

    res = chdb.query(query, format)
    return res.bytes()

@app.errorhandler(404)
def handle_404(e):
    return "Not found", 404

host = os.getenv('HOST', '0.0.0.0')
port = os.getenv('PORT', 8123)
app.run(host=host, port=port)
```

Data Gravity and Replication

Often analytical systems exist only in a single region or data center because analytical infrastructure like Snowflake tends to be costly. This forces all operational systems to send their data to a single region in a circumstance called *data gravity*.

Data gravity is the idea that data has mass, which is difficult to move or replicate as it grows in size and importance. This gravity impacts data creation and exchange and, in turn, also impacts applications, servers, and other data. The typical solution is to only replicate reduced amounts of analytical data.

By providing the changes from the materialized view to the operational plane systems, you can distribute replicas of the real-time analytics to all the regions where the user-facing applications are deployed.

Analytical Data Reduction

How do you reduce analytical data that represents petabytes of historical data? Reducing the analytical data to be served in the operational plane sounds hard but is easy because we've done it before. We can use the push and pull pattern for materialized views.

By creating the materialized view in the analytical system located in the analytical plane, we can stream the materialized view's changes to the operational plane. Proton can do exactly this. It can write changes to the materialized view into a topic. Said topic can be then consumed by an application with an embedded OLAP for analytical workloads. Likewise, OLTP streaming databases can also consume from the same topic and serve from their row-based storage. However, the row-based storage may increase the latency of analytical queries.

The near-zero-ETL approach can strike the right balance between complexity and scalability. For completeness, let's see what it takes to handle analytical data using a separate stream processor and OLAP database in a lambda architecture.

Lambda Architecture

The lambda architecture is a data processing architecture designed to combine both batch and real-time/streaming data processing. It was introduced by Nathan Marz in his 2011 book, *Big Data: Principles and Best Practices of Scalable Realtime Data Systems* (Manning), as a way to address the challenges of providing robust and scalable data processing for big data applications. The term "lambda" is inspired by the Greek letter, which looks like an inverted "y" and represents the dual processing paths for batch and real-time data.

The lambda architecture consists of three main layers:

Batch layer

This layer is responsible for handling large volumes of data in a batch-oriented manner. It precomputes results on the entire dataset and stores them in a batch serving layer, making it suitable for complex analytics and historical queries. Batch processing is typically done using technologies like Apache Hadoop, which can handle massively distributed data processing.

Speed layer

The speed layer deals with real-time data processing. It focuses on low-latency processing and handles recent data that hasn't yet been processed by the batch layer. The results from the speed layer are combined with the batch layer results to provide a complete, up-to-date view of the data. Technologies like Apache Storm or Apache Flink are commonly used for real-time processing in the speed layer.

Serving layer

The serving layer combines the results from the batch and speed layers to provide a unified view of the data. It serves queries and analytics requests from users or applications. The serving layer is often built using scalable NoSQL databases, like Apache HBase or Apache Cassandra, to handle the read-intensive workloads efficiently.

The lambda architecture's strength lies in its ability to handle both batch and real-time processing, providing a comprehensive solution for big data analytics. However, managing and maintaining two separate processing paths can introduce complexities, and ensuring consistency between batch and real-time views can be challenging. Some alternative architectures, such as the kappa architecture, propose a unified approach to stream and batch processing, aiming to simplify the overall system design.

Using a separate stream processor and OLAP database is also an option. For example, you can use Apache Pinot to serve petabytes of historical data with streaming data that was transformed using Flink (or Pathway, if you prefer Python).

In Figure 8-5, the lambda architecture is represented. On the left side of the diagram is the batch layer. On the right side of the diagram is the speed layer. The serving layer is Apache Pinot. In the past, merging streaming data with historical data in the data warehouse was difficult to accomplish using do-it-yourself coding. RTOLAP systems like Pinot can more conveniently solve the difficult task to provide a single view of all data.

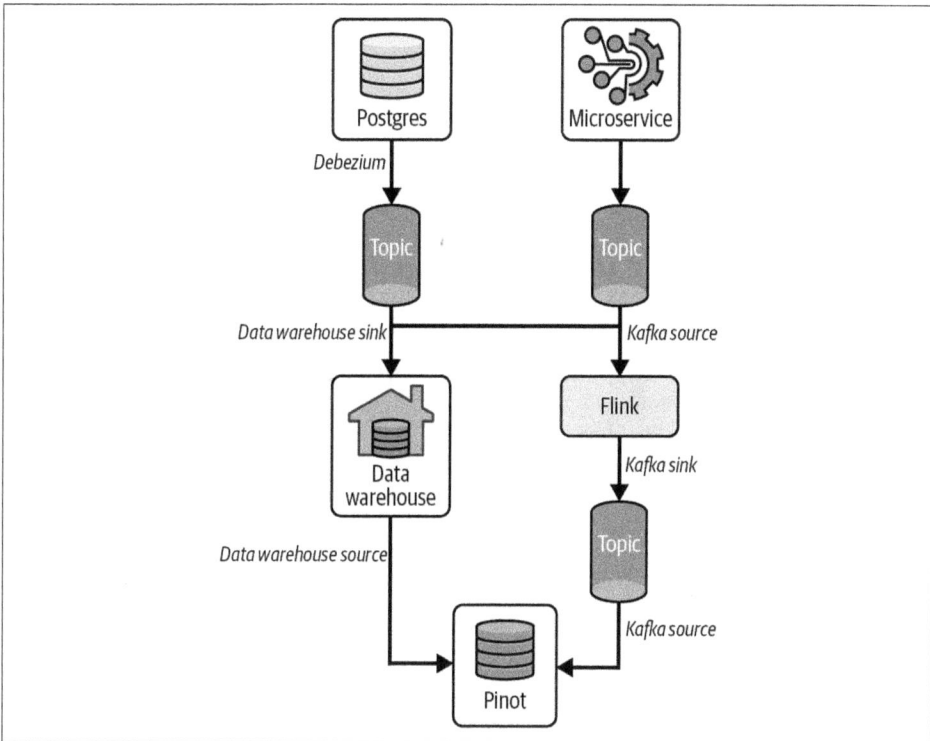

Figure 8-5. A more complex real-time data pipeline that can serve ad hoc queries on both streaming and historical data

Apache Pinot Hybrid Tables

A Pinot hybrid table is a table composed of two internal tables, one offline and one real-time, that share the same name. This is how Pinot can merge streaming and historical data.

Examples 8-10 and 8-11 are REALTIME and OFFLINE table definitions for a table called airlineStats, respectively.

Example 8-10. Pinot REALTIME table

```
{
  "tableName": "airlineStats",
  "tableType": "REALTIME",
  "tenants": {},
  "segmentsConfig": {
    "timeColumnName": "DaysSinceEpoch",
    "retentionTimeUnit": "DAYS",
    "retentionTimeValue": "5",
```

```
      "replication": "1"
   },
   "tableIndexConfig": {},
   "routing": {
      "segmentPrunerTypes": [
         "time"
      ]
   },
   "ingestionConfig": { ❶
      "streamIngestionConfig": {
         "streamConfigMaps": [
            {
               "streamType": "kafka",
               "stream.kafka.topic.name": "flights-realtime",
               "stream.kafka.decoder.class.name": "org.apache.pinot.plugin.stream.
                kafka.KafkaJSONMessageDecoder",
               "stream.kafka.consumer.factory.class.name": "org.apache.pinot.plugin.
                stream.kafka20.KafkaConsumerFactory",
               "stream.kafka.consumer.prop.auto.offset.reset": "smallest",
               "stream.kafka.zk.broker.url": "localhost:2191/kafka",
               "stream.kafka.broker.list": "localhost:19092",
               "realtime.segment.flush.threshold.time": "3600000",
               "realtime.segment.flush.threshold.size": "50000"
            }
         ]
      },
      "transformConfigs": [ ❷
         {
            "columnName": "ts",
            "transformFunction": "fromEpochDays(DaysSinceEpoch)"
         },
         {
            "columnName": "tsRaw",
            "transformFunction": "fromEpochDays(DaysSinceEpoch)"
         }
      ]
   },
   "fieldConfigList": [
      {
         "name": "ts",
         "encodingType": "DICTIONARY",
         "indexTypes": [
            "TIMESTAMP"
         ],
         "timestampConfig": {
            "granularities": [
               "DAY",
               "WEEK",
               "MONTH"
            ]
         }
      }
```

```
  ],
  "metadata": {
    "customConfigs": {}
  }
}
```

❶ The ingestion configuration from Kafka

❷ Streaming ingestion transformation

In Chapter 7, we noted that RTOLAP systems like Pinot are adding more stateful
stream processing and that next-generation OLAPs will look and act like streaming
databases. Pinot's star-tree index is an example of this trend, which we briefly covered
in Chapter 3.

Example 8-10 shows ingestion transformations that are typically needed when sourcing data from a publish-subscribe (pub-sub) system like Kafka. Data published to
a pub-sub system may be expected to support multiple subscribers and, therefore,
need to provide generic versions of the data that will satisfy many subscribers. Each
consumer will need to handle any additional transformations necessary for their
particular analytical workload.

Example 8-11. Pinot OFFLINE table

```
{
  "tableName": "airlineStats",
  "tableType": "OFFLINE",
  "segmentsConfig": {
    "timeColumnName": "DaysSinceEpoch",
    "timeType": "DAYS",
    "segmentPushType": "APPEND",
    "segmentAssignmentStrategy": "BalanceNumSegmentAssignmentStrategy",
    "replication": "1"
  },
  "tenants": {},
  "fieldConfigList": [
    {
      "name": "ts",
      "encodingType": "DICTIONARY",
      "indexTypes": [
        "TIMESTAMP"
      ],
      "timestampConfig": {
        "granularities": [
          "DAY",
          "WEEK",
          "MONTH"
        ]
      }
```

```
    },
    {
      "name": "ArrTimeBlk",
      "encodingType": "DICTIONARY",
      "indexes": {
        "inverted": {
          "enabled": "true"
        }
      },
      "tierOverwrites": {
        "hotTier": {
          "encodingType": "DICTIONARY",
          "indexes": {
            "bloom": {
              "enabled": "true"
            }
          }
        },
        "coldTier": {
          "encodingType": "RAW",
          "indexes": {
            "text": {
              "enabled": "true"
            }
          }
        }
      }
    }
  ],
  "tableIndexConfig": {
    "starTreeIndexConfigs": [ ❶
      {
        "dimensionsSplitOrder": [
          "AirlineID",
          "Origin",
          "Dest"
        ],
        "skipStarNodeCreationForDimensions": [],
        "functionColumnPairs": [
          "COUNT__*",
          "MAX__ArrDelay"
        ],
        "maxLeafRecords": 10
      }
    ],
    "enableDynamicStarTreeCreation": true,
    "loadMode": "MMAP",
    "tierOverwrites": {
      "hotTier": {
        "starTreeIndexConfigs": [
          {
            "dimensionsSplitOrder": [
```

```json
          "Carrier",
          "CancellationCode",
          "Origin",
          "Dest"
        ],
        "skipStarNodeCreationForDimensions": [],
        "functionColumnPairs": [
          "MAX__CarrierDelay",
          "AVG__CarrierDelay"
        ],
        "maxLeafRecords": 10
      }
    ]
  },
  "coldTier": {
    "starTreeIndexConfigs": []
  }
}
},
"metadata": {
  "customConfigs": {}
},
"ingestionConfig": {
  "transformConfigs": [
    {
      "columnName": "ts",
      "transformFunction": "fromEpochDays(DaysSinceEpoch)"
    },
    {
      "columnName": "tsRaw",
      "transformFunction": "fromEpochDays(DaysSinceEpoch)"
    }
  ]
},
"tierConfigs": [ ❷
  {
    "name": "hotTier",
    "segmentSelectorType": "time",
    "segmentAge": "3130d",
    "storageType": "pinot_server",
    "serverTag": "DefaultTenant_OFFLINE"
  },
  {
    "name": "coldTier",
    "segmentSelectorType": "time",
    "segmentAge": "3140d",
    "storageType": "pinot_server",
    "serverTag": "DefaultTenant_OFFLINE"
  }
]
}
```

❶ Star-tree index that preaggregates historical data to build a materialized view. Star-tree index can be used in both real-time and offline Pinot tables.

❷ Pinot has tiered storage that allows it to move data to lower tiers as it ages to free up more capacity (see Figure 8-6).

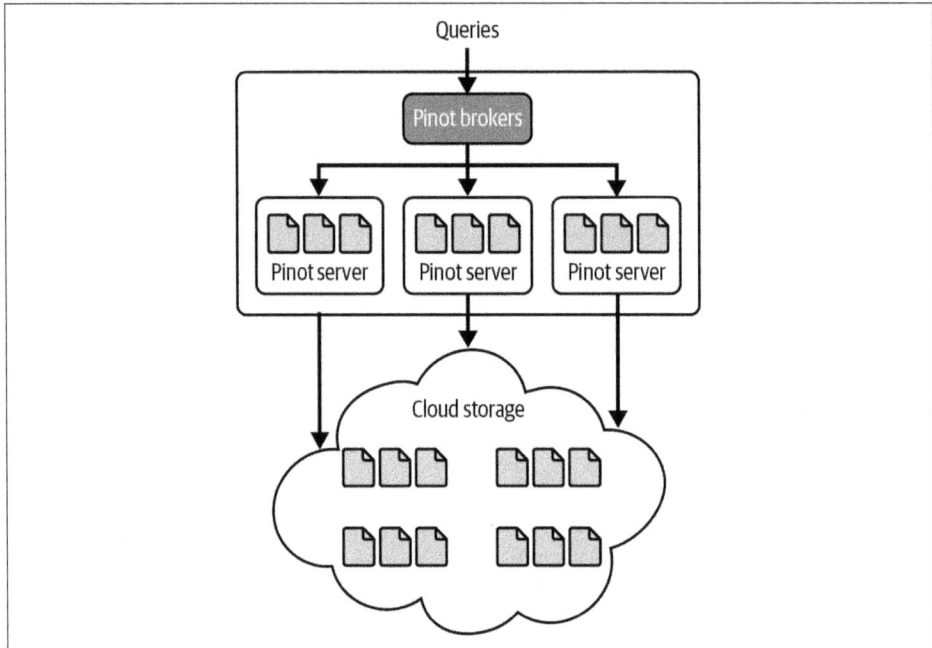

Figure 8-6. Pinot tiered storage

Unlike REALTIME table definitions, which include configurations to read from a topic from a streaming platform, OFFLINE tables do not have ingestion configurations. To make querying streaming data possible within milliseconds of publication, REALTIME tables are spread across multiple servers that store streaming data in volatile memory. REALTIME and OFFLINE tables are separated and are only brought together by the query engine.

REALTIME tables have a retention period after which data from the REALTIME servers is offloaded to the OFFLINE servers so that the capacity of the REALTIME servers is not exceeded.

The advantage of using an OLAP database is that you don't need to reduce the analytical data to fit within the capacity of an OLTP or HTAP database. Reducing the analytical data takes away flexibility for users who need to access all of the historical data. However, flexibility—like anything—comes with more complexity and infrastructure costs.

With Pinot's tiered storage, you can offload older data to lower tiers to free up more capacity in Pinot. If you need more historical data to perform ad hoc queries, it's best to leverage OLAP systems that can merge historical data with real-time data from a stream.

Pipeline Configurations

Pinot provides the solution for merging historical and real-time data. Before reaching Pinot, the lambda architecture data flow is started by sourcing data from an OLTP database like Postgres using a Debezium CDC connector. If you recall, Debezium captures change transactions from many types of transactional databases. Example 8-12 shows a Debezium Postgres configuration.

Example 8-12. Creating a Kafka source connector in Flink

```
{
    "name": "postgres",
    "config": {
        "connector.class": "io.debezium.connector.postgresql.PostgresConnector",
        "tasks.max": "1",
        "database.hostname": "0.0.0.0",
        "database.port": "5432",
        "database.user": "postgres",
        "database.password": "postgres",
        "database.dbname" : "postgres",
        "topic.prefix": "dbserver1",
        "schema.include.list": "inventory"
    }
}
```

This connector will write change data into a topic. We can use Flink SQL as the stream processor to transform the data. Example 8-13 shows Flink SQL sourcing streaming data from Kafka.

Example 8-13. Creating a Kafka source connector in Flink

```
CREATE TABLE KafkaSource (
  `id` BIGINT,
  `col1` STRING,
  `col2` STRING,
  `ts` TIMESTAMP(3) METADATA FROM 'timestamp'
) WITH (
  'connector' = 'kafka',
  'topic' = 'my_data',
  'properties.bootstrap.servers' = 'localhost:9092',
  'properties.group.id' = 'abc',
  'scan.startup.mode' = 'earliest-offset',
```

```
    'format' = 'json'
)
```

Once you've sourced data from a topic, you can perform transformations using SQL. In Flink, these are called pipelines. After the transformation is completed, the data can be written back to a topic using the code in Example 8-14.

Example 8-14. Creating a Kafka sink in Flink SQL

```
CREATE TABLE KafkaSink (
  `user_id` BIGINT,
  `col1` STRING,
  `col2` STRING,
  `ts` TIMESTAMP(3) METADATA FROM 'timestamp'
) WITH (
  'connector' = 'kafka',
  'topic' = 'my_data_transformed',
  'properties.bootstrap.servers' = 'localhost:9092',
  'properties.group.id' = 'testGroup',
  'scan.startup.mode' = 'earliest-offset',
  'format' = 'json'
)
```

Pinot gives you the ability to perform ad hoc queries on the real-time data from the topic along with historical data from a data warehouse or object store like Amazon S3. It's important to know that use cases involving the execution of ad hoc queries on real-time and historical data are not intended for user-facing applications. Ad hoc queries are intended for data analysts who are internal to the business and discovering insights from the data. This type of capability should not be exposed to external users, whose numbers could end up in the tens of thousands—they would put too much resource stress on the OLAP system.

Summary

The limitations of zero-ETL emphasize its inability to achieve real-time analytics and its tendency to impose batching semantics for push queries, lacking materialized views. In response to these drawbacks, we introduced alternatives that support near-zero-ETL. These also enable real-time analytics, for example, when employing Proton to reduce real-time and historical data into a materialized view that can be written out to a Kafka topic. We were required to build a Kafka consumer on the operational plane to build a local replica in the embedded OLAP database. The same approach can also be implemented with HTAP databases instead of an embedded OLAP.

The patterns proposed in this chapter depend heavily on the streaming plane of the Venn diagram introduced in Chapter 7. In Chapter 9, we delve deeper into the streaming plane and how it can be leveraged in architectural patterns like data mesh.

The Streaming Plane

In the previous chapter, we explored the existing real-time systems in today's ecosystem and introduced three distinct data planes: operational, analytical, and streaming. Both the operational and analytical planes predominantly deal with data at rest, emphasizing static information. In contrast, the streaming plane stands out as the sole realm characterized by data in motion.

In this chapter, we will be delving into the streaming plane and how data architects and engineers can begin to think about its role in simplifying real-time analytics.

We have consistently interlinked terms such as asynchronous, data in motion, and streaming, treating them as interchangeable expressions. They are synonymous with long-running processes that do continuous transformations, simplifying and quickening the retrieval of real-time analytical data for applications.

Figure 9-1 shows only the streaming plane portion of the Venn diagram shown throughout Chapter 7. We will refer to this diagram throughout this chapter.

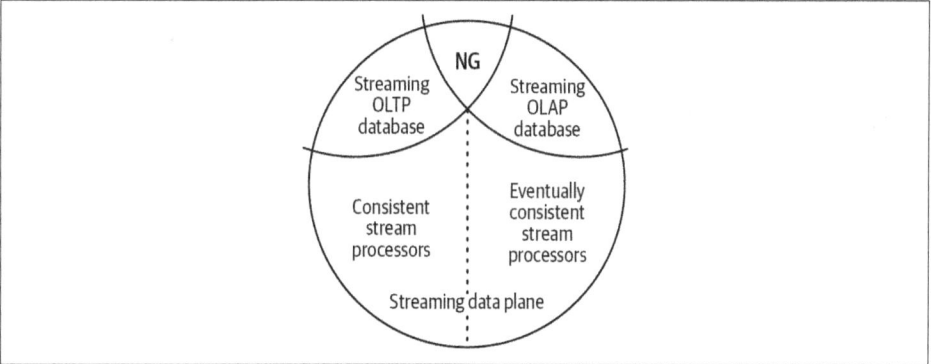

Figure 9-1. Streaming plane from the Venn diagram from Chapter 7

This chapter will examine several pivotal topics to understand the intricacies of real-time data processing on the streaming plane. Among the focal points is the concept of *analytics on the operational plane* (or operational analytics), which delves into the practice of performing analytical workloads near the applications in the operational plane. Furthermore, we will extend to the aspects of *data locality*, investigating how the geographical proximity of data to its processing environment impacts overall *system performance*. Understanding data locality is instrumental for optimizing resource utilization and minimizing latency in streaming analytics scenarios.

Another critical theme we'll explore is *data replication*, a fundamental strategy in the streaming plane. Data replication involves data duplication across multiple nodes or global regions, fostering *decentralization*. We will encompass the concept of *data products*, inspired by data mesh. We'll discuss how real-time analytics can be harnessed to generate valuable data products replicated globally for local consumption.

By navigating through these salient topics, readers will understand the multifaceted challenges and opportunities presented by the streaming plane, offering solutions crucial for designing resilient and efficient systems within the global landscape of streaming analytics.

Data Gravity

Think of data as a planet. As data builds mass, it attracts services and applications the same way gravity attracts the moon to the earth and keeps you from drifting off into space. For example, you create data when you post a message on social media. Your message was submitted to a service that attracts interactions from your friends and creates even more data.

In a typical data architecture that doesn't consider the streaming plane, the operational plane would push data directly to the analytical plane. Think of the operational plane as moons in orbit around a dense planet, which is the analytical plane. The operational plane moons push data to the planet. As more operational plane moons send data back to the analytical plane planet, the planet becomes a monolithic system of historical data. Workloads start to suffer from the effects of data size, which introduces latency.

As we stated in previous chapters, data movement from the operational to the analytical plane is a one-directional downstream flow. Forcing the data to flow in the opposite upstream direction is difficult. Another way of seeing this is the idea of data gravity.

Figure 9-2 depicts a typical data architecture without considering the streaming plane. The operational plane exists as nodes on the outside, publishing data to the analytical plane represented as the earth.

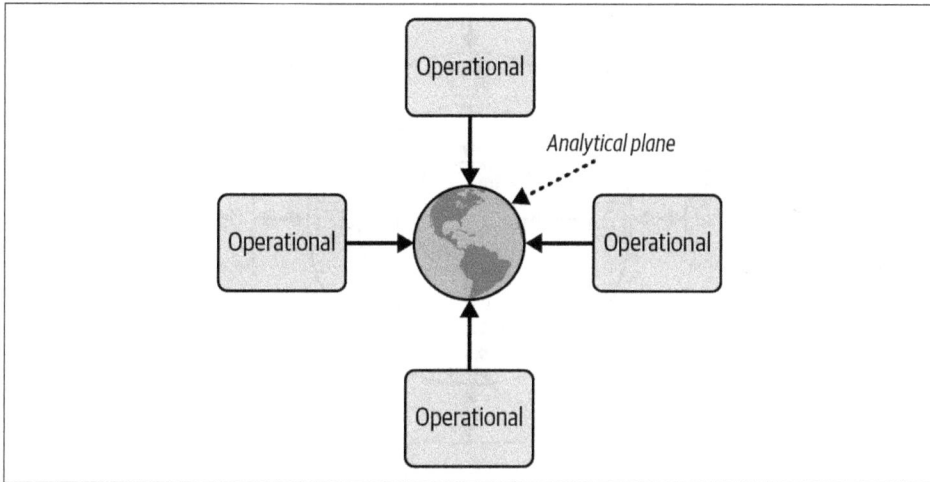

Figure 9-2. The effects of data gravity on data and infrastructure

As more operational systems send their data to the analytical plane, the analytical plane becomes a monolithic system of historical data. Workloads on the analytical plane start to feel the effects of data size, which introduces more latency to the analytics that it can no longer provide in real time.

The story is different if you have a data architecture with a streaming plane. Instead of having the operational plane moons push data directly to the planet, they instead push data to satellites within the streaming plane. These satellites provide a means to implement analytics closer to the operational plane moons while delivering data products to the planet. It dampens the effects of gravity. The streaming plane provides the fluidity needed to allow data to flow back into the operational plane for user-facing analytics.

In Figure 9-3, think of the data in materialized views in the streaming plane as satellites in orbit around a planet (or the analytical plane). You can consume real-time data from these materialized views like live television programs from a satellite. Similar to watching live television programs, data in the streaming plane can be served globally.

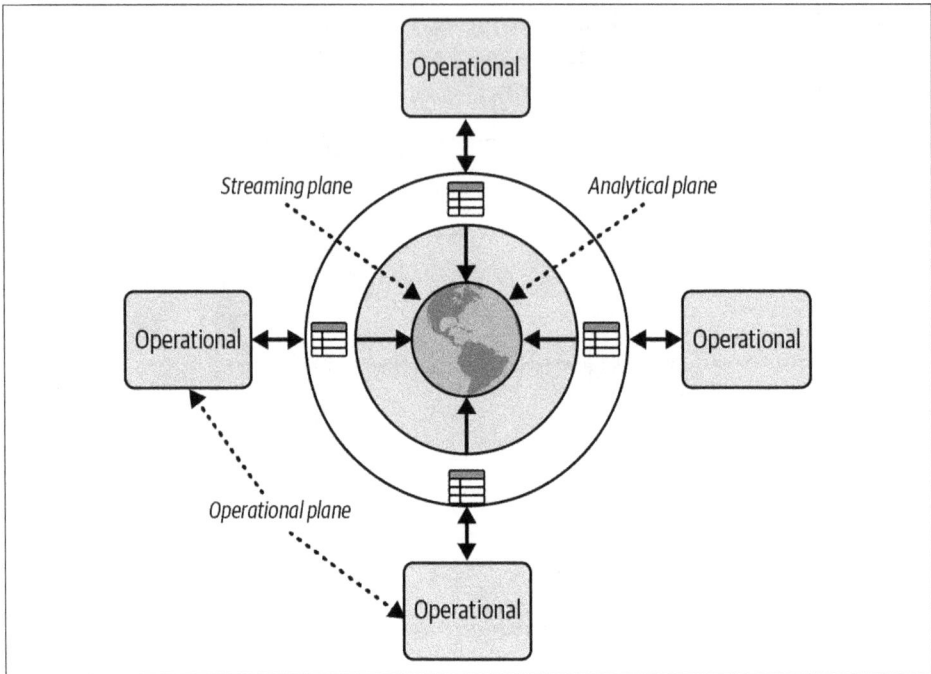

Figure 9-3. Materialized views orbiting the globe via replication

The streaming plane provides the means to implement analytics closer to the operational plane while delivering the data products that make up these analytics globally. It dampens the effects of data gravity while still providing the analytical plane with the incremental data it needs for archiving and extensive batch processing.

Components of the Streaming Plane

Figure 9-4 shows the multiple solutions and systems in the streaming plane today. Throughout this chapter, we will leverage this diagram to help describe the systems that compose the streaming plane and how they facilitate data decentralization and real-time analytics.

Figure 9-4 shows the familiar operational and analytical planes at opposite ends, separated by the streaming plane represented as a cloud. The streaming plane is supported by two components that comprise its foundation: a streaming platform like Kafka and source/sink connectors. The bidirectional arrow identifies them in Figure 9-4. It's this foundation from which the other components in the streaming plane consume real-time data.

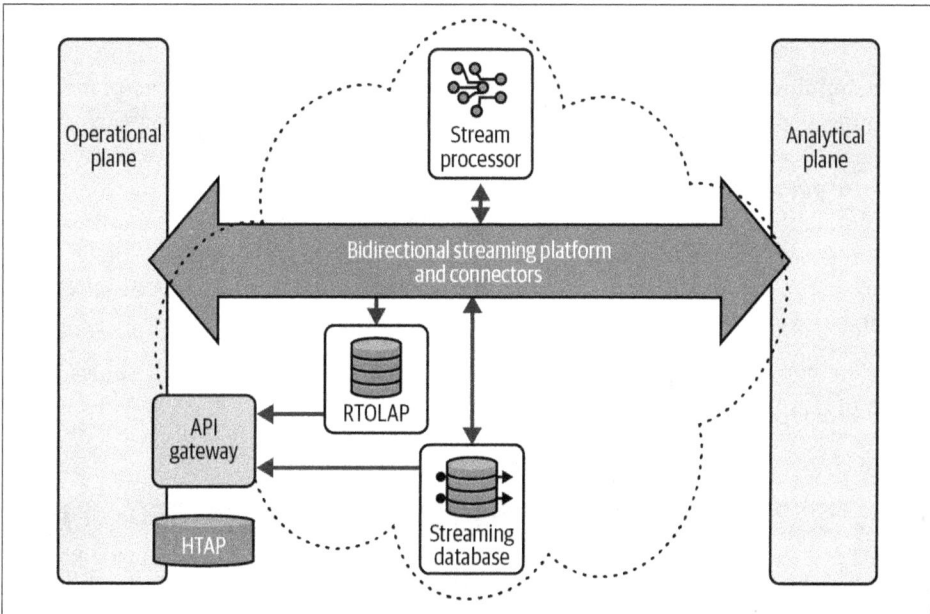

Figure 9-4. The streaming plane

Stream processors, RTOLAP databases, and streaming databases all read from Kafka to transform and serve real-time analytical data. Stream processors and streaming databases can also write analytical data back into Kafka, enabling them to build replicas of the analytical data in other planes.

The streaming plane is divided into consistent and eventually consistent streaming and real-time systems. Systems in the streaming plane migrate to their respective consistency positions and perform the workloads near their consuming planes. To the left of the streaming plane are operational analytics. To the right of the streaming plane, we have internal analytics that can tolerate eventual consistency and can access all historical data.

To summarize, here are the components of the streaming plane:

- Streaming platforms like Kafka
- Source and sink connectors
- Stream processors like Flink
- RTOLAP databases
- Streaming databases

When designing a data infrastructure for real-time analytics, architects need to account for consistency and the personas that consume the analytics.

Streaming Plane Infrastructure

When building the infrastructure of the operational plane, analytical plane, and streaming plane, architects should consider separate infrastructure for each plane. Having dedicated infrastructure for operational and analytical planes has always been standard practice. Since the streaming plane is a new concept introduced in this book, it might not be evident for architects to dedicate infrastructure to the streaming plane. Instead, architects may think of deploying streaming systems into the existing operational or analytical planes, especially since the streaming systems usually don't persist data for a very long time.

There are many reasons to dedicate infrastructure to systems. Table 9-1 shows just a subset of them.

Table 9-1. Reasons for dedicating infrastructure to data systems

Reason	Description
Scalability	As data volumes grow, architects need to design infrastructure that can scale to handle increased data loads without compromising performance. This involves selecting appropriate hardware, databases, and other components that can be easily scaled horizontally or vertically.
Performance	Dedicated infrastructure allows architects to optimize performance for specific data-related tasks. This includes considerations for data processing speed, query performance, and overall system responsiveness.
Reliability and availability	Architects design infrastructure to ensure that data systems are reliable and available when needed. This involves redundancy, failover mechanisms, and disaster recovery plans to minimize downtime and data loss.
Security	Protecting sensitive data is a top priority. Dedicated infrastructure allows architects to implement robust security measures, including access controls, encryption, and regular audits to safeguard data from unauthorized access and cyber threats.
Integration	In many organizations, data systems need to integrate with various applications, services, and platforms. Dedicated infrastructure facilitates seamless integration, ensuring that data can be shared and used across the organization efficiently.
Compliance	Depending on the industry, there may be regulatory requirements regarding how data is stored and handled. Architects must design infrastructure that complies with these regulations to avoid legal issues and penalties.
Cost efficiency	Allocating specific infrastructure resources for data systems allows architects to optimize costs. They can choose the most cost effective storage solutions, processing units, and networking components tailored to the specific needs of the data systems.
Data governance	Infrastructure plays a crucial role in enforcing data governance policies. Architects can design systems that track and enforce data quality, integrity, and consistency, ensuring that the data is reliable and accurate.

Dedicating infrastructure centers on effective management, storage, processing, and data accessibility. The streaming plane doesn't store data for a long time but processes and moves data at scale. Dedicating infrastructure to streaming systems is essential for ensuring the effective, secure, and reliable management of data in motion, supporting its various functions and strategic objectives.

Any data persisted in the streaming plane is ephemeral—temporary or short lived. The fluidity of the streaming plane keeps data fresh and limits the effects of data gravity. Its processing abilities provide analytical workloads to the operational plane.

Operational Analytics

Operational analytics refers to collecting, processing, and analyzing data near the source of data generation, typically at or near the user-facing application, rather than relying solely on analytical plane systems. Operational analytics refers to performing analytical workloads near the applications or microservices that generate the data. They do so by leveraging the streaming plane's ability to run asynchronous processes at scale.

You may think, "Why would you execute analytical workloads on the operational plane?" This question is reasonable, especially since there are many reasons why we separated these workloads, which we covered in Chapter 3.

Here are some reasons for moving analytical workloads to the operational plane:

Real-time decision-making
> Operational analytics enables organizations to derive insights from data in real time. This is crucial for making quick and informed decisions that impact ongoing operations.

Enhanced efficiency
> By embedding analytical capabilities into operational systems, organizations can streamline processes and reduce the need for manual intervention. Automated analytics within operational workflows can enhance efficiency and reduce processing time.

Improved customer experience or personalization
> Real-time analytics allows organizations to personalize interactions with customers based on their current behavior and preferences. This can significantly enhance the overall customer experience.

Proactive issue resolution and predictive analytics
> Operational analytics often includes predictive modeling, helping organizations identify potential issues before they escalate. This proactive approach allows for timely intervention and issue resolution.

Cost savings and resource optimization
> By integrating analytics into operational systems, organizations can optimize resource allocation, for example, human resources, inventory, or equipment. This can lead to cost savings and improved resource utilization.

Overall, moving analytical workloads to the operational plane is driven by the need for agility, real-time decision-making, and the desire to extract actionable insights directly within the context of ongoing business operations. This integration allows organizations to become more data driven and responsive to rapidly changing conditions in their operational environments.

The operational plane infrastructure would not have the storage capacity to hold all the historical data that the analytical plane infrastructure has. Analytical workloads executed on the operational plane have limited access to historical data. The operational systems would also be limited in scale, so even if they had access to historical data, they could only consume a small portion.

Getting historical data from the analytical plane to be consumed by systems in the operational plane for analytical workloads can be difficult. The effect of data gravity is significant and applies to more than just data. It also applies to the applications that process the data. Because of these effects, building a solution for operational analytics can get confusing. We will cover solutions to sourcing historical data in Chapter 10.

Despite these limitations, bringing analytics closer to the application and data source makes it a valuable pattern for the evolving real-time analytics landscape. Recalling the toy bank use case in Chapter 6, stream processors or streaming databases used as part of operational analytics need to be consistent. The likelihood of processing streams of transactions asynchronously that get consumed back into the application in real time is extremely high. The consequences of inconsistency can have drastic effects and a loss of trust in the application, as we demonstrated in Chapter 6.

Frank McSherry (a computer scientist and chief scientist at Materialize.io) talks about trusting streaming data. Trust unfolds into three characteristics[1]:

Responsiveness
Refers to synchronous interactive access to analytical data, measured by query latency, QPS, and concurrency (number of end users).

Freshness
Refers to how near real time the analytics results are. The freshness of data is a measure of its value as time moves forward. In Figure 9-5, the scale of the x-axis (time) is relative to the use case. It can be in hours, minutes, seconds, or milliseconds.

Consistency
We talked about consistency in detail in Chapter 6.

---

1 Frank McSherry. "A Guided Tour Through Materialize's Product Principles," Materialize, September 22, 2023 (*https://oreil.ly/jqfL1*).

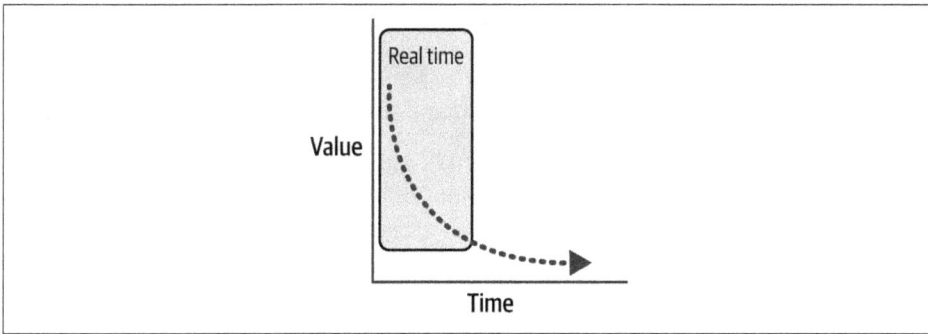

Figure 9-5. The definition of real time is based on how quickly or slowly value degrades as time progresses

In Figure 9-5, the real-time box contains data that hasn't lost all value due to time. The x-axis (time) scale will determine the types of systems you will need to employ. If the scale is in days or end-of-day, batch processing may suffice. If the scale is less than an hour, you must leverage streaming systems deployed on streaming plane infrastructure. If the scale is within 8 hours, streaming systems will prepare you for more aggressive timelines in the future.

The streaming plane gives the operational plane all the necessities for real-time analytical processing with streaming databases and stream processors. It provides real-time analytics in tabular structures for the applications and their users to consume. Moreover, a generic perspective of the streaming plane composed of a mesh of connections and tables resembles a streaming database. The implementation ideas of operational analytics align with a data mesh architecture that promotes the decentralization of data and reverses the effects of data gravity.

Data Mesh

Data mesh is a conceptual framework for data architecture introduced by Zhamak Dehghani in 2019. Departing from traditional centralized models, data mesh advocates for a decentralized approach, where data is treated as a product and ownership is distributed among different domains or business units. Each domain is responsible for its own data, fostering autonomy and accountability. Data teams function as product teams, managing the end-to-end lifecycle of the data they handle, including quality, documentation, and accessibility. The infrastructure is designed to be self-serve and empowers domain teams to independently access and manage their data. Federated computational governance ensures adherence to common standards and policies while allowing for localized control within each domain. This approach aims at addressing scalability challenges in large organizations, fostering agility and improving overall data quality.

Pillars of a Data Mesh

Data mesh comprises four key principles, or pillars. These pillars are foundational to designing and implementing a decentralized and scalable data architecture:

Domain-oriented decentralized data ownership
> This pillar emphasizes the distribution of data ownership among different domains or business units within an organization. Instead of having a centralized data team, individual domains take responsibility for the data generated and used within their specific context. This approach aligns data management with the organizational structure, fostering autonomy and accountability.

Data as a product
> The second pillar treats data as a product with its own lifecycle, quality standards, and documentation. Data teams function as product teams, responsible for the end-to-end management of the data they produce. This includes ensuring data quality, providing proper documentation, and making data easily accessible to others within the organization. Treating data as a product encourages a mindset shift toward delivering high-quality, usable data.

Self-serve data infrastructure
> The third pillar focuses on creating a self-serve data infrastructure that enables domain teams to autonomously access and manage their own data. This involves providing tools, platforms, and services that empower domain teams to work with data without heavy reliance on centralized data teams. A self-serve infrastructure supports agility and reduces bottlenecks, allowing teams to be more responsive to their specific data needs.

Federated computational governance
> The fourth pillar addresses governance by applying federated computational governance, which involves setting, using federated councils, common standards and policies while allowing local autonomy within each domain. This ensures there's a balance between enforcing organization-wide standards and providing flexibility for individual domains to govern their data according to their specific requirements. Federated computational governance helps maintain consistency and compliance across the organization.

These four pillars collectively form the basis of the data mesh framework, providing guiding principles for organizations to build scalable and agile data architectures.

By decentralizing data ownership and treating data as a product, data mesh aims to overcome the limitations of centralized models, promoting autonomy, efficiency, and improved governance. This approach acknowledges the dynamic and evolving nature of data management, aligning with the need for organizations to adapt to changing requirements and leverage data as a strategic asset.

Data mesh focuses primarily on the decentralization of data, including analytical data. Similarly, operational analytics focuses on moving analytical workloads to the operational plane, which has the inherited side effect of decentralizing data and analytical workloads.

Bringing analytical workloads closer to the operational plane aligns with data mesh concepts by promoting decentralized data ownership and improving the autonomy of domain-oriented teams. The key idea behind this alignment is to empower operational teams with direct access to analytics, enabling them to derive insights and make data-driven decisions in real time.

Here's how this alignment unfolds within the context of data mesh:

Domain-oriented decentralized data ownership

In a data mesh, data ownership is distributed among different domains or business units. Bringing analytical workloads closer to the operational plane extends this principle by allowing operational teams to own and analyze the data generated within their specific domain. This decentralization facilitates a more agile and context-aware approach to analytics, as operational teams have a deeper understanding of their data.

Data as a product

Treating data as a product implies that data is not only collected and stored but also analyzed and consumed as part of the overall data product lifecycle. Bringing analytical workloads closer to operations ensures that the insights derived from analytics are integrated seamlessly into operational processes. Operational teams become responsible for the end-to-end lifecycle of their data, including its analysis, interpretation, and application to drive business outcomes.

Self-serve data infrastructure

Analytical workloads often require specialized tools and platforms. By bringing these workloads closer to the operational plane, operational teams gain more autonomy in accessing and using analytical tools. This reduces dependencies on centralized data teams and empowers operational teams to perform ad hoc analyses, generate insights, and iterate on analytical processes without extensive external support.

Federated computational governance

Analytical workloads at the operational plane need to adhere to common standards and governance policies while allowing local autonomy. Federated computational governance is essential to ensure consistency, compliance, and security. This principle ensures that while operational teams have autonomy in their analytics, there are overarching standards that maintain the integrity and reliability of the organization's data.

In summary, aligning analytical workloads with the operational plane within the context of a data mesh supports the core principles of decentralization, autonomy, and treating data as a product. This alignment aims at making analytics more responsive to operational needs, fostering a culture of data-driven decision-making across different domains within an organization.

Challenge of a Data Mesh

However, implementing a data mesh is challenging due to the need for a significant cultural shift, technical complexity, organizational silos, and skill set gaps. The cultural shift involves transitioning from centralized control to a decentralized model, emphasizing domain-oriented ownership and collaboration. Technical challenges arise in building a self-serve data infrastructure aligned with data mesh principles, often requiring integration with existing systems. Overcoming organizational silos and fostering cross-functional collaboration is essential, as is addressing skill set gaps and ensuring teams adopt a product-oriented mindset. Data quality and governance pose challenges in balancing local autonomy with overarching standards. Effective communication and coordination are crucial, and the incremental adoption of data mesh practices while supporting existing infrastructure requires careful planning.

> *While promising, Data Mesh adoption may face hurdles related to expertise, necessitating advanced tooling and infrastructure for self-service capabilities.*
> —Roland Meertens et al., "InfoQ AI, ML, and Data Engineering Trends Report: September 2023" (*https://oreil.ly/MyvA2*)

Despite these challenges, the potential benefits, such as increased agility and improved data quality, drive organizations to navigate these complexities for a successful implementation of data mesh.

A simplified and familiar approach to data mesh can ease its adoption and simplify its implementation, which is how streaming databases can help. Streaming databases bring a familiar approach to data, enabling more data accessibility and a faster adoption of data mesh architecture. They allow data products to be consumed by multiple domains globally, accelerate iterative development, and refine data solutions quickly.

Streaming Data Mesh with Streaming Plane and Streaming Databases

A streaming data mesh implements all the pillars of a data mesh but is implemented using real-time streams. It enables real-time analytics for all domain consumers. By using streaming databases, domains can build streaming data products without needing to deeply understand streaming concepts—instead, they can leverage their database knowledge also for streaming databases.[2]

In Chapter 7, we defined a streaming database from a database perspective as "a database that can consume and emit streams as well as execute materialized views asynchronously."

Streaming databases have the unique ability to emit data as streams for other streaming databases to consume. You can build a network of connections between streaming databases that share data. As stated, the streaming plane can be treated as a streaming database stretched across all enterprise domains.

Figure 9-6 represents the goal of the streaming data mesh and how it's facilitated by the streaming plane. Streaming databases build materialized views based on replicated data from other domains. They also emit their data products for different domains to pick up.

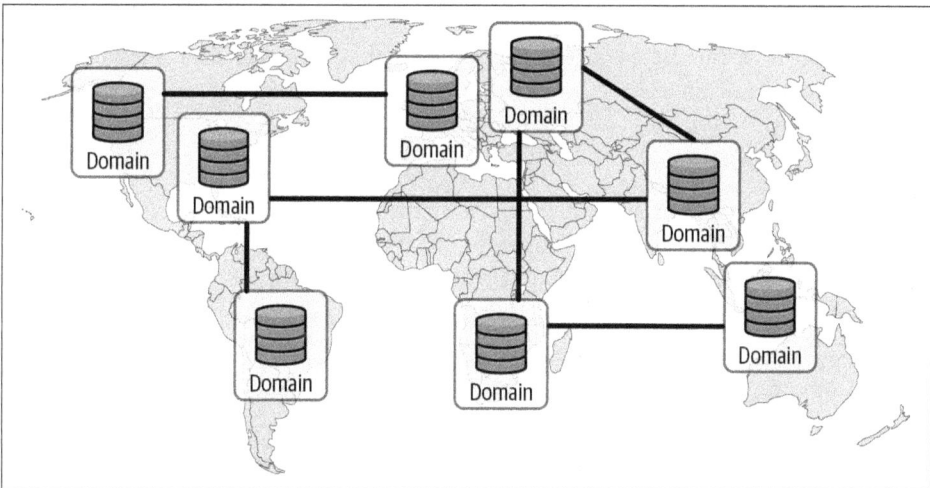

Figure 9-6. The streaming plane uses streaming databases to consume and produce data products as well as connectors and streaming platforms to replicate data products and analytics

Data Locality

Consuming data locally in a data mesh has implications for both performance and security. From a performance perspective, local consumption allows more efficient and faster access to data. Since data is replicated from remote domains and stored

---

2 For more information, see *Streaming Data Mesh* (O'Reilly) and "Kafka and RisingWave" (*https://oreil.ly/ 8LFpA*).

within the local domain where needed, teams can minimize latency and optimize data processing for their specific use cases. This can improve performance for analytical workloads, real-time processing, and other data-driven operations, as teams can tailor their data infrastructure to meet local performance requirements. Additionally, local consumption facilitates the scalability of data processing, as domain teams can independently scale their infrastructure based on their specific needs without impacting other domains.

On the security front, consuming data locally aligns with the principle of federated computational governance within a data mesh. Security measures can be implemented at the domain level, allowing each domain to enforce its own security policies and access controls. Furthermore, domain teams can focus on securing their data assets without compromising the entire organization's security. By implementing security measures at the domain level and adhering to common global standards, a data mesh improves the balance between local autonomy and the overarching security requirements of the organization.

To get data for local use in a domain, systems that replicate data are one of the cornerstones of a data mesh.

Data Replication

Replication is pivotal in implementing a streaming data mesh by ensuring data reaches its destinations for local consumption. In a streaming data mesh, data is distributed among different domains, and real-time replication mechanisms are crucial for maintaining data consistency and reliability.

Moreover, replication supports the scalability requirements of a streaming data mesh. As data volumes and processing demands vary across domains, replication allows for the efficient distribution of data processing workloads. By replicating relevant data streams to the domains where they are needed, organizations can optimize resource utilization and minimize latency, enabling each domain to scale its infrastructure independently based on its specific operational needs. This scalability is critical for accommodating fluctuations in data velocity and ensuring that the streaming data mesh can adapt to evolving business requirements with agility and efficiency.

Replication in the streaming plane works by building a network of connected streaming platforms. For example, Kafka has a mechanism called Mirror Maker 2.0 (MM2) that can mirror topics from one Kafka cluster to a different remote Kafka cluster.

Example 9-1 is a sample configuration for MM2 that will mirror topics between Kafka clusters.

Example 9-1. Mirror Maker 2.0 configuration for mirroring topics between two Kafka clusters

```
# specify any number of cluster aliases
clusters = source, destination ❶

# connection information for each cluster
# This is a comma separated host:port pairs for each cluster
# for example.
# "A_host1:9092, A_host2:9092, A_host3:9092"
# and you can see the exact host name on Ambari > Hosts
source.bootstrap.servers = kafka-source1:9092,kafka-source2:9092,kafka-source3:9092
destination.bootstrap.servers = kafka-dest1:9092,kafka-dest2:9092,kafka-dest3:9092

# enable and configure individual replication flows
source->destination.enabled = true

# regex which defines which topics gets replicated. For eg "foo-.*"
source->destination.topics = foo ❷
groups=.*
topics.blacklist="*.internal,__.*"

# Setting replication factor of newly created remote topics
replication.factor=3

checkpoints.topic.replication.factor=1
heartbeats.topic.replication.factor=1
offset-syncs.topic.replication.factor=1

offset.storage.replication.factor=1
status.storage.replication.factor=1
config.storage.replication.factor=1
```

❶ The names for the source and destination Kafka clusters

❷ The topics to mirror in the destination Kafka cluster

MM2 mirrors topics only between two Kafka clusters. The streaming plane can comprise many Kafka clusters, possibly 1 to 2 per region where domains exist. One instance of MM2 must be deployed for additional regions that want to consume real-time data locally.

MM2 is usually implemented as a connector that runs in a Kafka Connect cluster. As mentioned earlier in this chapter, the streaming plane is built upon a foundation of streaming platforms and connectors. It is these components that create the mesh of streaming data.

An alternative to MM2 is a proprietary solution called Cluster Linking (CL) provided by Confluent. CL connects Kafka clusters and mirrors topics between them. Unlike MM2, CL doesn't require a Kafka Connect cluster. MM2 and CL provide solutions to keep data in motion to minimize the effects of data gravity.

Summary

Streaming databases abstract away a significant amount of complexity of the streaming plane with a simple and familiar database experience. Any operational domain can participate in a data mesh and produce and consume real-time data products with other domains without deep knowledge about stream processing. In the next chapter, we will review different deployment models that will serve as a blueprint for your real-time analytical needs.

Deployment Models

This chapter will cover several deployment models for a spectrum of use cases. A key aspect of our exploration will be to find out where leveraging streaming databases is most advantageous and when alternative approaches might be more suitable. We will account for all the streaming attributes we covered in the past chapters, including consistency, workload types, storage formats, and the ideas about the streaming plane introduced in Chapter 9.

We will focus on unraveling various architectural patterns facilitating real-time analytics in the streaming plane. The streaming plane's dynamic nature exposes a unique set of strategies to harness its potential effectively. It can support a spectrum of real-time use cases:

- At one end of the spectrum are the use cases that interact with the application deployed in the operational plane. These streaming solutions require consistency but have limited access to historical data.

- On the other end of the spectrum are the use cases that only deal with real-time analytics without the need for interaction with application logic. These streaming solutions can be eventually consistent and have access to all historical data.

Of course, different degrees of consistency and historical data can be met along the spectrum. We'll cover the entire real-time analytical spectrum from left (consistent/internally consistent solutions) to right (analytical only).

It's important for us to stress that the solutions in this chapter will leverage streaming solutions as they come "out of the box." This is especially important when it comes to consistency. For streaming databases and stream processors that are eventually consistent, it's possible to "emulate" stronger consistency guarantees by, for example, adding extra fields and adding them to the join logic. Implementing this also requires deeper knowledge of the streaming platform that goes beyond the scope of this book. However, engineers who are familiar with databases but new to streaming will expect a higher degree of consistency without the need to mimic it or bolt it on afterward. With this understanding, more consistent solutions can provide the highest value with less effort.

Consistent Streaming Database

When you need a database that can run complex asynchronous/stream processing that participates in your application logic, you can build it with a consistent streaming database. Moreover, since it's also a database, you can query the output of the asynchronous process directly from the streaming database. A consistent streaming database can simplify your infrastructure without requiring deep streaming knowledge. Solutions that satisfy this are RisingWave and Materialize.

In Figure 10-1, a consistent streaming database like RisingWave or Materialize shows its hybrid characteristics by sitting on the border between streaming and operational planes.

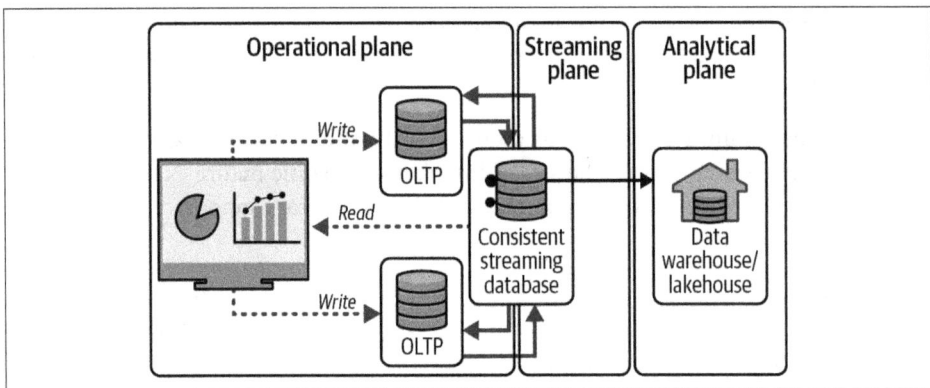

Figure 10-1. Operational analytics using a consistent streaming database

The solid arrows in Figure 10-1 represent streaming data. The dashed arrows represent the read-and-write interaction between the application and databases. The consistent streaming database consumes from the OLTP database and executes analytical transformations via stream processing. The results are saved in row-based storage in the streaming database.

This solution allows the application to write directly to the OLTP database and read from the streaming database. It also enables the separation of resources between reading and writing data.

The streaming database also provides the ability to consume and aggregate data from multiple OLTP databases and send transformed data to the data warehouse or lakehouse (the analytical plane). The data warehouse would be used for internal business analytics.

This solution is limited when the user-facing application needs historical data from the data warehouse or lakehouse. Because of data gravity, receiving historical data from the analytical plane is difficult.

The consistent streaming database also gets to its limits when complex analytical queries are required. Those are better suited for a columnar database. Here is a consolidated table of pros and cons associated with this solution:

Pros	Cons
• Provides data freshness in milliseconds. • There is a separation of read and write resources that can be independently and explicitly scaled up and down. • You can combine inputs from multiple OLTP databases (even from different vendors) into a single, consistent streaming database. • Transformations can be performed incrementally, before the data is sent to the analytical plane. • Push and pull queries are supported in the streaming database using the same query engine/interface.	• Lacks columnar storage, which is better for faster analytical queries. • Consistent streaming databases need help receiving historical data from the analytical plane because they cannot source it themselves. • Can struggle when the data size starts to become too large.

Use this solution for use cases that need consistent stream processing that takes part in the application logic but does not need (too much) historical data from the analytical plane. It's also an excellent way to aggregate data from multiple OLTP databases from different applications.

Consistent Streaming Processor and RTOLAP

Alternatively, you can use a consistent stream processor like Pathway if you prefer to output the stream to a columnar database. Consistent stream processors can execute push queries near the operational plane and participate in the application's logic. They write their output into a streaming platform like Kafka, from which a RTOLAP database (like Pinot) can consume data and then serve it.

Figure 10-2 shows how to transform data in the stream processor and write the results to a data warehouse/lakehouse and a RTOLAP database. The RTOLAP can also read historical data from the data warehouse/lakehouse (analytical plane), join it with the real-time data from the consistent stream processor, and make it available to the operational plane as low-latency pull queries. Here are the pros and cons associated with this solution:

Pros	Cons
• Can provide data freshness in milliseconds to seconds. • User-facing analytics can include all historical context without storing it on operational infrastructure. • The columnar format in the RTOLAP database provides fast analytical workloads to the application. • The RTOLAP and stream processor can reuse many topics on the streaming platform. • A consistent stream processor can play a dual role by participating in the application's business logic and preparing real-time analytics.	• Push and pull queries are separated between stream processor and OLAP database, respectively. Separation of these queries often requires separate engineers and strict coordination between them that may prove hard to achieve in practice.

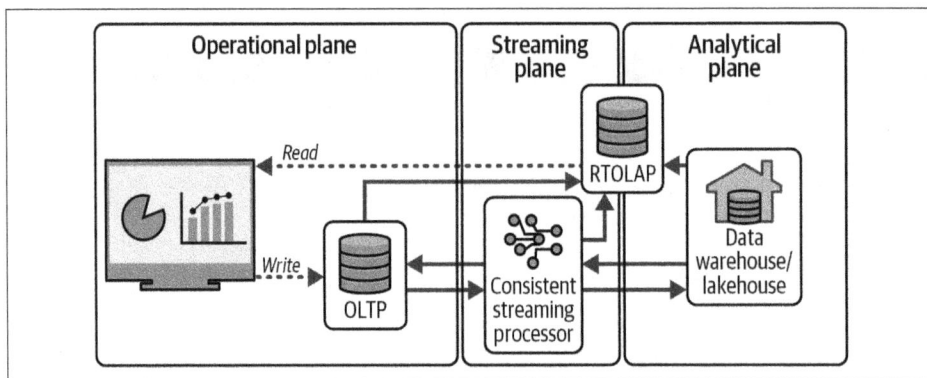

Figure 10-2. Consistent stream processor

Use this solution if your use case requires most or all historical data to be available for user-facing analytics and a consistent stream processor to participate in the application logic.

Eventually Consistent OLAP Streaming Database

If having a separate stream processor and OLAP database is making infrastructure too complex, leveraging a streaming OLAP database like Proton is a great way to consolidate all analytical workloads into one solution. But, because of its eventually consistent characteristics, it shouldn't participate in the application's logic. In Figure 10-3, the data movement between the OLTP and the streaming database is one directional. Applications can take advantage of the OLAP's columnar store for low-latency queries.

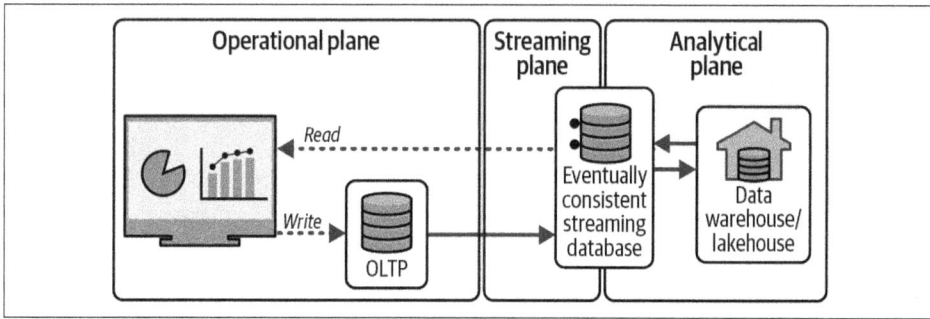

Figure 10-3. Eventually consistent streaming OLAP database

Since Proton is a streaming database, it has the ability to write its stream processing output to Kafka. This allows other databases to consume the analytical stream to build replicas in other databases. But since Proton embeds ClickHouse (an RTO-LAP), it already has columnar storage and can serve analytical queries with low latency. Outputting analytics to Kafka has the added feature of distributing analytics to other global regions in real time. Here's an overview of the pros and cons:

Pros	Cons
• Data freshness in milliseconds to seconds. • Provides more or even all historical data, providing more context to real-time data. • Proton can emit analytical changes to allow developers to build replicas of the analytical results. • Simpler solution that converges stream processing and OLAP technologies. • Provides a single SQL engine to build push and pull queries. • Is less bulky.	• Only eventually consistent; should not take part in the application logic.

The greatest benefit gained when using a streaming OLAP database is its ability to balance push and pull queries from within a single query engine and interface. It reduces the work to a single engineer, unlike the solution incorporating a separate stream processor and an OLAP database. Proton provides a simple solution for real-time analytics.

Use this solution to reduce the infrastructure and engineering complexity and to allow access to more historical data for user-facing analytics.

Eventually Consistent Stream Processor and RTOLAP

This solution is probably the most common in providing real-time analytics today. It often involves Flink and an RTOLAP database like Pinot. See Figure 10-4.

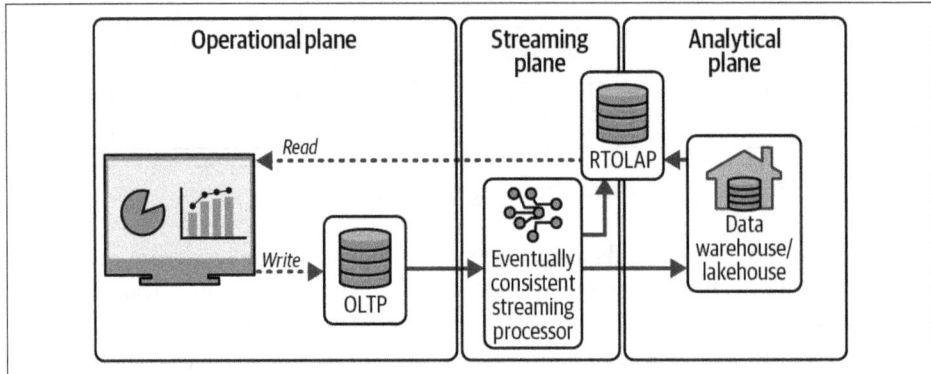

Figure 10-4. Eventually consistent stream processor and RTOLAP

This solution has been proven in many high-scale, real-time applications today:

Pros	Cons
• Data freshness can be achieved in in milliseconds to seconds. • Historical data + real-time data can be joined together to provide a complete view of analytics.	• This is a complex and bulky solution that can lead to higher cost. • Because Flink is eventually consistent, it should not take part in application logic. • Since the stream processor and real-time OLAP execution engines are separated, this solution doesn't provide a single SQL engine for push and pull queries, which can lead to higher engineering and organizational stress.

Use this solution when your use case requires more historical data for user-facing analytics in your application. Consistency should not be a significant concern when enriching fact streams with dimensional streams.

Eventually Consistent Stream Processor and HTAP

In cases where you want to keep analytical workloads near or in the operational plane, using an HTAP database along with an OLTP database can be convenient. You can add an eventually consistent stream processor to capture historical data to be sent to your data warehouse or lakehouse. See Figure 10-5.

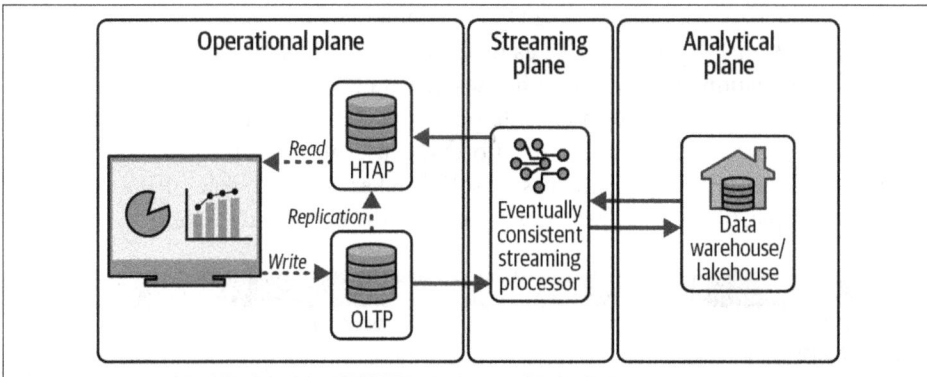

Figure 10-5. Eventually consistent stream processor and HTAP

The stream processor can source limited historical data from the analytical plane and provide it to the HTAP database. Because of its columnar format, it has the ability to serve low-latency analytical queries. The amount of historical data the HTAP database holds is typically limited and/or comes with a limited retention time. Here are the pros and cons:

Pros	Cons
• Provides data freshness in milliseconds.	• Limited historical data.
• HTAP databases have columnar storage for fast analytical queries.	• Complexity increases when implementing retention for the historical data held in the HTAP database.
• Low infrastructural complexity.	• The stream processor cannot take part in the application logic.

Use this solution if your use case requires data to be fresh in milliseconds and only requires a small subset of historical data for user-facing analytics.

ksqlDB

In Chapter 6, we discussed the consistency guarantees provided by ksqlDB ("continuous refinement," similar to "eventual consistency"). ksqlDB is based on the underlying JVM library Kafka Streams built for deployment inside microservices. Microservices are deployed in the operational plane as part of an application backend.

We recommend using Kafka Streams and ksqlDB only for simpler stream processing operations. JOINs are hard to get right, especially when combining append-only "streams" and changelog-like "tables." ksqlDB only supports a subset of SQL syntax and semantics (e.g., no self-JOINs, no nested JOINs). The risk of implementing inconsistent logic is high, even though it's possible to harness ksqlDB if you have a team of well-versed stream processing experts at your disposal.

As a result, the best use cases for ksqlDB are simpler stream processing operations on Kafka (ksqlDB only supports Kafka as its data source and sink) that prepare data for analytical destinations like data warehouses or data lakes. It's also possible to use the materialized views of ksqlDB to execute point queries, for example, for destinations that only support batch and cannot afford the use of a full-fledged, continuously running Kafka consumer. In this case, ksqlDB takes over the role of the consumer that, for example, filters and preprocesses data for the batch-only system:

Pros	Cons
• Data freshness.	• Only supports Kafka as source/sink.
• Stream processing capabilities.	• High amount of stream processing expertise required.
• Enables point queries using materialized views (TABLEs) to support batch-only destinations.	• Complex stream processing operations hard to implement correctly.
	• No support for full SQL syntax and semantics.

Incremental View Maintenance

Solutions supporting IVM, such as Feldera, PeerDB, or Epsio, can also be used to support batch-based point queries on preprocessed, fresh data. Contrary to ksqlDB, these solutions are more closely integrated with operational databases such as PostgreSQL and do not require the use of Kafka as an intermediary layer.

In addition, these solutions allow for more complex preprocessing of the data using full and consistent SQL semantics. The downside is that they tend to be more inflexible than solutions based on Kafka. You are essentially restricted to those data sources and sinks that are supported by the respective vendor, whereas if you use Kafka as an intermediary layer, your choice of data sources and sinks is significantly higher.

IVM solutions can also increase the understanding of asynchronous and continuous processing of data to IT organizations and act as a "gateway drug" for them to the world of streaming, stream processing, and streaming databases. They can still be operated in the same manner (e.g., PeerDB and Epsio), or even from inside the Postgres ecosystem, but their way of operation is already close to streaming, stream processing, and streaming databases—which might become necessary to integrate larger architectures in larger organizations:

Pros	Cons
• Data freshness.	• Restricted to the sources/sinks supported by the respective vendor.
• Full SQL syntax and semantics.	
• Consistency.	
• Enables point queries.	
• Sneaks in streaming aspects into the database world.	

Postgres Multicorn Foreign Data Wrapper

Multicorn is a PostgreSQL 9.1+ extension meant to make *foreign data wrapper* (FDW) development more convenient by allowing the programmer to use the Python programming language. This enables programmers to build, for the operational plane, FDWs for non-Postgres databases, for example, for RTOLAP databases such as Apache Pinot, and make the data available inside a PostgreSQL database.

If your databases on the operational plane are Postgres based, FDWs for Postgres are definitely an option to bring the operational and the analytical planes closer together without incurring the complexity of using, for example, a streaming platform like Kafka and stream processing in between. However, similar to IVM in the previous section, the problem with Multicorn is that it's restricted to one vendor. In larger organizations, in 99% of the cases you'll have a plethora of database technologies on the operational plane—not only Postgres. Hence, you'd have to establish Postgres as the central operational database, which is, in larger organizations, not achievable in practice. Again, using a streaming platform such as Kafka as an intermediary layer could help—if you can afford the additional complexity that this entails:

Pros	Cons
• Full SQL syntax and semantics. • Consistency. • Access to both OLTP (Postgres), other non-Postgres OLTP databases, and (real-time) OLAP databases within the Postgres ecosystem (operational plane).	• Requirement to use Postgres as the central database technology (impractical if deployed at large scale/in large organizations).

When to Use Code-Based Stream Processors

The processing and querying of the data can also be implemented with technologies other than streaming databases. Classical stream processing technologies such as Kafka Streams and Flink are still useful, especially for "hardcore" streaming use cases such as fraud detection or inside a microservices architecture, which are typically located on the operational plane.

The zoo of technologies for code-based stream processing has also grown considerably over the past years. Now, in addition to the classical technologies, you can also choose, for example, Quix Streams (Python, C#), Bytewax (Python), and Pathway (Python), where, interestingly, both Bytewax and Pathway are based on the same underlying stream processing engine used in Materialize (timely dataflow/DD). Other new and interesting technologies in this segment are Deephaven and a Python-based framework, GlassFlow.

When to Use Lakehouse/Streamhouse Technologies

Lakehouse technologies such as Databricks' Delta Tables, Apache Iceberg, or Apache Hudi also increasingly lean into the streaming space and offer streaming and/or stream processing features. Databricks has actually offered these features since the beginning (Spark Structured Streaming). The new Streamhouse architecture proposed by Ververica with Apache Paimon offers an even closer integration of stream processing and processing on the data lake. A little later, Confluent announced the feature Tableflow, which allows them to expose data on their Kafka-based streaming platform, Confluent Cloud, as Iceberg tables. Similar to Paimon, Confluent uses Flink to seamlessly integrate stream and batch processing.

A solution similar to Tableflow comes from the startup Streambased.io. It has built a solution for querying Kafka topics that is, on the one hand, closely intertwined with Kafka and, on the other, offers a database-like SQL interface based on the Trino SQL query engine. If you use Trino on Kafka without Streambased, the performance of the SQL queries can be painstakingly low since the query engine reads from the Kafka topics directly. Streambased adds a Bloom filter–based index to the Kafka topics, which is used to speed up the performance of the Trino-based queries 10× or more (the company claims 39× on its website).

Compared to RTOLAP databases such as Pinot, Druid, or ClickHouse, Streambased doesn't replicate the Kafka data but only creates additional indexes—and those indexes take up far less disk space than the actual data. The added performance gained from the indexing then allows you to query Kafka topics "almost directly" with very low latency. This could be another solution that enables "downward compatibility" of streaming and batch; you can actually query Kafka topics via REST or JDBC (Java Database Connectivity) as if they were database tables. This can make streaming much more accessible by making it almost invisible to the end user.

Essentially, all these developments increase the data gravity of the streaming plane. More processing can and will be done closer to the stream, or data in motion, and less processing has to be implemented late in the data warehouse/data lake. If data freshness/latency is not the main concern, the processing of the data can be seamlessly migrated from the streaming plane back to the analytical plane (and vice versa if latency becomes more important).

Caching Technologies

There is more to choose from, of course. If you need extremely low latency, more so than you can get with a streaming platform such as Kafka, you might also look into caching tools such as Redis or Hazelcast. These can be located either on the operational plane or the streaming plane, depending on how close they are integrated with the streaming platform. Solutions like Hazelcast even offer functionalities akin to stream processing using, for example, SQL-like syntax.

Where to Do Processing and Querying in General?

Over the course of this book, we have brought a large number of technologies into the spotlight, some of them living on the operational plane, some on the analytical plane, some on the streaming plane, and most of them somewhere in between.

You, as a reader of this book, are likely a practitioner. You have a task to accomplish, and you might read this book to get new ideas about how to do that. Now can we, the authors of this book, help you with that? Is there some more general advice that we can give to help you select the right method and technology—and how to distribute and scale it?

Of course, the safe answer to questions like these is to say, "it depends." And it does, but we'd love to be a bit more helpful. This section is about what "it depends" on and what consequences you can expect from choosing particular technologies for your task at hand.

The Four "Where" Questions

When you think of a certain task or use case, what are the most crucial factors determining the choice of the technology to accomplish this task? Let us hark back to our "map" or "landscape" of the data space, arranged in a Venn diagram of the overlapping operational, analytical, and streaming planes. This map might prompt us to think more of locations first and go from there.

As a result, when you consider your task or use case, try to pose yourself the following four "where" questions:

1. Where is my use case located?
2. Where is the data I need for my use case?
3. Where do I process it?
4. Where do I query it?

An Analytical Use Case

Figure 10-6 represents a typical example. Consider an analytical use case where data originally coming from operational systems needs to be queried in a business-facing dashboard application. Hence, the answer to the first question ("Where is my use case located?") is "the analytical plane." Let's assume the second question is also easy to answer—the origin of the data is on a streaming platform on the streaming plane. In the diagram, observe the arrow from the origin of the data (the answer to question 2) to the use case (the answer to question 1).

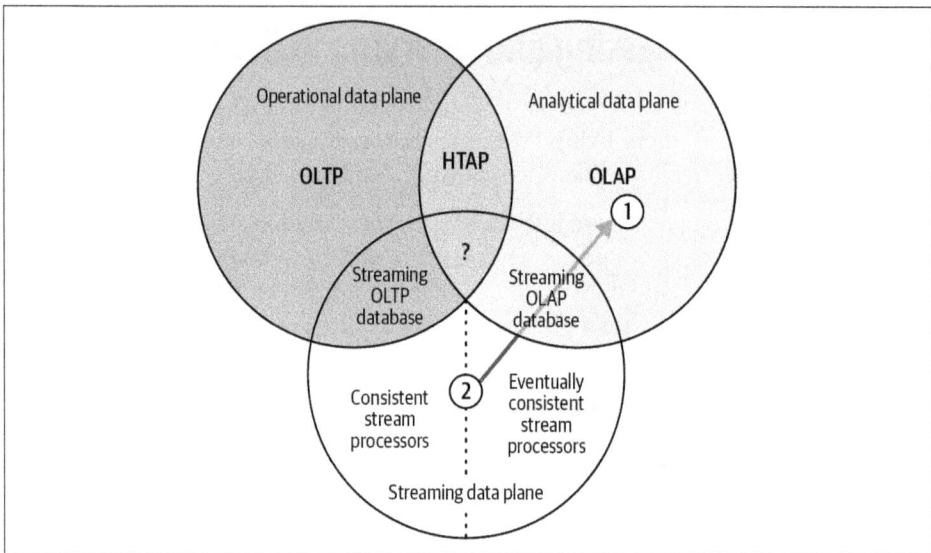

Figure 10-6. A continuum of locations

Let's usher in the following two "where" questions: Where do I process the data, and where do I query it? Typically, in today's world, the answer would be to "do both on the analytical plane," for example, in a data warehouse like Snowflake or a lakehouse technology like Databricks.

But maybe such a simple (and possibly costly) answer is not for you. For us, it isn't, because there is, of course, not just one answer to questions 3 and 4. In fact, there is a continuum of answers.

Let's focus on the straight line or "path" from 2 to 1. This path signifies the continuum of answers to questions 3 and 4. Of course, you could give simple answers and both process and query the data on the analytical plane as well, as shown in Figure 10-7.

However, you might also consider other options. For example, you could answer question 3 ("Where do I process the data?") with a technology that enables you to do the processing on the streaming plane, for example, with a stream processor like Flink or a streaming database. And you could even push the querying of the data (question 4) to the streaming plane if you use a streaming database, as shown in Figure 10-8.

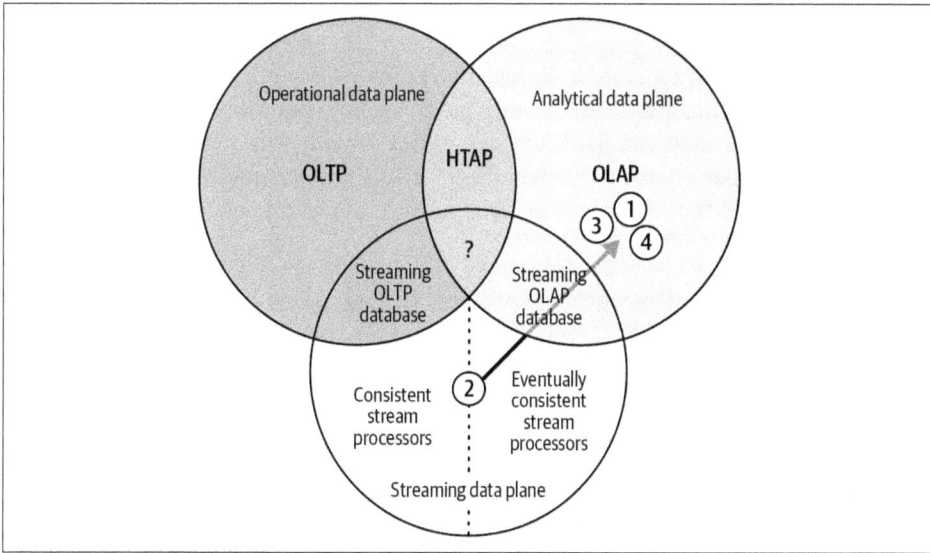

Figure 10-7. Doing the processing and querying both on the analytical plane

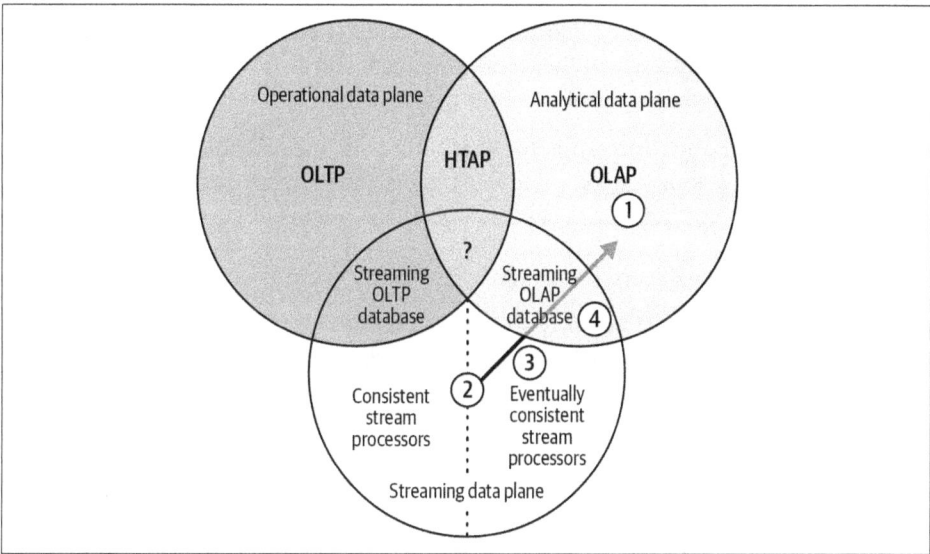

Figure 10-8. Doing the processing and querying closer to/on the streaming plane

So basically, the path connecting the location of your use case with the origin of the data for your use case specifies the continuum or set of possible locations and, therefore, also technologies you can use to address your task. You can do the processing and querying on any location on that path, but your choice will always have positive and negative consequences.

Consequences

What are those consequences? In theory, the further away from the source of the data you do the processing (question 3) and the querying (question 4) of the data, the more disadvantages you get. This, of course, ties in with what we wrote about data gravity in the earlier chapters. For example, if you answer questions 3 and 4 as in Figure 10-7 and do both on the analytical plane, close to the analytical use case, the following will be difficult:

- Keeping the data fresh because it needs to first travel to the analytical plane before it can be processed and then queried.

- Sharing the processed data because the processing is executed too closely to the use case.

- Processing incrementally. On the analytical plane, batch processing is prevalent. For processing to work, it'll have to go through the same data repeatedly, which is inefficient and can prove costly, especially when using cloud data warehouse technologies.

So why is the vast majority of the industry still doing this? Why are the answers to questions 3 and 4 most often, "Do it on the analytical plane"? Why is, for this very common use case, the gravity of the streaming plane still so low and the gravity of the analytical plane so high in light of the disadvantages that we have listed?

We think one of the main reasons for that otherwise inexplicable acceptance of an architecture with a long list of disadvantages is that stream processing (and also querying streams) is still hard. It's hard in at least three aspects:

- A lot of streaming expertise is required—which is often not readily available.

- Even if streaming expertise is available, stream processing will still be cost-intensive—so much so, in fact, that it outweighs the potential cost savings of earlier and incremental processing.

- Even with streaming expertise, it's difficult to get consistent results from stream processing.

To turn around what we said earlier, the earlier you can do the processing, the fresher the data will be, the more you'll be able to share the processed data, and the more incrementally you can process your data. But before the advent of streaming databases, using stream processing was often not practical for very pragmatic reasons.

Streaming databases have the potential to change this because they work a lot more like ordinary databases. For example, Materialize and RisingWave even use the Postgres wire protocol. The new stream processing engine in MongoDB can be easily used by MongoDB experts. Hence, in both cases, much less streaming expertise is required. Basically, you can put your existing database/data warehouse experts on the job, which can significantly reduce the cost of implementation of stream processing: no additional experts have to be hired.

Turning to the fourth "where" question about querying the data, next-generation streaming databases even offer capabilities to almost directly query streaming data by providing materialized views. Constantly updated materialized views make for fresher data, and by using incremental stream processing under the covers, they can also bring down the cost of implementing your use case: since only new data needs to be processed (and then materialized). Running queries against materialized views avoids the need to painstakingly traverse through the same old data points again and again. Especially for high-frequency queries, this can decrease the compute requirements and, thus, also reduce cost significantly.

As a result, streaming databases can actually act as a game changer for the adoption of streaming and have the potential to increase the data gravity of the streaming plane. For a lot of use cases, at least the processing (question 3) can be moved to the streaming plane in a way that was not possible before streaming databases surfaced.

When you combine this train of thought with the recent advent of technologies like Streamhouse (Ververica) and Tableflow (Confluent), the data gravity of the streaming plane will increase even further, and the lines between the three planes in our Venn diagram will continue to blur.

Summary

This chapter discussed the various deployment and architectural models for streaming databases and other hybrid technologies meandering between the operational, analytical, and streaming planes, as well as the pros and cons of basing your architecture on them.

We continued with a discussion of technologies that are less closely related to the overarching topic of this book but still related enough to be worth mentioning. This included code-based stream processing solutions, new developments around streaming in the lakehouse, and caching technologies.

We generalized our recommendations of deployment models by using a set of "where" questions. Based on the Venn diagram used throughout the later chapters of this book, we developed these questions to help you delineate a continuum of possibilities for locating the processing and the querying of your data.

We concluded that streaming databases could actually lead to a democratization of stream processing and the use of streaming in general. As a result, they have the potential to considerably increase the data gravity of the streaming plane. This is amplified by the increasing number of features of streaming vendors (Ververica's

Streamhouse and Confluent's Tableflow, etc.) and nonstreaming vendors (MongoDB, Databricks, etc.), which position these vendors more and more in those sections of our Venn diagram that overlap with the streaming plane.

In the next—the last—chapter, we continue this exciting train of thought about the convergence of streaming and databases in more detail.

Future State of Real-Time Data

The cave you fear to enter holds the treasure you seek.
—Joseph Campbell

After delving deeply into the deployment options for streaming databases, this chapter takes a step back and looks into the future state of real-time data, shaped by one of the central topics of this book: the accelerated convergence of streaming and databases. Streaming databases are one of the manifestations of this trend. But there's so much more evidence worth at least touching upon here.

We start out with graph databases and their ongoing journey toward the streaming realm (e.g., Memgraph, thatDot), followed by nowadays, after the ChatGPT GenAI breakthrough, super-popular vector databases (e.g., Milvus, Weaviate). We continue our travels through the converging lands of streaming and databases with tools for bringing one central aspect of streaming databases, namely, Materialized Views, aka IVM, to classical databases (Feldera, PeerDB, and Epsio). Toward the end of this chapter, we examine the streaming functionalities of established database vendors such as MongoDB and slowly turn our focus to the analytical plane with data warehouses like BigQuery, Redshift, and Snowflake that are also consequently extending their streaming functionalities. We close this chapter by surveying the confluence of streaming and lakehouse architectures driven by Apache Iceberg, Apache Hudi, Delta Lake, and Apache Paimon—one of the most promising macro trends not only in the streaming space but also in the big data space as a whole.

The Convergence of the Data Planes

Before we start our journey, let's set the context by having another look at the Venn diagram from Chapter 7 (Figure 11-1).

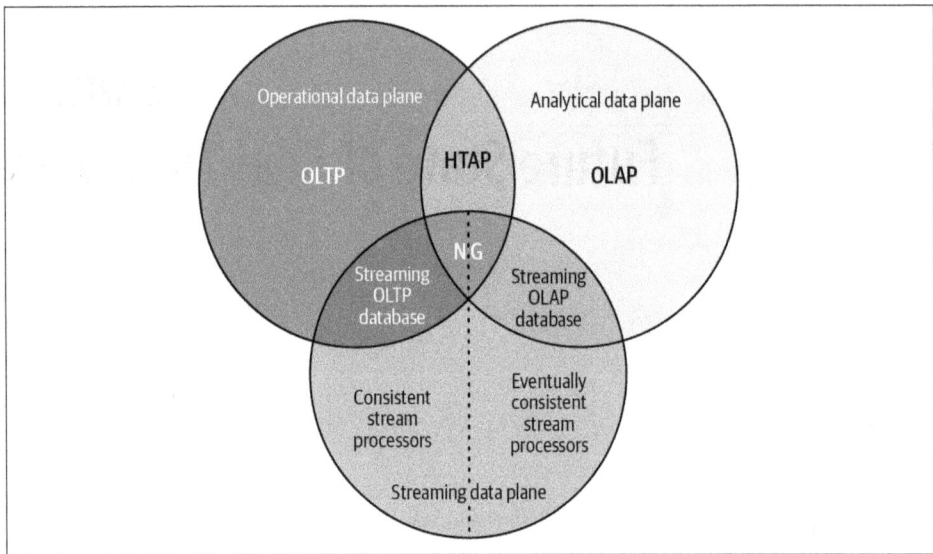

Figure 11-1. Venn diagram of next-generation databases

The diagram illustrates the convergence of the three data planes:

- Operational data plane
- Analytical data plane
- Streaming data plane

In the first sections of this chapter, we will focus on the operational data plane, that is, databases that are most commonly used in an operational rather than analytical setting. We will elaborate on how various kinds of operational databases are making their way toward the streaming data plane, namely, the shaded area where the operational and the streaming data planes overlap.

After that, we take a look at the efforts of vendors from the analytical data plane, including data warehouses (e.g., Snowflake) and lakehouses (e.g., Databricks) to augment their portfolio with streaming functionalities—and thereby getting closer to the shaded area where the analytical and the streaming data planes meet. Especially intriguing in this context is the ongoing convergence of lakehouse and streaming architectures—this is destined to become one of the major topics in the big data space in the years to come and will, therefore, act as the climax of this chapter.

Graph Databases

Graph databases use underlying graph structures to enable queries on graphs that would otherwise be hard to implement efficiently in a relational database. They formed an important part of the NoSQL movement from the 2000s and 2010s, which significantly broadened the database space. Popular graph databases are Neo4J, ArangoDB, and TigerGraph. Graph databases are clearly part of the operational data plane; they are typically used for operational applications, setting them apart from *graph compute engines*, which have their place on the analytical plane.

Typical use cases for graph databases are:

Social networks
> Graph databases excel in modeling and querying social networks and are widely used, for example, by Meta, X, or LinkedIn. The typical setup is that nodes represent users and edges represent relationships between them, such as "user A follows user B" or "user A is a friend of user B."

Recommendations
> Here, relationships between users and products/content are modeled and queried to extract personalized recommendations based on the preferences of the users.

Knowledge graphs
> In this use case, graphs are employed to model relationships between pieces of knowledge to facilitate more accurate semantic search.

Fraud detection
> If combined with AI/ML, the accuracy of fraud detection mechanisms can be noticeably improved by graph databases to improve the analysis of patterns of connections between entities.

Supply chain
> Here, nodes represent, for example, locations, products and entities, and edge relationships and movements within the supply chain. In this context, graph databases can be used to significantly optimize supply chains.

While established graph databases such as Neo4J and ArangoDB can be connected to streaming platforms, for example, using Kafka Connect, newer vendors like Memgraph and thatDot have begun to offer features that allow for an even tighter integration.

Memgraph

Memgraph offers features that enable it to directly connect to streaming platforms such as Kafka and Pulsar to ingest the data, and it even offers support for so-called *transformation modules* to transform incoming messages to consume them correctly. Transformation modules can either use the C API or the Python API.

Example 11-1 shows how Memgraph allows direct ingestion of data from Kafka.

Example 11-1. Directly ingesting data from Kafka in Memgraph streams

```
CREATE KAFKA STREAM <stream name>
  TOPICS <topic1> [, <topic2>, ...]
  TRANSFORM <transform procedure>
  [CONSUMER_GROUP <consumer group>]
  [BATCH_INTERVAL <batch interval duration>]
  [BATCH_SIZE <batch size>]
  [BOOTSTRAP_SERVERS <bootstrap servers>]
  [CONFIGS { <key1>: <value1> [, <key2>: <value2>, ...]}]
  [CREDENTIALS { <key1>: <value1> [, <key2>: <value2>, ...]}];

START STREAM <stream name> [BATCH_LIMIT <count>] [TIMEOUT <milliseconds>];
```

Example 11-2 exhibits a transformation module using the Python API.

Example 11-2. Using the Memgraph Python API for transforming incoming messages from a streaming platform

```
import mgp

@mgp.transformation
def transformation(context: mgp.TransCtx,
                   messages: mgp.Messages
                   ) -> mgp.Record(query=str, parameters=mgp.Nullable[mgp.Map]):
    result_queries = []

    for i in range(messages.total_messages()):
        message = messages.message_at(i)
        payload_as_str = message.payload().decode("utf-8")
        result_queries.append(mgp.Record(
            query=f"CREATE (n:MESSAGE {{timestamp: '{message.timestamp()}', payload:
            '{payload_as_str}', topic: '{message.topic_name()}'}})",
            parameters=None))

    return result_queries
```

thatDot/Quine

Quine is an open source graph (database) from the vendor thatDot. Quine allows the combination of multiple event streams into a single graph, querying for complex event relationships, and taking action on them in real time. The Quine messaging leaves out the "database" in the product name: the company actually calls its technology "Streaming Graph for Data Pipelines." In the sense of this book, Quine fully qualifies as a (graph-based) streaming database, though:

- It offers (graph-based) stream processing (standing queries), reading from streams, and writing the results of the processing out to streams.
- It provides materialized views (graphs).

Quine enables graph processing on a far larger scale than existing graph databases, such as Neo4J or TigerGraph, since it's a completely distributed system based on the concept of *actors* (implemented using the Scala library *Pekko*, a fork of Akka 2.6.1 under the covers). It also provides a pluggable storage layer supporting RocksDB, MapDB (locally), and Cassandra (remotely).

In Example 11-3, we depict an example for using a "server-side events" ingest stream to connect to the live stream of page revisions on Wikipedia.

Example 11-3. Ingesting a stream of "server-side events" of page revisions on Wikipedia with Quine

```
curl -X "POST" "http://127.0.0.1:8080/api/v1/ingest/wikipedia-revision-create" \
     -H 'Content-Type: application/json' \
     -d $'{
  "format": {
    "query": "CREATE ($that)",
    "parameter": "that",
    "type": "CypherJson"
  },
  "type": "ServerSentEventsIngest",
  "url": "https://stream.wikimedia.org/v2/stream/mediawiki.revision-create"
}'
```

In the next step (Example 11-4), we create an ingest query using the Cypher graph database language from Neo4J to load the individual events into nodes in the streaming graph database.

Example 11-4. Ingest query written in Cypher to load the individual events into nodes in the Quine graph database

```
MATCH (revNode),(pageNode),(dbNode),(userNode),(parentNode)
WHERE id(revNode) = idFrom('revision', $that.rev_id)
  AND id(pageNode) = idFrom('page', $that.page_id)
  AND id(dbNode) = idFrom('db', $that.database)
  AND id(userNode) = idFrom('id', $that.performer.user_id)
  AND id(parentNode) = idFrom('revision', $that.rev_parent_id)

SET revNode = $that,
    revNode.bot = $that.performer.user_is_bot,
```

```
    revNode:revision

SET parentNode.rev_id = $that.rev_parent_id

SET pageNode.id = $that.page_id,
    pageNode.namespace = $that.page_namespace,
    pageNode.title = $that.page_title,
    pageNode.comment = $that.comment,
    pageNode.is_redirect = $that.page_is_redirect,
    pageNode:page

SET dbNode.database = $that.database,
    dbNode:db

SET userNode = $that.performer,
    userNode.name = $that.performer.user_text,
    userNode:user

CREATE (revNode)-[:TO]->(pageNode),
       (pageNode)-[:IN]->(dbNode),
       (userNode)-[:RESPONSIBLE_FOR]->(revNode),
       (parentNode)-[:NEXT]->(revNode)
```

After setting up the graph from a streaming source, Quine allows setting up of a *standing query* to monitor the stream for specified patterns. Based on the recognition of these patterns, actions can be taken, such as updating the graph itself by creating new nodes or edges, writing results out to Kafka or Amazon Kinesis, or posting the results to a webhook. One of the crucial features of standing queries in Quine is that they do not require the specification of time windows such as in, for example, Flink. Standing queries essentially correspond to graph-based stream processing.

We show a standing query in Example 11-5. Standing queries consist of a pattern and an output. The pattern defines what should be matched, and the output defines the actions to take. Standing queries are, again, written in Cypher.

Example 11-5. Standing query written in Cypher match a pattern and take action on it (using a file sink)

```
{
  "pattern": {
    "query": "MATCH (n)-[:has_father]->(m) WHERE exists(n.name) AND exists(m.name)
    RETURN DISTINCT strId(n) AS kidWithDad",
    "type": "Cypher"
  },
  "outputs": {
    "file-of-results": {
      "path": "kidsWithDads.jsonl",
      "type": "WriteToFile"
    }
```

```
    }
}
```

To get the last 10 `revision-create` event nodes, you could now query Quine as in Example 11-6.

Example 11-6. Get the last 10 `revision-create` event nodes from Quine

```
MATCH (userNode:user {user_is_bot: false})-[:RESPONSIBLE_FOR]->(revNode:revision
  {database: 'enwiki'})
RETURN DISTINCT strid(userNode) as NodeID,
  revNode.page_title as Title,
  revNode.performer.user_text as User
LIMIT 10
```

We show the result of that query in Figure 11-2.

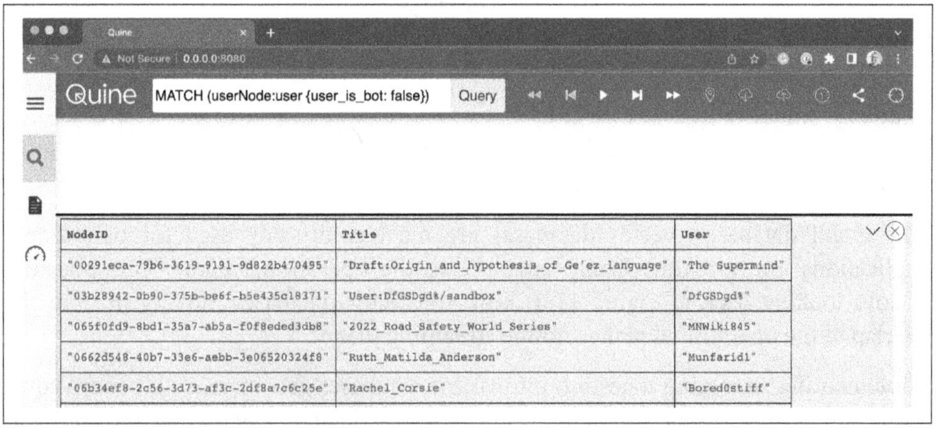

Figure 11-2. Result of the "not-a-bot" query

Memgraph—and especially thatDot/Quine—are at the forefront of the ongoing convergence of graph databases and streaming and, therefore, form a perfect example for the confluence of the operational plane and the streaming plane.

Vector Databases

In a nutshell, vector databases are optimized for storing and querying vectors, that is, fixed-length lists of numbers (typically, 50–1,500 per vector). Queries in a vector database typically amount to a similarity search implemented by approximate nearest neighbor (ANN) algorithms. The vectors stored in a vector database are high dimensional and represent features of unstructured data such as text, sound, and video. Popular vector databases include Milvus, Weaviate, Pinecone, Vespa, and Qdrant. Interestingly, an increasing number of existing databases have adopted vector database functionality as well, e.g., ClickHouse, Rockset, PostgreSQL, Cassandra, Elastic, Redis, and SingleStore.

The idea of turning unstructured data such as text, sound, and video into vector embeddings can be traced back as far as to Ludwig Wittgenstein's "language game."[1] In the 2010s, the two successful approaches, Word2vec from Google Research and GloVe from Stanford University,[2] pushed vector embeddings into the mainstream— and, indirectly, brought about the new category of vector databases. Large Language Models (LLMs) like OpenAI's GPT models can also generate vector embeddings.

Here is a list of use cases for vector databases:

Recommendations
> Similarity search can be used inside recommendation engines, for example, of online shops to find products similar to what the user was looking for. Similarity search can even be multimodal (e.g., textual similarity and graphic similarity).

Fraud detection
> Here, similarity search is used to flag, for example, fraudulent transactions.

Chatbots/generative AI
> Vector databases are useful, for example, for intent classification, retrieval-augmented generation (RAG), etc.

Like graph databases, vector databases are most commonly used for operational applications and are thus firmly attached to the operational plane. Our question is now, looking back at Figure 11-1, how are vector databases moving in onto the overlap of the operational plane and the streaming plane?

Implementing streaming ingestion into vector databases gets increasingly more common, for example, using Kafka Connect for vector databases like Pinecone and Milvus. But there are other touchpoints of vector databases and streaming. Milvus 2.x, for instance, was a complete architectural redesign from Milvus 1.x, even including a streaming platform under the covers. On the other hand, a number of RTOLAP databases, such as ClickHouse and Rockset, are increasingly adding support for vector search.

Milvus 2.x: Streaming as the Central Backbone

Compared to its first, rather monolithic, "single-binary" versions, Milvus 2.x is a complete architectural redesign build with horizontal scalability and cloud readiness

---

1 Ludwig Wittgenstein, *Philosophical Investigations*, Translated by G. E. M. Anscombe. New York: MacMillan, 1958 (1953).

2 Tomas Mikolov et al., "Efficient Estimation of Word Representations in Vector Space," 2013. Jeffrey Pennington et al., "GloVe: Global Vectors for Word Representation," 2014.

in mind. A very interesting aspect of the new architecture is the addition of a "message storage" or "log broker" responsible for streaming data persistence, execution of reliable asynchronous queries, event notification, and return of query results. It also ensures integrity of the incremental data when the worker nodes recover from system breakdown. Milvus goes as far as to follow the "log as data" principle: it does not maintain a physical table but guarantees data reliability through logging persistence and snapshot logs (Figure 11-3).

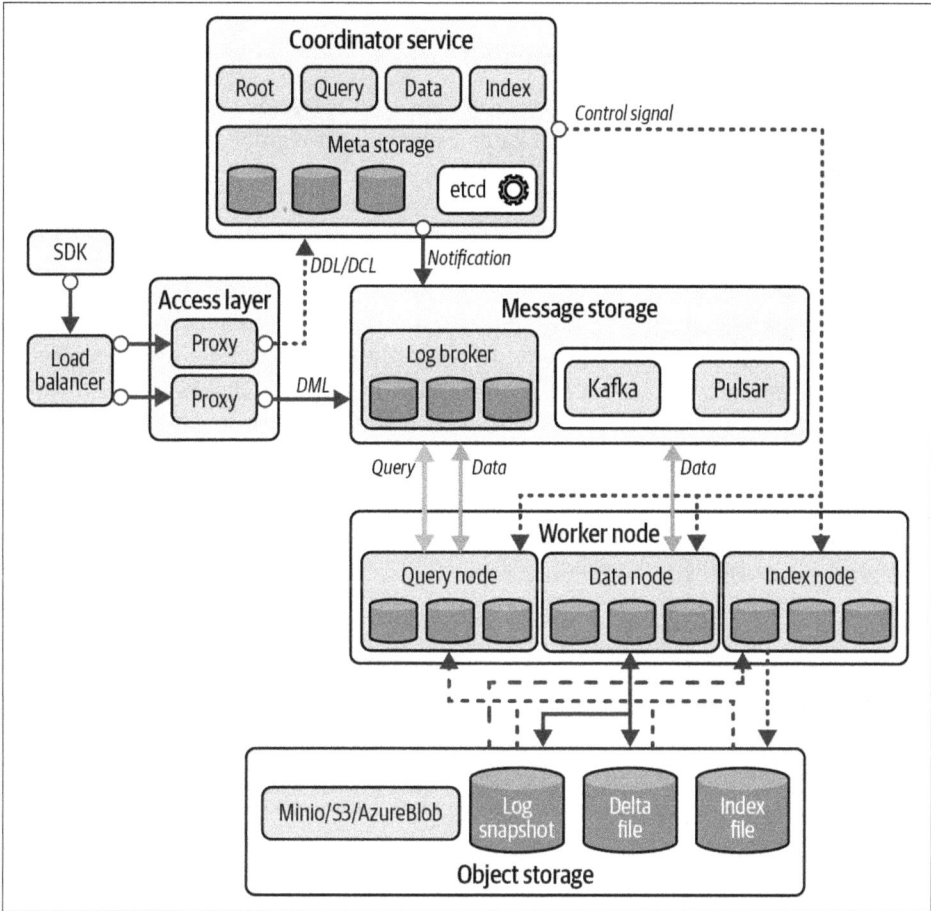

Figure 11-3. Milvus 2.x architecture with streaming ("message storage") as the central backbone

Milvus 2.x also boasts unified batch and stream processing by implementing a lambda architecture integrating the processing of incremental and historical data. To break unbounded (stream) data down into bounded windows, Milvus embraces a new watermark mechanism, which slices the stream data into multiple message packs according to write time or event time, and maintains a timeline for users to query by time.

Taken together, Milvus 2.x shows in an exciting way how even the design of newer databases can make deep inroads into the streaming plane. In the Milvus 2.x architecture, streaming/pub-sub is the backbone of the entire system, guaranteeing the scalability and resilience of the vector database. It will be exciting to see other vector databases follow suit in the near future.

RTOLAP Databases: Adding Vector Search

An increasing number of database vendors are adding vector search functionalities to their existing database products. Examples include MongoDB, Elastic, and Single-Store. This trend is also followed by RTOLAP databases, such as ClickHouse and Rockset.

ClickHouse

ClickHouse uses an array column type (`Array<Float32>`) to model vector embeddings and provides functions to compute the distance between a search vector and column values, such as `cosineDistance` and `L2Distance`. ClickHouse also offers specially optimized ANN search algorithms such as *Annoy indexes*.

Contrary to specialized vector databases, ClickHouse and other RTOLAP databases allow the combination of vector search with additional metadata filtering or aggregations on metadata. An example use case would be to perform vector search on images that are noncopyrighted—combining vector search with filtering based on copyright metadata.

We display an example ClickHouse SQL query combining vector search and metadata filtering in Example 11-7.

Example 11-7. Combining vector search and metadata filtering in ClickHouse

```
SELECT
        url,
        caption,
        L2Distance(image_embedding, [<embedding>]) AS score
FROM laion_100m
WHERE (width >= 300) AND (height >= 500) AND (copyright = '') AND similarity > 0.3
ORDER BY score ASC
LIMIT 10
FORMAT Vertical
```

As you can see, ClickHouse allows seamless combination of metadata filtering (here, the width and height of the images searched plus the copyright metadata) with vector search (using `L2Distance`).

Rockset

Rockset is another RTOLAP database offering support for vector search, including simpler KNN (K-nearest neighbors) and ANN search. In Rockset, an ANN index can be set up as in Example 11-8.

Example 11-8. Setting up an ANN index in Rockset

```
CREATE SIMILARITY INDEX book_catalog_embeddings_ann_index
ON FIELD commons.book_dataset:book_embedding DIMENSION 1536 as 'faiss::IVF256,Flat';
```

Here we are creating an index named `book_catalog_embeddings_ann_index`. We specify the dimension of the input vectors along with the type of index to create (in this case, an IVF [inverted file] index from Faiss).

Querying Rockset using this index looks as depicted in Example 11-9.

Example 11-9. Using vector search for querying in Rockset

```
SELECT
    book_dataset.title,
    book_dataset.author
FROM
    book_dataset ds
    JOIN book_metadata m ON ds.isbn = m.isbn
WHERE
    m.publish_date > DATE(2010, 12, 26)
    and m.rating >= 4
    and m.price < 50
ORDER BY
    APPROX_DOT_PRODUCT(:target_embedding, ds.book_embedding) DESC
LIMIT
    30
```

The interesting part here is in the `ORDER BY` clause, where the similarity search is used to order the results of the query based on the similarity of their content.

Incremental View Maintenance

IVM is a way to keep materialized views in a relational database up-to-date in an incremental way, where changes are continuously computed and applied on views instead of recomputing the contents of the views from scratch. IVM can update materialized views more efficiently than recomputation since only small parts of the view are changed at one time.

There are two approaches with regard to timing of view maintenance: *immediate* and *deferred*. In immediate maintenance, views are updated in the same transaction that its base table is modified. In deferred maintenance, views are updated after the transaction is committed, for example, as a response to an explicit user command like REFRESH MATERIALIZED VIEW, or periodically in the background, or only when the view is accessed.

IVM, in its immediate maintenance form, is another road crossing the operational and the streaming plane. In the last couple of years, a number of solutions have come into existence in this domain, for example, pg_ivm (a plug-in for PostgreSQL), Hydra, PeerDB, Epsio, and, to a certain extent, also Feldera/DBSP.

pg_ivm

pg_ivm adds immediately maintained materialized views to PostgreSQL. Materialized views are updated immediately in AFTER triggers when a base table is modified. An example is provided in Example 11-10.

Example 11-10. Create immediately maintained materialized view in PostgreSQL with pg_ivm

```
SELECT create_immv('myview', 'SELECT * FROM mytab');
```

pg_ivm has the advantage of being perfectly integrated with the underlying database—so no additional, externalized system needs to be set up and maintained.

On the other hand, the close coupling of pg_ivm with the operational database (PostgreSQL) also means that it has to share the resources (compute, memory) with the database itself. Because incremental materialized view maintenance can be expensive, it might be more sensible to externalize it into a separate system. For use cases where a columnar table format might be more useful, the row-based table setup of PostgreSQL might, in addition, cause performance issues.

Hydra

Hydra supports traditional materialized views using both row and columnar tables, as well as incremental materialized views powered by pg_ivm. Example 11-11 shows how to set up both row-based and columnar materialized views in Hydra.

Example 11-11. Create immediately maintained materialized view in PostgreSQL with pg_ivm

```
CREATE TABLE heap_table (...) USING heap;
CREATE TABLE columnar_table (...) USING columnar;
```

The additional flexibility of Hydra means that it can serve both use cases requiring a row-based table structure and those requiring columnar storage. It's also possible to create an externalized table in PostgreSQL and sync back to Hydra in a way mimicking zero-ETL.

Epsio

Epsio is a tool for incremental materialized view maintenance that plugs into existing PostgreSQL databases and constantly and incrementally updates results for queries whenever the underlying data changes. With its incremental mode of operation, Epsio never has to recalculate the entire dataset—allowing it to provide instant and always up-to-date results for complex queries. Epsio supports a large subset of SQL syntax, including most types of JOINs, CTEs, subqueries, GROUP BY, etc.

How does Epsio work in practice? In Example 11-12, we define a simple Epsio materialized view.

Example 11-12. Define a materialized view in Epsio

```
CALL epsio.create_view('epsio_view',
  'SELECT SUM(SALARY), d.name FROM employee_salaries e
    JOIN deplartments d on e.department_id = d.id
    GROUP BY d.name');
```

In Example 11-13, you can see how querying the materialized view works (exactly as it does directly in a PostgreSQL database).

Example 11-13. Query a materialized view in Epsio

```
SELECT * FROM epsio_view;
```

The advantages of using a separate system, such as Epsio, instead of querying PostgreSQL directly are manifold:

- The materialized views in Epsio are constantly incrementally updated without having to recalculate the entire dataset.
- The performance of the source database is not impacted by its own materialized view maintenance or continuous queries.

Feldera

Feldera is a "Continuous Analytics Platform" that allows users to run continuous queries directly on streaming data. Essentially, it processes queries and produces output continuously: whenever changes arrive, Feldera recomputes the query results incrementally and only then sends the changed query results to its outputs.

In a sense, it's a real-time ETL platform based on stream processing—driven by the DBSP (Database Stream Processor) engine. In many ways, Feldera overlaps with streaming databases, such as Materialize or RisingWave, but with an emphasis on bringing data from sources to targets and without offering support for materialized views. It can also be likened to a pure stream processing system, such as Flink, but offers additional consistency guarantees such as, for example, Materialize (DBSP is in many ways similar to the stream processing engine underlying Materialize, Differential Dataflow).

Let's see how Feldera works in practice. First, in Example 11-14, we declare some input tables.

Example 11-14. Declare input tables in Feldera

```
create table VENDOR (
    id bigint not null primary key,
    name varchar,
    address varchar
);

create table PART (
    id bigint not null primary key,
    name varchar
);

create table PRICE (
    part bigint not null,
    vendor bigint not null,
    price decimal
);
```

The declarations do not specify the concrete data sources. Records for the VENDOR, PART, and PRICE tables could come from a Kafka stream, a database, or an HTTP request. The "SQL program" can be instantiated with a data source (or even multiple data sources) in the Feldera UI later.

In the second step, we can now write continuous queries on the input data. We show this in Example 11-15.

Example 11-15. Write continuous queries in Feldera

```
-- Lowest available price for each part across all vendors.
create view LOW_PRICE (
    part,
    price
) as
    select part, MIN(price) as price from PRICE group by part;
```

```
-- Lowest available price for each part along with part and vendor details.
create view PREFERRED_VENDOR (
    part_id,
    part_name,
    vendor_id,
    vendor_name,
    price
) as
    select
        PART.id as part_id,
        PART.name as part_name,
        VENDOR.id as vendor_id,
        VENDOR.name as vendor_name,
        PRICE.price
    from
        PRICE,
        PART,
        VENDOR,
        LOW_PRICE
    where
        PRICE.price = LOW_PRICE.price AND
        PRICE.part = LOW_PRICE.part AND
        PART.id = PRICE.part AND
        VENDOR.id = PRICE.vendor;
```

In Feldera, queries are written as SQL views, which can be defined in terms of tables and other views. In Example 11-15, the PREFERRED_VENDOR view is defined in terms of the LOW_PRICE view. This flexibility enables Feldera to express, for example, deeply nested queries.

PeerDB

PeerDB is an open source tool for streaming data from PostgreSQL to data warehouses (Snowflake, BigQuery), queues (Azure Event Hubs), and storage engines (S3, GCS). Like Feldera, PeerDB does not offer materialized view maintenance directly, but you can achieve a similar effect by synchronizing PostgreSQL databases in real time with, for example, Snowflake, where the "materialized view" then resides in Snowflake.

PeerDB has four modes of replication:

- Log-based
- Cursor-based (timestamp or integer)
- XMIN-based
- Streaming query

In the log-, cursor-, and XMIN-based modes, PeerDB picks up table changes from PostgreSQL (the "source peer") tables and brings them to the "target peer." Contrary to similar CDC tools, PeerDB claims to be much more performant (10× faster). PeerDB also supports "streaming query" replication for more complex replication requirements. In this mode, you can do complex transformations of the source peer data before sending it over to the target peer.

Let's look at an example of how PeerDB works. The first step is to create a source and a target peer (Example 11-16).

Example 11-16. Create source peer and target peer in PeerDB

```
CREATE PEER source FROM POSTGRES WITH
(
  host = 'catalog',
  port = '5432',
  user = 'postgres',
  password = 'postgres',
  database = 'source'
);

CREATE PEER target FROM POSTGRES WITH
(
  host = 'catalog',
  port = '5432',
  user = 'postgres',
  password = 'postgres',
  database = 'target'
);
```

In Example 11-17, we then kick off log-based CDC by creating a "mirror."

Example 11-17. Set up log-based CDC in PeerDB

```
CREATE MIRROR cdc_mirror FROM source TO target
WITH TABLE MAPPING (public.test:public.test);
```

This "mirror" now takes care of replicating all DML commands (INSERT, UPDATE, DELETE) from the source to the target and makes use of a table mapping.

Setting up a streaming query is a bit more involved (Example 11-18).

Example 11-18. Set up a streaming query in PeerDB

```
CREATE MIRROR qrep_mirror FROM source TO target
FOR $$
    SELECT id, hashint4(c1) hash_c1, hashint4(c2) hash_c2, md5(t) AS hash_t
    FROM test WHERE id BETWEEN {{.start}} AND {{.end}}
$$ WITH (
    watermark_table_name='public.test',
    watermark_column='id',
    num_rows_per_partition = 10000,
    destination_table_name='public.test_transformed',
    mode='append'
);
```

This streaming query masks the columns c1, c2, and t by hashing them prior to sending them to the target.

Data Wrapping and Postgres Multicorn

In Chapter 7, we talked about PostgreSQL's rise to ubiquity, which we attributed to several factors, like its open source nature, developer community, and extensibility, like pg_ivm. In addition, a key factor in PostgreSQL's ubiquity is its exceptional extensibility. This refers to its ability to be customized and expanded beyond its core functionality, which includes features like these:

FDWs
> Allow seamless integration with external data sources, making it a central hub for diverse data.

Multicorn extension
> Simplifies building custom FDWs in Python, further lowering the barrier to entry for data integration. These features, combined with a strong community fostering extension development, empower users to tailor PostgreSQL to their specific needs, making it a valuable tool for many use cases.

PostgreSQL FDWs allow you to access data residing outside PostgreSQL itself, as if it were a regular table within your database. FDWs empower you to combine data from various sources, like other databases, files, APIs, streaming platforms, and columnar-based databases, all using familiar SQL queries.

Multicorn is a Postgres extension used to create custom FDWs using Python. It provides a user-friendly framework, abstracting away the complex low-level details of FDW implementation. With Multicorn, you can focus on the specific logic required to interact with the external data source, leaving the communication with Postgres to the framework. Together, FDWs and Multicorn unlock flexible data integration and streamlined development for working with diverse data sources within your PostgreSQL environment.

Here's a breakdown of how to implement real-time analytics using PostgreSQL, the Multicorn extension, and an OLAP database:

1. Set up PostgreSQL and Multicorn:

   a. Install PostgreSQL. Ensure you have PostgreSQL installed and running on your system. You can find installation instructions on the official PostgreSQL website (*https://postgresql.org*).

   b. Enable Multicorn extension. Once PostgreSQL is set up, enable the Multicorn extension using the following command:

      ```
      CREATE EXTENSION IF NOT EXISTS multicorn;
      ```

2. Implement a data ingestion pipeline:

   a. Establish a connection. Create a connection between your application and the PostgreSQL database using an appropriate library like psycopg2 for Python or *pg* for Node.js.

   b. Capture data in real time. Implement logic in your application to capture data in real time. This could involve:

      i. Streaming data. Use libraries/frameworks that support real-time data ingestion from various sources like Apache Kafka or message queues like RabbitMQ.

      ii. WebSockets/Server-Sent Events (SSEs). Establish real-time connections with clients and receive data updates through WebSockets or SSEs.

      iii. API calls. If data originates from external APIs, make periodic API calls to retrieve and update the database.

3. Queue, process and store data:

   a. Queue data. Consider using temporary tables or queues within the PostgreSQL database to buffer incoming data before processing.

   b. Process in-memory. For faster processing of real-time data, explore in-memory databases or techniques like materialized views within PostgreSQL. However, this might not be suitable for large datasets.

   c. Transform and store data. Within your application or using triggers in PostgreSQL, transform the received data into the desired format and store it in appropriate tables. This might involve dimension tables for storing static attributes and fact tables for storing measures/metrics.

4. Connect to an OLAP database:

   a. Choose an OLAP solution. Select an OLAP database like Apache Druid, Apache Kylin, or ClickHouse that aligns with your specific needs and data volume.

b. Establish a connection. Use the provided libraries/connectors from your chosen OLAP solution to connect to the database from your application.

c. Periodic data transfer. Set up scheduled tasks or use triggers within PostgreSQL to periodically transfer the processed data from your PostgreSQL database to the OLAP database. This ensures the OLAP database remains updated with the latest data for efficient analytical queries.

Be sure to consider the following as well:

Error handling and logging
Implement proper error handling mechanisms to ensure data consistency and data quality throughout the pipeline.

Monitoring and scaling
Monitor the performance of your system and OLAP database as the data volume increases. Consider scaling your infrastructure as needed to handle the real-time data flow.

Security
Secure your data pipeline by implementing authentication, authorization, and encryption mechanisms where necessary.

Remember, this is a general guideline, and the specific implementation details will vary based on your chosen tools, technologies, and the specific requirements of your real-time analytics use case.

Classical Databases

The recurring topic of this chapter—and the whole book—is the ongoing convergence of streaming and databases, or, in other words, the unification of data in motion with data at rest. One of the most recent indicators for this convergence is a new feature called *Atlas Stream Processing* from MongoDB, an already "classical" NoSQL database. Atlas Stream Processing extends MongoDB with stream processing capabilities such that MongoDB is getting close to becoming a streaming database itself. In our Venn diagram (Figure 11-1), the location of this convergence is the overlap of the operational with the streaming plane—which is exactly where streaming databases such as Materialize and RisingWave fit in.

Atlas Stream Processing adds stream processing functionalities to MongoDB that can read from streaming platforms like Kafka and also write back the processed data to a streaming platform. In addition, Atlas Stream Processing allows the use of MongoDB collections as materialized views of the processed data. We display a rough architectural diagram in Figure 11-4.

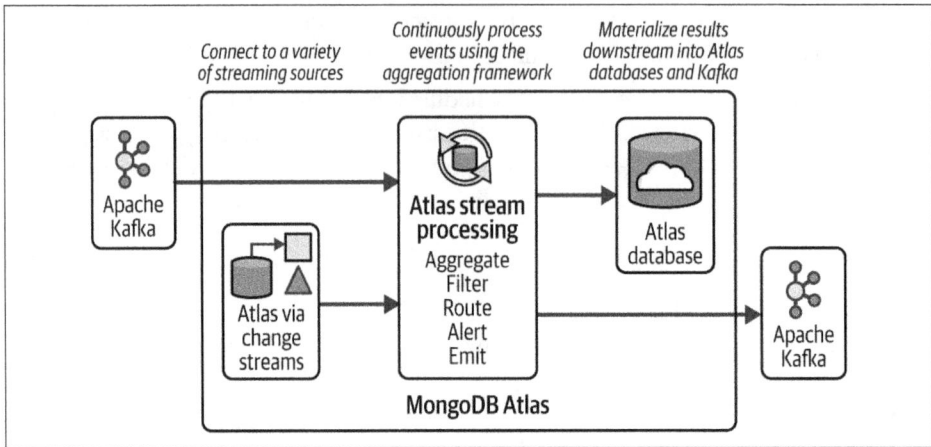

Figure 11-4. MongoDB Atlas Stream Processing architecture

By being embedded in MongoDB, Atlas Stream Processing allows for a seamless integration of using data in motion (through stream processing) and data at rest (using MongoDB collections as before). The similarity of messages (typically in JSON format) and MongoDB documents (also in a JSON-like format) makes for an even more seamless integration—much more compared to when streaming is integrated with a relational model, as in the SQL-based streaming databases introduced in Chapter 5. However, Atlas Stream Processing is still in its early stages, as can be seen from the feature matrix available on the MongoDB homepage. JOINs of any sort, for example, aren't yet supported. It remains to be seen how it can encroach upon the stream processing market with established solutions like Flink, and how it can become a direct competitor to streaming databases like Materialize and RisingWave.

Let's see a few glimpses of Atlas Stream Processing in practice. The JavaScript code using the MongoDB Query API shown in Example 11-19 exemplifies how to query a Kafka topic and bring the results into a MongoDB collection.

Example 11-19. Querying a Kafka topic and sinking the result into a MongoDB collection using Atlas Stream Processing

```
// define a source from the connection registry
var source = { $source: {
connectionName: 'kafkaprod',
topic: 'stocks'
} }

// create some other stages
var match = { $match: { 'exchange':'NYSE'} }

// create a sink
var sink = { $merge: {
```

```
into: {
connectionName: 'mongoprod',
db: 'StockDB',
col: 'TransactionHistory'

} }

// try it!
var myProcessor = [source, match, sink]
sp.process(myProcessor)
```

Here, the source stage connects to the Kafka topic stocks, the match stage matches only those Kafka messages whose exchange field matches with the string NYSE, and the sink stage brings the matched messages to a materialized view, aka MongoDB collection called TransactionHistory. The last line, beginning with sp.process, actually starts the stream processor.

Another example shows how to use Atlas Stream Processing for windowed aggregations (Example 11-20).

Example 11-20. Executing a windowed aggregation in Atlas Stream Processing

```
// define a tumbling window
{
  $tumblingWindow: {
    interval: {
      size: NumberInt(60), unit: 'second'},
      pipeline: [{
        $group: {
          _id: '$ip_source',
          count_connection_reset: { $sum: 1 }
        }
      }]
    }
  },


// output has projections for convenience
{
  _id: '127.0.0.1',
  count_connection_reset: 60,
  _stream_meta: {
    sourceType: 'kafka',
    windowStartTimestamp: 2023-05-18T17:07:00.000Z,
    windowEndTimestamp: 2023-05-18T17:08:00.000Z
  }
}
```

In the code snippet in Example 11-20, we first define a tumbling window of 60 seconds and use it to count the messages of a Kafka topic.

Data Warehouses

Streaming is making large inroads not only into the database but also into the data warehouse space. In this section, we look into three of the major players: BigQuery, Redshift, and Snowflake—located in the overlapping section between the analytical and the streaming plane in our Venn diagram (Figure 11-1).

BigQuery

Google's BigQuery also supports streaming ingestion through its SDK. Similar to Redshift, this enables BigQuery to also cover near-real-time analytics use cases where low latency is of paramount importance. Data coming into BigQuery through streaming ingestion is available for real-time analysis within a few seconds of the first streaming insertion into a table.

Contrary to Redshift, streaming ingestion in BigQuery is not implemented via SQL, but via an SDK for Java and Python. In Example 11-21, we show Python code inserting table data in this fashion.

Example 11-21. Streaming ingestion (inserting rows) into BigQuery using its Python SDK

```
def stream_data(dataset_name, table_name, json_data):
    bigquery_client = bigquery.Client()
    dataset = bigquery_client.dataset(dataset_name)
    table = dataset.table(table_name)
    data = json.loads(json_data)

    # Reload the table to get the schema.
    table.reload()

    rows = [data]
    errors = table.insert_data(rows)

    if not errors:
        print('Loaded 1 row into {}:{}'.format(dataset_name, table_name))
    else:
        print('Errors:')
        pprint(errors)
```

Google Cloud Platform (GCP) also features integrations of BigQuery with its product, Cloud Dataflow, based on Apache Beam. Data can be written to BigQuery using Cloud Dataflow, and data from BigQuery can be sinked out to Cloud Dataflow as well. In addition, Google has recently announced *Apache Kafka for BigQuery* to easily deploy Apache Kafka in conjunction with BigQuery in a serverless fashion.

Redshift

Redshift supports streaming ingestion for low-latency ingestion of streaming data from Kinesis or Kafka (Amazon Managed Service for Apache Kafka, or MSK) into materialized views. The materialized views can be configured using SQL statements and make up the *landing area* for the data coming from the input stream. The data is processed as it arrives—for example, JSON values from the Kinesis data streams or Kafka topics can be consumed and mapped to the data columns of the materialized views.

This feature even enables Redshift to cover near-real-time analytics use cases where data that's continuously streamed must be processed within a short period of its generation. Example sources are Internet of Things (IoT) devices, system telemetry data, or clickstreams. Compared to sourcing data only indirectly from a streaming platform by using Kinesis Data Firehose to stage it in S3 first, direct streaming ingestion results in less complexity and lower latency.

Here is how streaming ingestion in Redshift works in practice. The crucial part is to set up a materialized view to consume data from, for example, a Kafka topic as displayed in Example 11-22.

Example 11-22. Creating a materialized view to consume data from a Kafka topic in Redshift

```
CREATE MATERIALIZED VIEW MyView AUTO REFRESH YES AS
SELECT
    kafka_partition,
    kafka_offset,
    kafka_timestamp_type,
    kafka_timestamp,
    kafka_key,
    JSON_PARSE(kafka_value) as Data,
    kafka_headers
FROM
    MySchema."mytopic"
WHERE
    CAN_JSON_PARSE(kafka_value);
```

Materialized views and streaming ingestion in Redshift can be likened to materialized views in streaming databases, such as Materialize and RisingWave, especially when using AUTO REFRESH instead of MANUAL REFRESH. However, as the underlying architecture of Redshift is not streaming based, this still is not strictly the same—contrary to streaming databases, the refresh is still done periodically, not continuously, which drives up the latency of Redshift compared to a streaming database, which works fully incrementally.

Snowflake

Snowflake has invested a lot into building features around streaming recently. As a result, Snowflake now provides the following streaming-based capabilities:

Continuous data loading
> This is about streaming ingestion, similar to Redshift and BigQuery. For that, Snowflake provides Snowpipe Streaming and the Snowflake Connector for Kafka Connect.

Continuous data transformation
> Snowflake has introduced a feature called dynamic tables for declaratively implementing automated data pipelines that simplify data ingestion coupled with processing.

Change data tracking
> This is a feature implementing CDC for normal Snowflake tables and also dynamic tables.

Let's first look a bit deeper into Snowpipe Streaming for streaming ingestion. Similar to BigQuery, Snowflake provides an SDK (for Java) to do that. Hence, to implement streaming ingestion, the user needs to come up with a Java application. In Example 11-23, we show a simplified example of how this looks in practice.

Example 11-23. Streaming ingestion (inserting rows) into Snowflake using its Java-based SDK

```
[package, imports]

public class SnowflakeStreamingIngestExample {
  [setup]
      // Insert rows into the channel (Using insertRows API)
      final int totalRowsInTable = 1000;
      for (int val = 0; val < totalRowsInTable; val++) {
        Map<String, Object> row = new HashMap<>();

        // c1 corresponds to the column name in table
        row.put("c1", val);

        // Insert the row with the current offset_token
        InsertValidationResponse response = channel1.insertRow(row, String.valueOf(val));
        if (response.hasErrors()) {
          // Simply throw if there is an exception, or you can do whatever you want
          // with the erroneous row
          throw response.getInsertErrors().get(0).getException();
```

```
      }
   }

   // If needed, you can check the offset_token registered in Snowflake to
   // make sure everything is committed
   final int expectedOffsetTokenInSnowflake = totalRowsInTable - 1;
   // 0 based offset_token
   final int maxRetries = 10;
   int retryCount = 0;

   do {
      String offsetTokenFromSnowflake = channel1.getLatestCommittedOffsetToken();
      if (offsetTokenFromSnowflake != null
         && offsetTokenFromSnowflake.equals(String.valueOf
         (expectedOffsetTokenInSnowflake))) {
         System.out.println("SUCCESSFULLY inserted " + totalRowsInTable + " rows");
         break;
      }
      retryCount++;
   } while (retryCount < maxRetries);

   [close]
      }
   }
}
```

Snowflake has introduced dynamic tables for declaratively building data ingestion pipelines with SQL. Dynamic tables are similar in many ways to the materialized views of Redshift's streaming ingestion, and to materialized views in streaming databases such as Materialize and RisingWave. Again, as for Redshift the underlying architecture is batch- and not streaming-based. Hence, even the automatic refresh of dynamic tables is still done periodically and not strictly continuously, as in streaming databases, resulting in far higher latency.

Lakehouse

There's an enormously quickly growing trend of streaming engines and stream processing systems offering more seamless support for data lakes/lakehouses. Streaming engines like Confluent, Redpanda, and WarpStream are moving toward offering streaming data from their "cold" object storage layer directly, using open table formats like Apache Iceberg. Open Source Kafka is moving there too (*https://oreil.ly/ nEBfP*), and Apache Paimon, an offspring of Apache Flink, is bringing Flink-based stream processing to the data lake, aka "Streamhouse." Confluent has already started offering Iceberg support directly in its proprietary Confluent Cloud/Kora streaming platform and coined the term *multimodal stream* to describe their ability to offer data in both streaming and table format. With this feature, Tableflow, Flink can also be used to access both streaming and table/batch data. Data on Delta Lake, another open table format, can also be processed using stream processing (Spark Structured Streaming).

In this section, we further explore this form of convergence of the analytical plane and the streaming plane (see our Venn diagram in Figure 11-1) and close with a discussion of the present and future relationship of streaming technologies and the lakehouse.

Delta Lake

Like the other two most popular open table formats (Apache Iceberg and Apache Hudi), Delta Lake is based on the columnar Parquet file format. In addition to Parquet files, it offers a file-based transaction log for implementing ACID transactions and scalable metadata handling. Since it's compatible with the Apache Spark APIs (Spark and Delta Lake are both mainly developed by Databricks), Delta Lake is also tightly integrated with Spark Structured Streaming for streaming and batch processing of the data at large scale. Note that Spark Structured Streaming is using microbatches under the hood, so strictly speaking, it's not pure stream processing.

The open table format underlying Delta Lake is called Delta Table. In Delta Lake, Delta Tables can serve both as sources and sinks—and in conjunction with Spark Structured Streaming, it's possible to implement stream processing on Delta Lake. In Example 11-24, we display a simple example for how this looks.

Example 11-24. Using Delta Lake (Delta Tables) as a source using Spark Structured Streaming

```
spark.readStream.format("delta")
  .load("/tmp/delta/events")

import io.delta.implicits._
spark.readStream.delta("/tmp/delta/events")
```

In the example, the Delta table /tmp/delta/events is read as a stream using Spark Structured Streaming. You could now add queries using arbitrary stream processing logic, and the query would process all of the data present in the table as well as any new data that arrives going forward.

Writing processed data back from Spark Structured Streaming to Delta Tables works analogously (Example 11-25)

Example 11-25. Using Delta Lake (Delta Tables) as a sink using Spark Structured Streaming.

```
events.writeStream
  .outputMode("append")
```

```
        .option("checkpointLocation", "/tmp/delta/events/_checkpoints/")
        .toTable("events")
```

Apache Paimon

Apache Paimon aims to be similar to Delta Lake, but instead of using microbatching such as Delta Lake/Spark Structured Streaming, it's built on "pure" stream processing based on Apache Flink. The main vendor behind Paimon, Ververica, also refers to Paimon as a *Streamhouse* (as opposed to a lakehouse) solution.

Contrary to Delta Lake, Iceberg, and Hudi, Paimon does not use Parquet as the underlying columnar data format—instead, its files are based on its own format based on an LSM (log-structured merge) tree structure. In addition to Flink, Paimon also supports reading these files by other computation engines like Apache Hive, Apache Spark, and Trino. Although Paimon is based on a streaming-first architecture, it also supports a batch mode for reading and writing data.

In Example 11-26, we show how to create the Paimon tables customers and Orders, where the latter is based on a source Kafka topic (we omitted the catalog setup for brevity).

Example 11-26. Creating the tables customers and the temporary table Orders based on a Kafka topic in Apache Paimon

```
CREATE TABLE customers (
    id INT PRIMARY KEY NOT ENFORCED,
    name STRING,
    country STRING,
    zip STRING
);

INSERT INTO customers ...

CREATE TEMPORARY TABLE Orders (
    order_id INT,
    total INT,
    customer_id INT,
    proc_time AS PROCTIME()
) WITH (
    'connector' = 'kafka',
    'topic' = '...',
    'properties.bootstrap.servers' = '...',
    'format' = 'csv'
    ...
);
```

Now this table can be queried, for example, with the lookup JOIN query in Example 11-27.

Example 11-27. Querying the table Orders using a lookup JOIN query in Apache Paimon

```
SELECT o.order_id, o.total, c.country, c.zip
FROM Orders AS o
JOIN customers
FOR SYSTEM_TIME AS OF o.proc_time AS c
ON o.customer_id = c.id;
```

Apache Iceberg

Apache Iceberg is a very popular open table format, originally coming from Netflix, and supported by many vendors like Spark, Flink, Presto, Trino, Hive, Impala, StarRocks, Doris and Pig, and Snowflake. Streaming platforms like Redpanda, WarpStream, and open source Kafka also plan to include Iceberg/Parquet support to directly access their cold data through the Iceberg APIs. Confluent Cloud/Kora has already started to expose Kafka topics as Iceberg tables with Tableflow.

Streaming databases are also following this trend. RisingWave already supports Iceberg as a sink, as we exhibit in Example 11-28, where sink data is, for example, upserted into an Iceberg table (RisingWave also supports an append-only mode).

Example 11-28. Sinking the table s1_table into an Apache Iceberg table in RisingWave

```
CREATE SINK s1_sink FROM s1_table
WITH (
    connector = 'iceberg',
    warehouse.path = 's3a://my-iceberg-bucket/path/to/warehouse,
    s3.endpoint = 'https://s3.ap-southeast-1.amazonaws.com',
    s3.access.key = '${ACCESS_KEY}',
    s3.secret.key = '${SECRET_KEY},
    database.name='dev',
    table.name='table',
    primary_key='seq_id'
);
```

As Iceberg is also supported by Spark Structured Streaming, in Example 11-29, we provide an example where data is brought into an Iceberg table using Python and Spark.

Example 11-29. Using Spark Structured Streaming to ingest data into an Apache Iceberg table

```
df.writeStream \
    .format("iceberg") \
    .outputMode("append") \
    .trigger(processingTime=WINDOW_SIZE) \
    .option("path", table_id) \
```

```
    .option("fanout-enabled", "true") \
    .option("checkpointLocation", checkpointPath) \
    .start()
```

Iceberg tables can also be sources for Spark Structured Streaming (Example 11-30).

Example 11-30. Using Spark Structured Streaming to read data from an Apache Iceberg table

```
spark.readStream \
    .format("iceberg") \
    .load(basePath) \
    .start()
```

Apache Hudi

Apache Hudi is another popular open table format, originally developed at Uber. Hudi also supports a number of query engines such as Apache Spark, Apache Impala, Apache Hive, Presto, and Trino. Contrary to Iceberg, Hudi has a feature called *incremental query* based on its support for record-level change streams, which can be used to bring data from Hudi to, for example, Spark Structured Streaming (Example 11-31).

Example 11-31. Using Spark Structured Streaming to read data from an Apache Hudi table

```
spark.readStream \
    .format("hudi") \
    .load(basePath) \
    .start()
```

Data from, for example, Spark Structured Streaming can also be brought into Hudi, similar to the Iceberg example in Example 11-30. The Hudi example is shown in Example 11-32.

Example 11-32. Using Spark Structured Streaming to write data to an Apache Hudi table

```
df.writeStream
    .format("hudi") \
    .options(**hudi_streaming_options) \
    .outputMode("append") \
    .option("path", baseStreamingPath) \
    .option("checkpointLocation", checkpointLocation) \
    .trigger(once=True) \
    .start()
```

OneTable or XTable

OneTable or XTable is a new open table format built with the aim of making the different open table formats interoperable. In that sense, it's a meta open table format. Currently, OneTable or XTable supports Apache Iceberg, Apache Hudi, and Delta Lake.

OneTable or XTable is especially useful for companies that use multiple open table formats at the same time, such as Iceberg and Delta Lake—and yields an abstraction layer that avoids copying the data back and forth between the different lakehouses. As OneTable or XTable has been put out into the open source, support for Apache Paimon's table format could also be built.

The Relationship of Streaming and Lakehouses

Redpanda, WarpStream, and open source Kafka (*https://oreil.ly/LkExc*) are paving the way for an increasingly tight integration of streaming platforms, stream processing, and lakehouses with their upcoming additions offering cold data from tiered storage layers (or, for WarpStream, its only layer) directly using columnar table formats (e.g., Iceberg/ Parquet) and the "Streamhouse" idea from Apache Paimon.

As we write this book, the integration of lakehouses and streaming is still often restricted to pure streaming ingestion. The tighter integration of streaming platforms and open table formats on the near horizon is going to change this state of affairs quite dramatically. One possible outcome is that a lot of data currently only stored in the lakehouse could be moved over to the streaming platforms—avoiding additional copying/ingestion from the streaming platform into the actual lakehouse. This would also mean that the streaming platforms, instead of the lakehouses, would increasingly become the "single source of truth" of the data. Or, technologies like Confluent's Tableflow could offer two APIs—one streaming and events, one batch and tables—to access the same, nonduplicated data directly on the streaming platform.

In general, many SaaS data services are going the route of using cloud object stores as lower-tier storage (or tiered storage). Using tiered storage helps enterprises offload colder data, which saves storage costs. Many have extrapolated this idea by suggesting using the cloud object store as the interface by which data can be served and stored— and not the SaaS interface itself. For example, if your SaaS provides a database and it offloads data to the object store for cheap cold storage, why can't it just read that data directly from said object store? Likewise, your SaaS database should be able to read from the cloud object store. Why not then use the data I already have in the cloud object store to be served by your SaaS database?

What would all that mean for the technology this book is mainly about—streaming databases? We see this as a big opportunity for them to grow. If streaming platforms like Kafka grow more and more into the role of becoming the single source of truth, the data processing pipelines so far only executed on the lakehouse could also move toward the streaming platforms. And, especially for operational applications where low end-to-end latency is of paramount concern—but actually for all use cases where huge amounts of data have to be processed—stream processing systems and streaming databases that are "streaming-native" can yield far better performance and also enormous cost savings compared to systems like data warehouses (e.g., Snowflake) or lakehouses (e.g., Databricks) that are built on a batch-based architecture.

Conclusion

We've come a long way in this book. You learned how streaming technologies were influenced by features already implemented in databases. You learned that by turning the database inside out, we were able to scale the individual parts beyond the capacity of a single database. Most of all, you learned that bringing these technologies back into the database (in other words, bringing database technologies outside in) helped consolidate infrastructure and simplify the interface for engineers without losing the scalability we learned from decomposing the database.

We have seen a plethora of indications for the ongoing convergence of streaming and batch (databases/data lakes/lakehouses), starting with the increasingly overlapping operational and streaming planes. Not only do more and more vendors supporting graph and vector databases offer features for more direct integration with streaming platforms, but a number of vendors are also providing support for incremental materialized view maintenance. Established database vendors like MongoDB are even, in part, evolving into full-fledged streaming databases.

Even more interesting is the ongoing convergence of the analytical plane with the streaming plane. Here, data warehouse solutions such as BigQuery, Redshift, and Snowflake are offering more and more interesting features to directly support streaming. The most interesting convergence at the moment, however, is that of streaming and lakehouses. Here, we have observed strong pushes from both sides, from streaming into the lakehouse and also vice versa, to seamlessly combine streaming with lakehouse architectures, leading to new concepts like multimodal streams, driven by open table formats like Apache Iceberg. We have observed that this confluence could also be a big driver for the adoption of purely streaming-based stream processing solutions and, of course, streaming databases.

At the time of writing this book, we are just at the beginning. We're looking forward to finding out how this story of the convergence of the operational, analytical, and streaming planes will actually unfold.

Index

About the Authors

Hubert Dulay is a systems and data engineer at StarTree. A veteran engineer with over 20 years of experience in big and fast data and MLOps, Hubert has consulted for many financial institutions, healthcare organizations, and telecommunications companies, providing simple solutions that solve many data problems. He is the author of *Streaming Data Mesh* (O'Reilly).

Ralph M. Debusmann is a former AI/natural language processing researcher–turned–software engineer, solution architect, and technologist, now acting as Enterprise Kafka Engineer at Migros-Genossenschafts-Bund in Zürich, Switzerland. He received his PhD in computer science focusing on natural language processing and AI in 2006 (Saarbruecken University and University of Edinburgh) and has spent 15 years at SAP, Bosch, and Forecasty.AI/BASF SE before joining Migros-Genossenschafts-Bund in 2023.

Colophon

The animal on the cover of *Streaming Databases* is a huchen fish (*Hucho hucho*), a large fish in the *Salmonidae* family found throughout the Danube River basin and the Balkans also known as the *Danube salmon*. The species is migratory and spawns in shallow freshwater. Mature huchen measure about 55 inches long and weigh anywhere from 55 to 100 pounds. They eat other fish and insects.

Hucho hucho was classified Endangered due to habitat loss in 2008 by the IUCN Red List. Many of the animals on O'Reilly covers are endangered; all of them are important to the world.

The cover illustration is by Karen Montgomery, based on a black and white engraving from *Lydekker's Royal Natural History*. The series design is by Edie Freedman, Ellie Volckhausen, and Karen Montgomery. The cover fonts are Gilroy Semibold and Guardian Sans. The text font is Adobe Minion Pro; the heading font is Adobe Myriad Condensed; and the code font is Dalton Maag's Ubuntu Mono.

O'REILLY®

Learn from experts.
Become one yourself.

Books | Live online courses
Instant answers | Virtual events
Videos | Interactive learning

Get started at oreilly.com.